Praise for *Social Locati*

"Too many people are running around ___al media experts.' Simon doesn't call himself that. His clients do. And they're right. I'll read anything this man writes."

Peter Shankman, Founder, Help a Reporter Out
Entrepreneur, Social Media Investor

"Location-based services are becoming increasingly crucial to brands, marketers and their agencies. Social consumers are sharing their locations—and how they feel about them—with these applications. This book is a vital head start for marketers who are seeking to incorporate these new capabilities into their plans (and that should be everyone)."

Adam Keats, Senior Vice President, Weber Shandwick

"Have you checked-in to the new reality of business? Simon shows you how to engage the social consumer and compete for tomorrow's future, today."

Brian Solis, Author of *Engage, The Complete Guide for Businesses to Build and Measure Success in the Social Web*

"This book offers a revolutionary idea: that you can win by timing your marketing to reach people who are actively sharing their location online instead of trying to blast them with irrelevant marketing at every hour of the day. Many now-defunct companies could have been saved by heeding this deceptively simple idea."

Rohit Bhargava, Author of *Personality Not Included* and EVP of Strategy & Planning at Ogilvy

Social Location Marketing

Outshining Your Competitors on Foursquare,
Gowalla, Yelp & Other Location Sharing Sites

Simon Salt

800 East 96th Street,
Indianapolis, Indiana 46240 USA

Social Location Marketing: Outshining Your Competitors on Foursquare, Gowalla, Yelp & Other Location Sharing Sites

Copyright © 2011 by Simon Salt

ISBN-10: 0-7897-4721-9

ISBN-13: 978-0-7897-4721-1

Library of Congress Cataloging-in-Publication data is on file.

Printed in the United States of America

First Printing: January 2011

Trademarks

All terms mentioned in this book that are known to be trademarks or service marks have been appropriately capitalized. Que Publishing cannot attest to the accuracy of this information. Use of a term in this book should not be regarded as affecting the validity of any trademark or service mark.

Warning and Disclaimer

Bulk Sales

Que Publishing offers excellent discounts on this book when ordered in quantity for bulk purchases or special sales. For more information, please contact

U.S. Corporate and Government Sales
1-800-382-3419
corpsales@pearsontechgroup.com

For sales outside of the U.S., please contact

International Sales
international@pearson.com

Associate Publisher
Greg Wiegand

Acquisitions Editor
Rick Kughen

Development Editor
Rick Kughen

Managing Editor
Sandra Schroeder

Project Editor
Mandie Frank

Copy Editor
Barbara Hacha

Indexer
Cheryl Lenser

Proofreader
Leslie Joseph

Technical Editor
Thomas Myer

Publishing Coordinator
Cindy Teeters

Designer
Anne Jones

Compositor
Mark Shirar

Reviewers
Julie Cary
Aaron Strout

TABLE OF CONTENTS

About the Author

Simon Salt—With a M.S. in Information Systems and a B.S. in Behavioral Science, Simon has been at the intersection of technology and human interaction for more than a decade. He has been a part of three successful startups and currently leads his own marketing communications company IncSlingers. As a social media influencer, Simon has been sought out by both large brands and international PR companies as an advisor and social media advocate. He also served as technical editor for Peter's Shankman's book, *Customer Service: New Rules for a Social-Enabled World*, published by Que. He describes himself as less of a writer and more of a talker who types fast. He can be found on most social media sites as "Incslinger."

Dedication

This book is dedicated to three women whose location is always known to me:
Alicia Helen Salt—March 1931-December 2008—In Memoriam
Gemima & Tessa Salt—two truly amazing daughters who inspire me always.

Acknowledgments

While only my name appears as author on this book, no book is a work of one individual. I am truly grateful to all of the following people.

Rick Kugen for being an amazing editor and making my first book so painless.

Thomas Myer for being not only a great technical editor but a friend and inspiration for actually committing to this book.

Michelle Lemire for being my original editor, my supporter, head cheerleader, and believing in me even when I didn't.

BJ Emerson at Tasti-Di-Lite, Amy Bradley Hole, the team at AJ Bombers, Kathy Mandlestein at IBM, Blair Smith at Austin Dirty Dog, and all the others who provided or directed me to case study material.

Haley Odom for sending me iPhone screenshots when I needed them in a rush.

To my own social network, in Austin and across the world, who have constantly supported my efforts to bring this book to life and have sent me words of encouragement without which I would never have made it to the end.

To the teams at Foursquare, Gowalla, SCVNGR, Yelp, Brightkite, Booyah, Whrrl, and all the other platforms for creating so much fun for the rest of us oversharers.

Aaron Strout, CMO at Powered, and Julie Cary, CMO at La Quinta, for their reviews of the initial concept and helping shape it into a more useful book.

We Want to Hear from You!

As the reader of this book, *you* are our most important critic and commentator. We value your opinion and want to know what we're doing right, what we could do better, what areas you'd like to see us publish in, and any other words of wisdom you're willing to pass our way.

As an associate publisher for Que Publishing, I welcome your comments. You can email or write me directly to let me know what you did or didn't like about this book—as well as what we can do to make our books better.

Please note that I cannot help you with technical problems related to the topic of this book. We do have a User Services group, however, where I will forward specific technical questions related to the book.

When you write, please be sure to include this book's title and author as well as your name, email address, and phone number. I will carefully review your comments and share them with the author and editors who worked on the book.

Email: feedback@quepublishing.com

Mail: Greg Wiegand
         Associate Publisher
         Que Publishing
         800 East 96th Street
         Indianapolis, IN 46240 USA

Reader Services

Visit our website and register this book at informit.com/register for convenient access to any updates, downloads, or errata that might be available for this book.

Introduction

A vision of the future:

Footsteps ring out on an empty street; a lone individual stalks the evening in search of a distraction. Unbidden, his hand slides into his pocket. His fingers caress the smooth edges of the weapon he is carrying. The engineers did a good job this time. Small but powerful was what he needed, small and powerful was what they delivered. Something that would pass unobtrusively in daily life. Something that would pass unnoticed and yet be very noticeable when used, that would separate him from the crowd as a connoisseur, as someone who knew what he is doing.

The sounds of music, voices, people enjoying themselves flood from doorways as the searcher passes them. Will they still be as happy if he chooses this location as his destination? Will this place meet his needs? He has an idea of what he is looking for, but as yet his prey is unclear. There is a certain thrill in this hunt, knowing as he does that he is armed with the device he is carrying: he has already won this battle in his mind.

He slows as he approaches each opportunity, pausing slightly to try to decide from the sounds emanating from within whether this is the location he is seeking. Door staff eye the individual, assessing him, not knowing that he has the power in his hands to decide their fate. Half beckoning, half rejecting him as he slows outside each, allowing the lights, music, and conversation to wash over him. These sensory indicators are mere distractions. They no longer factor into his decision; he is able to reject them as such, given the power from the device he is carrying they no longer concern him.

Searching is time consuming, but finding the right location is an essential part of his plan; it must have all the right elements and in the right mix. He is very selective, not just anywhere will do. He is confident that he will find just what he is looking for. He knows that both he and his device will find their target. After all, that is why he bought it, because with it he never need be lured to the wrong target again.

He arrives at a venue that seems, on the surface, to meet his needs: it's the right location, and the people inside seem to fit his image of what they would be like. He reaches again into his pocket, his hand finding the device. The door staff stiffens at the action. They have seen this before; they are wary, they don't want to react too quickly, but react they must.

He is armed, and fearless in his use of the weapon he carries, he will be merciless in its use. It gives him that power, and that power gives him the right to choose. Slowly withdrawing it, revealing the sleek black casing, he levels it at the front of the building. Taking careful aim, he zeros in on the sign above the door.

The screen on the weapon he has produced, only a few square inches in size, provides him with all the information he needs. Instantly he can see who he knows that is already inside, read their reviews and the reviews of critics, get the menu, the drinks list, and decide in a moment if this is where he will spend his hard-earned money. He is armed with a Smartphone, *the* weapon of the information age.

The year is 2011.

No, you are not reading a science-fiction novel, nor a wild hypothesis on what might be. Everything described in the preceding scenario is already available and already being used in its individual elements by consumers. Foursquare, Gowalla, Yelp, Layar, Google Goggles, and other tools are already empowering consumers to make more informed buying choices on a location-by-location basis. Mobile information-empowered consumers can make informed decisions as quickly as they can walk across the street. They can leave your location behind because of a lack of information and instead choose your competitor because their friends and trusted strangers have already been there and left enough data behind to enable consumers to make an informed buying decision.

This is the reality facing marketers in the modern age. You no longer get to control the message, the content, or the information that buyers see about your product, service, or location. This applies equally to the family owned corner store as it does to the multinational chain. Each location is seen as a separate and disparate entity by the consumer. The information being shared is not just about your brand but about the individual experience encountered by a users' network of trusted informants. People buying from people has always been the reality, especially in the small business space. In the information-powered age, it is even more so, because the people that users are buying from might not be your people but their own network, based on the information that network provides them. Long before they see your messaging they have received the messaging about your organization from their network and have already started to form an opinion as to whether you are a fit for their needs.

Influencing the buyer is not enough. Now you must influence the potential buyer's network; the organization must expand its vision beyond simple messaging to potential customers or users to be inclusive of those who are already users or customers and persuade them to make recommendations, to become advocates for your organization. The organization must be prepared to provide incentives and rewards for these advocates, whether they are active or passive advocates and be able to differentiate between the two.

Social location marketing is bringing businesses closer to their customers and potential customers than any other marketing tool in recent history. It is more powerful than any other form of social media and has higher rewards for a lower cost than any other form of digital marketing. Ignoring it will bring equally higher risks. Social location sharing is happening to your product, service, venue, and location whether you are active or not. This is not something you have the choice to opt in or out of. Unlike Facebook, Twitter, or LinkedIn, you don't get to decide your point of entry, no launch dates, no collateral marketing around it. Users have already decided whether you should join in.

By reading this book, you are taking the first steps in ensuring that your organization is a part of that new future and not losing customers to more information enabled environments. This future has already arrived and is accelerating in its empowerment of consumers daily as new applications and tools are launched to the market, all of which are free to use.

What's in This Book

This book is designed to be a how to book for marketers interested incorporating social location sharing platforms such as Foursquare and Gowalla into their marketing mix. In addition it includes real world case studies of companies that have already achieved success by doing so.

The book will take you through the following stages:

Chapter 1

Why Should I Bother?—Why people want to share their location with others and what is in it for them when they do. What is in it for businesses both large and small.

Chapter 2

Square Pegs and Round Holes: Where Does This All Fit?—Where does social location marketing fit into the broader scope of social media and how does it benefit the organization that is using it.

Chapter 3

Games People Play—Understanding the motivations of users through game theory. Why game play fits with sharers and how to design marketing campaigns that take advantage of this.

Chapter 4

Introduction to Location Sharing Tools—What are the platforms, what do they do, who uses them and which one should you use.

Chapter 5

Industries Making it Work—Which industries are already making social location marketing an active part of their marketing plans and what successes are they experiencing in doing so.

Chapter 6

Get Set, Go—Walk through setting up accounts on the major platforms, tips and tricks for getting the most out of them as a user and as a marketer.

Chapter 7

Marketing to Social Location Sharers—How different venues/locations can utilize social location sharing platforms as part of their marketing strategy, including single venue organizations, multiple venue organizations, organizations without a venue and business to business organizations.

Chapter 8

We're Here All Week—Event marketing with social location sharing platforms.

Chapter 9

Socially Speaking: The Social Business—Integrating all the pieces into one plan. Incorporating customer service into the plan and how it impacts social location marketing.

Chapter 10

Plan, Plan, Plan—What does a social business really look like, how to align an existing business and how to create one from scratch.

GEOSOCIAL NIGHTMARES

1

Why Should I Bother?

Social location sharing is the latest addition to the realm of social media/social networking and as such has a lot to offer individuals and businesses alike. The focus of this book is to illustrate how marketers can make use of the growing trend among the social-media savvy of sharing their location and their opinions about those locations.

The process of utilizing social location sharing tools as a marketing channel is known as social location marketing. Throughout the book I will use both social location sharing (SLS) and social location marketing (SLM). Social location sharing refers to the platforms and applications—such as Gowalla and Foursquare—as used by those sharing their locations. Social location marketing refers to the methods of marketing to those users.

This book examines why people would want to share their locations, the implications of doing so as an individual, and what is in it for those who do. It also offers insight into how businesses, both small and large, with and without physical locations, as well as those organizing events can use these tools as part of their marketing efforts.

The most popular of the social location sharing tools are examined in depth, with guides on how to set them up to benefit your business. Real-world case studies are included throughout the book, which illustrate how different businesses are already using these tools to gain competitive advantage and increase their revenues.

Social location marketing has the ability to impact the purchase decision cycle at all points—brand awareness, brand elevation, brand consideration and purchase. The concept of the purchase decision cycle is best defined as the continuous loop through which customers become aware, consider, select and finally reconsider purchases.

In the pre-social media market place, the purchase decision cycle involved much less influence from strangers. Purchasers were influenced by a closer network of people. Purchasers were also unable to take part in the level of comparison shopping that they are able to do now. Comparison shopping took time, it took effort and in the pre-Internet world, it actually involved travel. With the advent of the internet the travel requirement declined but it still took time to visit all the websites and make notes on which product had which features and which site was offering the best prices.

Price comparison sites quickly became popular with members posting coupon codes and special offers as they became aware of them. Social media took all of this to the next level. Twitter and Facebook users can post a question and receive hundreds of responses about the best deals, perhaps even getting responses directly from brands themselves.

Now social location sharing not only adds location but immediacy to the mix of that purchase decision cycle.

This is unlike most other forms of marketing communication channels, and as such is a major reason why marketers should be taking it very seriously. Given the low cost of entry, the returns have the potential to be much greater than many other forms of marketing communication and are achievable for all sizes and types of organizations—from the Fortune 500, through the small and medium business to the nonprofit and event-based organization. All of these can, are, and should benefit from taking part in social location marketing. What differentiates social location sharing from much of the rest of social media marketing is that it is specific to a location. It happens as someone becomes or is in the process of becoming a customer, visitor, or user. It is this immediacy that makes it so different, for both the

**Social Location Marketing plays a
part in every stage of the purchase decision cycle**

Figure 1.1   *Social location marketing's role in how your customers make buying
decisions.*

user and the business. This makes the data generated by social location sharing
tools incredibly valuable.

In Figure 1.1 you can see that the impact of social location marketing is extremely
broad. How can this be so? How can the simple act of a user checking in at a location have such a broad impact on a business and on the purchase decision cycle?

When users check in at a specific location, they are publicly declaring an affinity
with that location. Wittingly or unwittingly, they are making the statement that they
use this location as part of their lives. Whether it is a grocery store, a clothing shop,
a restaurant, or a hair salon, the effect is the same. They are telling the people in
their networks, all of whom they have selected to share with, that this is a place they
go to. Some of these places will have a certain cache attached to them, and therefore
the reason for sharing has an element of selfishness to it. Some users want their network to be aware that they can afford, gain entry to, or otherwise be associated with
a certain location—more because of what it says about them as a person than what
it says about the location.

At other times, users will have more altruistic motivations. For example, perhaps
they want to promote a local business because of the great service they have received
from them. They believe that by announcing this location and its great service, they
are helping to promote and prolong the business (which, of course, they are).

Event attendees have their own motivators for checking in. Checking in at a conference that has a desirability factor among peers and that is known for being a place at which to meet important figures within an industry is a way of establishing credibility. This shows that the user knows where it is important to be and who it is important to be seen with and learn from. Foursquare, in particular, leverages this "cool by association" factor in that it announces who else the user is checking in with at the same time (or within a certain time frame). Likewise, a music performance, festival, or even a flashmob can all have a cache of "being there" that adds credibility to the user. What would Woodstock have looked like with social location sharing?

All of these motivators can be leveraged by marketers and all have their place within the purchase decision cycle. In the following list, I have broken down the purchase decision cycle and explained how social location marketing affects each stage.

- **Brand Awareness:** Making the target audience aware of the existence of the brand. This is traditionally something that is associated with advertising, but in the current environment of a society that is more "word of mouth aware," getting existing customers to be your advertisers/advocates is a much more common effort. Social location sharing tools are most definitely achieving that. These tools broadcast the fact that the user is not only grocery shopping but is shopping at a specific grocery store. Regardless of whether it is a chain or a local store, the fact that a user is telling his network that he shops there calls attention to that brand and places it in the awareness of others who might not have encountered it before.

- **Brand Elevation:** Making the target audience aware of a brand is not usually enough to trigger a purchase. Rather, having made the target audience aware of the brand, the next step is to move the brand into the consideration stage of the purchase decision cycle. To do that, the brand needs to position itself as a better choice than its competitors. Again, social location sharing tools play their part here. Given that most brands face some kind of competition and that most customers have several choices for their purchase, positioning against those competitors and having more reasons for a purchase is extremely valuable to any business. Having an advocate in the form of a social location sharer share her decision to make a purchase at a location immediately aids that business in providing a reason why it is different from its competitors. Given that the people in the user's network are faced with the same, sometimes dizzying, array of choices, information that helps them make a decision quickly is considered valuable. A recommendation from a friend, whether delivered in person or via a social tool is very likely to move a business into the consideration phase for a new or returning buyer.

- **Consideration:** This stage can be immediately before purchase or can be several months, even years ahead of purchase. Much of this depends on the immediate need of the purchaser, the price point of the product or service, and the amount of information available. A customer looking to buy a pair of jeans is unlikely to spend the same amount of time in the consideration phase as a customer buying a new car or even a home. However, social location sharing tools can and do play a part in all these decisions. Users checking in at the Apple store, for example, are stating a preference for a particular brand, but they are also stating a preference for a particular type of technology. Among their networks will be people who are in the consideration phase of buying new technology. Seeing someone from their network whose opinion they value might give them an additional incentive to investigate a brand that they might otherwise have dismissed. By moving a brand, product, service, or location into the consideration phase a business has a much greater opportunity to convert a browser to a customer.

SOCIAL NETWORK ADVICE

Notice that Figure 1.1 has an additional phase from the traditional purchase path—social network advice. The ability for potential customers to gain recommendations, comparisons, even reviews of products, services, and so on from their networks has expanded exponentially with the increasing use of social networking/social media tools. Reaching out on Twitter, Facebook, LinkedIn and so on has become a normal part of the consideration process. Businesses that are a part of this community are more likely to be included in the final consideration set than those that are not. This is true of both businesses that are actively involved and those that are passively involved, especially when it comes to social location sharing. Many businesses whose venues are being checked in at are still—at least at the time of this writing—unaware that these tools even exist or that they are being used to promote, discuss, or rate their products and services. That said, more and more businesses are starting to incorporate social location marketing into their overall marketing plans. As overall awareness increases, so too will more imaginative rewards for customers.

- **Purchase:** Checking in at the time of purchase, and announcing that a purchase has been made, is obviously the most powerful use of these tools. Each of the tools allows for this in different ways, but at the most basic users can tag their check-in and in doing so start a conversation on other platforms such as Twitter. Because these conversations are happening at the time of a purchase, they provide the best opportunity for businesses to get feedback and join the conversation. Everything from a simple "Thank you" to a more detailed conversation shows that the brand is a part of the community, and that the company values its customers and wants more business from like-minded users.

Who Cares Where I Am?

As with most new technologies, the very early adopters are enthusiasts. They already understand the concept and some of the benefits of the new technology. They might even have a vision or share the vision of the creators as to where the new technology might go. As more people begin to adopt a new technology, a common question is asked: "So What?"

When Twitter started to gain popularity it was certainly the most common question, along with "Why would anyone want to know I am <insert banal activity here>?" So it is with social location sharing. Why should I bother telling people where I am? Who is really interested? And why would they care?

An additional concern that has been raised with social location sharing is that of safety. Is it a good idea to broadcast your location? Aren't you inviting stalkers to find you? Telling burglars that you are away from your home? Especially for women, these questions have become prominent among those who are both trying to raise genuine concerns and those who are against the general "over sharing" trend. We will discuss the safety implications of these tools later in the book, from both the perspective of the user and of the locations.

So why does anyone want to share their location with the world, and what would make them want to continue to do so in the face of all of these concerns? Competition, rewards, and incentives are definitely part of the answer, as is the ability to share when they are somewhere that has a "cool" factor attached to it. Knowing the why's makes it easier for the marketer to appeal to the users and create reasons for their location, event, or business to be included in the free publicity that social location sharing provides. Chapter 3, "Games People Play," explores the motivations behind why people get involved in these types of games and activities. This is important for marketers and business owners to understand so that they can ensure they are including the right type of offers, targeted at the right type of user, on the right platform.

What's in It for the Individual?

From a user perspective, social location sharing appears, on the surface, to be nothing more than a game. Check in more times than your friends and claim the title of "Mayor" of a location, visit a cool bar and collect a funky guitar, visit your favorite restaurant and buy it virtually. So what? In much the same way that new Twitter users are stumped by the question "What are you doing?" new social location sharing users find the act of checking in at a location somewhat pointless. As a friend of mine says, "other than enabling stalkers, what exactly are you getting out of it?"

Although some early adopters think that the current value of social location sharing to the average user is minimal, this is mainly isolated to users who stay mostly in their home towns. If a user checks in at the same restaurant as her friends, she might get a recommendation for an alternative restaurant, but that's it. Although this was certainly true at the end of 2009 and early 2010—before businesses became aware of the marketing implications of these tools—it is less true now and will become decreasingly relevant as a criticism of these tools as adoption from the business community increases and the rewards offered by them increase. Users who travel have been realizing different benefits from these tools almost since joining these communities. Mostly these have come in terms of recommendations for places to visit, things to do, and the potential of meeting other users—the core of social media. It is this last element, the ability to connect individuals (the core of good social media platforms) that adds real value to users. New friendships are created, new business is agreed, and new networks are strengthened and grown.

Just as Twitter has spawned numerous add-on services and applications, social location sharing tools are doing the same thing by opening up their APIs. As these new tools start to appear, the value of the social location sharing tools increases. Also, as marketers start to realize the real potential of these tools, the user benefit increases accordingly. Already we are starting to see the appearance of some very innovative tools that leverage the use of social location sharing and reward users for sharing their locations. The case studies in this book include some good examples of how both companies and users can benefit from a little imaginative thinking—from small business tools to integration with point of sale systems. These are only the beginning.

 Note

Want to see a definitive list of add-on services and applications spawned by Twitter? Go to: OneForty (www.oneforty.com).

The organizations that are providing the best user rewards are those that already have some form of customer loyalty program in place. Cafes, bookstores, gas stations, airlines, and so on have all been leveraging the concept of "frequent visitor" loyalty for a long time. Social location sharing now allows the customer to not only take part in a social game but be rewarded for doing so. As more industries start to see this benefit to them, we, as users, can expect to see more places offering rewards. Businesses need to start realizing the benefit of knowing that they have regular customers and believing that it really is easier—or at least less expensive—to keep a customer than to obtain a new one. As is often the case in marketing communication, small businesses are early to realize the truth of this. They do not have the luxury of ignoring customers. They have to fight for each one and in doing so realize that the closer they make the customer feel, the better the chances are that the customer will return.

Industries such as the airlines have had multi-tiered reward programs in place for a long time, and by combining it with social location sharing they can not only provide added rewards but can use these tools to be more in touch with their customers. It's one thing for an airline to sell you a ticket, to know that you have checked in for your flight, but quite another for them to see, in real–time, what you think of the gate where you are sitting, the service you received from the staff, and what you thought of the flight attendants.

This level of sharing not only benefits users in that they feel more empowered to be able to tell their friends, followers, and so forth about their experiences, but it allows the organizations concerned to respond in a more timely fashion.

Currently, rewards tend toward the lower value. This is appropriate given that the technology still lends itself to being "gamed," and why would a marketer want to risk a high-value reward for someone who has cheated the system? As these bugs get worked out, we can expect to see more high-value rewards being offered for loyalty. Hotels offering a free night's accommodation, free upgrades, and all things they offer in other marketing promotions will start to find their way into social location sharing.

Competitions based around social location sharing are already starting to appear. Time-limited offers based on frequency of check in, number of different locations checked in at, and even the platform used are all being rewarded in various ways. Because of the nascent state of social location marketing, organizations are still very much in the stage of trail and error. Users of social location sharing tools will be the ones who benefit from the additional offers and marketing efforts that appear because of social location marketing. Also, as the accuracy of the software reading your location from the GPS chip increases, so too are marketers gaining confidence in offering prizes with real-world value. Adobe partnered with Gowalla to place virtual versions of their new software release (CS5) at various locations across the United States. For example, when the Gowalla user found the virtual copy, the user was informed that he or she had in fact won a copy of the actual software, a $1500 value. This is certainly a great way to both promote a product and gain users of the social location sharing platform at the same time.

So what is really in it for you as the individual? As an early adopter, it is primarily a sense of competition. If competition isn't something that you are motivated by, then the rewards that are increasingly being offered by businesses through social location sharing tools will certainly attract you. These rewards will overshadow the competitive nature of social location marketing and lead to a broader adoption.

Of these secondary features, the most compelling—and the one that is greatly overlooked at the moment because of its nascent state—is rich content. Being able to view not only friends' thoughts on a product, service, or venue but also "expert" opinion drawn from valued sources is going to become a compelling reason why these tools will see a greater adoption rate. Imagine being able to read a venue's menu, critic reviews, and friend reviews and suggestions all on one screen before entering and ordering a meal.

As we see the convergence of existing data on various platforms being drawn together into these tools, the time each individual spends with the tool will increase. We will see a transition from simply checking in to actually reading, annotating, and making decisions based on the information provided. Why would someone go to a venue that their friends have dismissed, even if the critics love it? Combining both network opinion with valued "expert" opinion and even "informed stranger" opinion into one information stream is the direction that the major players in social location sharing are taking us. This makes the need for search capability obvious.

The ability to get recommendations for alternatives will also be a compelling feature of these platforms as they evolve. Having a friend tell you that you probably won't like a particular restaurant is one thing. Having a friend recommend an alternative restaurant is even better. Better still is a recommendation that comes with a map showing how to get there, a menu, and of course the reviews of the new location. It can start to sound all a little too sci-fi—a cross between Big Brother and *Minority Report*—and I'm sure the conspiracy theorists are having kittens reading about the new data that is being captured about an individual's movements. The reality is, the technology has been unboxed—no one is going to repack and return it, and those who adopt early will benefit early.

The benefits of these services are likely to expand to include notification of special deals, available only to users of these tools. This will also increase adoption and will ultimately fuel even more of these types of offers. So even for those who aren't game players, getting involved early on and deciding which of the various tools to use could ultimately lead to much greater rewards in the near future.

What's in It for the Small Business?

Small businesses have long had an advantage in the social media space. They are traditionally much closer to their customers and have become used to developing relationships and handling feedback at a personal level. Social media is simply another tool in the small business arsenal and allows the businesses to do what they have already been doing in a more organized, trackable, and measurable way.

Social location sharing is no exception to this. Knowing when their customers are at one of their locations, knowing which of their customers are regulars, and which are first timers is all extremely valuable information to any small business, regardless of the type of business. The TV show *Cheers* comes immediately to mind when thinking of a location that knows its regulars. In the show, the patrons were greeted by name and the bar staff knew their favorite drinks, what was going on in their lives and were considered friends. Many small businesses do operate that way.

However, not all small business have embraced social location marketing, and not all are even able to do so. A busy café might not have the bandwidth to be able to pick out regulars from semi-regulars from first timers. However, using social location sharing tools allows them to gain that insight, even if it is after the fact. Whereas it might not come as a surprise to a small business who becomes "Mayor" of its location, it might surprise that business to learn who the other regulars are that are sharing the location with others and what types of comments they are making about that location. It is the sharing aspect that many venues overlook. As the term implies, if users share their location, they must be sharing it with someone. In fact, in the case of social location sharing tools, users are likely to be sharing it with a lot of someones (via the user's personal network—many of whom live in the same geographic location). The simple act of sharing a location, without even adding a comment, validates that location among the user's network. The people in this user's network see where the user is, think about the activity that takes place at that location (coffee, food, music, and so on), and include that venue in their consideration phase the next time they are looking to take part in the same activity.

Getting on the radar is incredibly important for any small business. Most do not have the budget for advertising campaigns, and when they do it tends toward the mass communication type, such as Yellow pages, local newspapers, and perhaps radio. What is more powerful is word of mouth. The referral to their business by a satisfied customer has long been the way most small businesses grow.

In marketing terms, being a part of the consideration phase of the purchase decision cycle is essential to being chosen as a vendor. People have to know you exist first (brand awareness) before they can consider you. To be considered, they must attach some value to the business—something must prompt them to increase their value judgment of the business (brand elevation). When this occurs the potential customer can then place the business into the consideration phase, which is what ultimately leads to sales.

Social location sharing achieves brand awareness and elevation for the small business in a way that is not possible at the same price point for many other communication channels. In many cases, it is happening without the business even knowing, just as it has before the creation of these social location sharing tools, through word of mouth. However, social media in general, and social location sharing tools in particular, allow the business owner to become aware of these conversations and, time permitting, even join them.

All other forms of awareness and elevation activity undertaken by small businesses lack the feedback that social media in general and social location sharing in particular give access to. Although having lots of Twitter followers is nice, it is ultimately just that, a number. The number of check ins at a venue has a direct effect on the money at the checkout. These are more than just followers or fans—they are real customers who are at the location. They are spending money with the business, and they are telling others about their activity. This is a huge opportunity to both reward and take advantage of that behavior. Reinforcing this behavior with positive rewards for customers will encourage them to do it more often.

The rewards can be simple, low cost, or even free. Recently a friend of mine became Mayor of a coffee shop that was an outlet of a national chain. However, the staff at that outlet treat it as though it were the only one of its kind and treat their customers the same way. When they noticed that the customer had become Mayor, they put up a whiteboard sign, which they produced at her next visit, congratulating her on becoming Mayor and gave her a free coffee that day. Simple, cheap, and the reason I know of this story is because she took a picture of the sign and shared it with her network. Free promotion for that coffee shop. Notice the correlation here between having the information and acting on it. No point in having all this rich data if you don't use it to both improve the customer experience and increase affinity with the location.

Being armed with this information allows venues to provide a better experience for customers, regardless of whether those customers are regulars. Read the case study on AJBombers in Chapter 6, "Get Set, Go" on how they adapted their menu based on feedback left via Twitter. This type of inclusion, although possible before, is now not only possible but desired by customers. Social location sharing tools provide customers with both the ability and the outlet to give valuable feedback to the venue.

Social location sharing tools can bring other benefits to small businesses beyond simply understanding their customer's behavior. With the creation of open APIs and the advent of third-party applications utilizing the data captured by social location sharing tools, information that would have been extremely difficult and costly for a small business to capture is now becoming available.

One type of application that is being developed mixes Foursquare data with that of Google maps to produce heat maps of check ins, like the one shown in Figure 1.2.

While still in development as of April 2010, this type of tool has many applications beyond producing pretty pictures for individual users. As you can see in Figure 1.2, the heat map (which is for my check ins in Austin) gives an immediate picture of where I am most likely to check in and which parts of town hold the most appeal for me as an individual user. Applying this to the small business space, we can extrapolate the following example:

Figure 1.2   *This map mixes Foursquare data with Google maps data to show a heat map of check-ins.*

A service call business providing air conditioning services for homes or businesses could have technicians use Foursquare to check in at each call. Using a heat map service, they can then see exactly which part of town their most frequent calls are from, and more importantly which part of town they are not getting calls from. This would allow them to make very targeted marketing efforts instead of simply blanketing the city with their message. If doing so achieves nothing else, it helps reduce the cost of materials and the time distributing them, depending on how they are acquiring new business. Even if they don't decide to go after this area of town, they can at least get a sense of where their best customers are and the ones that give them only occasional business. Again this information aids the business in building greater affinity with customers when combined with other information that the business already has.

Previously, this type of technique would have been cost prohibitive for most types of small business. However, with free tools like this, small businesses are able to compete with much more sophisticated software used by larger companies. Now instead of wondering where their next customer is coming from, they can specifi-cally market to an area that is currently not using their service and may not be aware that their company exists.

Social location sharing for this type of company just became more than a game. Again, this is all a part of the brand awareness, brand elevation, consideration, purchase paradigm that larger companies operate on all the time but that many small businesses have previously not had the tools to use or even the knowledge to implement. Social media is not only bringing customers closer to all businesses, large and small, but it's leveling the playing field between different sized organizations.

This type of tool shows that social location sharing is not just for the business-to-consumer market, but can be leveraged by the business-to-business market as well. It is the broad spectrum adoption that will ensure that these tools become an essential part of the marketer's general arsenal. The business-to-business space has struggled with how to successfully use most social media tools, and social location sharing is no exception. Small businesses in this space, who are often service/product providers to much larger organizations, struggle with how to use these tools to communicate with their customers and potential customers.

However, as you can see in detail in the Ideaworks case study in Chapter 8, "We're Here All Week," social location sharing can become a valuable method of communicating to potential clients and increasing your business network in a way that leads to more business. Using social location sharing tools as part of an organization's outreach to its local business community is a great method of providing awareness of the services/products provided by the company.

For example, perhaps you operate a catering service company that provides the hardware used in coffee shops, restaurants, and bars. Checking in at your potential client's premises and leaving a tip or comment that highlights a particular need—a need that your organization can fulfill—can be a way to introduce your services without actually cold calling the owner. You have planted a seed—one that other customers will no doubt comment on and one that, providing the establishment is listening (and they should be) will have to take action on. Why not call on them to say that you have noticed the comments about their wobbly chairs? Tell them about your great deals on café chairs. It's a conversation starter.

What's in It for Larger Businesses?

Scaling social media, as with any marketing effort is always a challenge. Just because the local coffee shop has managed to increase its customer base using social location sharing doesn't mean a chain of stores can translate that activity into new customers. The economies are different; the ability to connect at an individual customer level is a much greater challenge. The fact that marketing departments are often siloed in large businesses doesn't aid these efforts. Social media is often the red-headed stepchild of the marketing world. In some organizations, everyone wants to own it because it is seen as new and impactful. In others, no one wants it, because it is seen as unproven and a waste of time. Does it belong in PR, advertising, customer support, online marketing, or general marketing? Different answers are found in every organization.

Where it fits into an organization has to be somewhere that can leverage the information that is going to flow into the organization. That information is going to be a stream that requires some analysis. Some of it will contain sales opportunities, some of it will contain customer support opportunities, some of it will be advocacy data, and some will be simple mentions in various social networks. All of this needs to be routed to the appropriate departments and acted upon. All this also has to happen without creating analysis paralysis, which is the state achieved when an organization is facing so much information it simply can't act on it.

Later in the book we will explore strategies that work in large-scale environments that enable organizations to make use of the data in ways that leverage the competitive advantage the data can bring and feed back to the bottom line.

Automation is certainly one solution, and companies like Tasti-di-Lite have made some very good inroads in this area (see the Tasti-di-lite case study in Chapter 10, "Plan, Plan, Plan"). By making it easier for customers to take part in social location sharing, rewarding them for doing so and tying them into a customer loyalty program in one action, larger organizations can definitely benefit from and utilize social location sharing tools.

Where larger organizations have an advantage in social location sharing—as they do in all aspects of business—is volume. A local café might see between 20 to 100 customers in a day. A big box store might see somewhere in the order of 100 times that many people in a day. By giving those customers an incentive to use social location sharing as part of a customer loyalty program, these stores can produce a wealth of data and a flood of consumer-generated content that is broadcast across multiple social media platforms. Leveraging this data, observing trends and frequencies, is something that large companies already do. Having real-time data will make these observations even more powerful.

Leveraging existing partnerships, especially those that offer market development funds is another avenue that is primarily open to the larger businesses. Because they are volume buyers and sellers, organizations without physical locations—such as manufacturers who sell through resellers or retail outlets—can still take part in social location sharing. For example, a beverage company might run an incentive for stores that work with them on a promotion in which customers check in when purchasing their product and add that information to their check in. The beverage company could take that one step further and extend the offer if the beverage is then included in pictures of other locations where the user checks in.

Social location sharing data combined with sales data can add an extremely useful dimension. Knowing that running a 10% off discount on a Tuesday leads to increased sales is great, but knowing who among those buyers are regulars and who among them are first timers is even more powerful, especially when tied into the marketing communications effort that enveloped the offer. Now a company has a sense of who they are reaching and whether these buyers are already brand aware— or are they new to the brand? Add to that the geographic data, and regional targeting becomes an even more powerful marketing method. Perhaps Tuesdays work in New York but Wednesdays are better in Los Angeles for bringing in new customers. Existing customers prefer Mondays and Wednesdays, so maybe a loyalty card incentive would work well for them. The possibility to, appear closer to the customer increases customer affinity. As customers, we find ourselves liking a brand that wants to communicate with us in a way we understand, in much the same way we do with those who are not native speakers of our own language. We applaud their efforts, make allowances for the odd mistake in phrasing because at least there is an effort being made.

TYING CUSTOMER LOYALTY TO SOCIAL LOCATION SHARING

An example of how large businesses can put social location sharing tools to work for them is to create a customer loyalty program for a chain of clothing stores that is tied into social location sharing tools. Customers who check in at the store are rewarded by the social location sharing tool that they use. However, if they tie their account to their store-based customer loyalty account, they not only receive rewards from the social location sharing tool but from the store as well. If they receive a special discount and agree to connect their social location sharing account with their other social media accounts (more on the discussion of privacy later) then they not only get their discount but now they are broadcasting that discount to their network. For example, "I just earned 20% off at XYZ stores, you can too" might be their Twitter status update or a Wall post on their Facebook page. All of this is automated at the point of sale, so the customer does nothing other than make a purchase and use their loyalty card to earn rewards.

Making it easy for the customer, through the use of technology is and always has been an advantage of larger businesses over small ones. Think about devices such as the self-service checkout installed in so many chain grocery stores. These are beyond the scope of most small business, but also a method by which the customer can avoid interacting with store staff and thus being drawn into an affinity situation. Social location sharing data means that larger companies can still offer this "hands-off," one step removed advantage to those of their customers who prefer it, while still building affinity.

Whereas smaller businesses rely on the customer to do the work, larger businesses are often in a position to take most of this burden away from the customer, which increases adoption and frequency of use. By increasing the adoption rate and the use of these tools, businesses can build ever-larger amounts of user data. Remember that it is not just the real-time nature of the data but the fact that these tools also store historical data along with the competitive data that makes them powerful to organizations.

Knowing when someone stops becoming Mayor of a location is just as useful as knowing when they become the Mayor. Sending them a message to invite them back to regain their mayorship is a quick and easy way of reminding them that they have been a frequent customer and that they should come back. Giving them an incentive to do so may well hasten the visit. This also plays on the competitive nature of these platforms. A sliding scale of rewards that includes not only becoming Mayor but "ousting" an existing Mayor definitely makes people want to take part.

Likewise, for Gowalla users, being aware of which items are currently at your locations and promoting those items is a simple and free way of joining in the game without increasing marketing spending. Rewarding the players who collect items or leave items at your locations, especially items that have a connection to the venue, is a way to give players an incentive to include the location in their gaming behavior. Later in the book we will look at specific cases where doing this pays off, and also how partnering with the various companies behind the platforms can produce interesting elements to campaigns, along with some examples of the costs associated with running these campaigns.

As with so much of social media, companies are only starting to scratch the surface of the ways in which they are able to connect with their customers and answer the overwhelming question, "What's in it for me?" asked when a customer is approached by a business. Customers do not willingly give up their information for no gain, whether that gain is real or virtual. By combining a sense of "joining in" and exceptional marketing, the customer is more likely to not only give up information but continue to do so across other platforms.

Social location marketing, like any channel, should not be considered a standalone activity. To be truly effective it needs to be part of a much more integrated marketing communications strategy. We'll discuss some of these options in Chapter 2, "Square Pegs and Round Holes: Where Does This All Fit?" when we look at where social location marketing fits as part of the broader social media strategies. But it is worth noting that a strategy that doesn't pull the data from social location marketing and incorporate it into other elements is a waste. Email, direct mail, and so on can all benefit from the data drawn from these tools.

As you explore this book, keep in mind that all the strategies and ideas are not meant to stand alone. Make sure that you're thinking of how to incorporate them into your existing and planned activities. Just as with social media in general, social location marketing is not a silver bullet. It is not a recipe for overnight success for your ailing business. If you have things to fix in your organization, social location marketing—or for that matter, social media in general—is not something you should be doing. Go fix your issues first, and then come back and join in the fun and games.

2

Square Pegs and Round Holes: Where Does This All Fit?

Social media has become the next greatest business savior in the past 3–5 years. In actuality, the technology has been around for more than a decade, but like so many technology stories it takes a while for the business applications to finally appear and be adopted on a broad enough scale that they are taken seriously. Of course, its real ability to save a company is highly suspect. Social media is not a silver bullet (I will repeat that mantra throughout this book).

This might seem strange coming from someone who makes a living from selling social media consultancy to organizations. But I am nothing if not honest about the capability of social media to save a company. If your products, services, or your organization generally faces major issues, social media is unlikely to be able to save it on its own, although it can be a part of communicating the solutions that you have found. An example that was very relevant at the time this book was written was with the BP oil spill in the Gulf of Mexico. Although BP could have used social media as one part of a much larger strategy to regain public trust, it would not have been able to change public opinion about the damage from the spill via social media alone. While a formidable tool, social media doesn't have that kind of massive impact. Real-world action has to accompany it. Social media is a communication channel, not a magic wand.

While many companies are still pondering the pros and cons of blogs, others are wondering if they can really achieve sales via Twitter. However, other companies have successfully incorporated these technologies (and more) into what they do and how they do it to the point where it no longer needs a special status.

What is Social Media?

Social media can be described as services, tools and platforms such as Twitter, Facebook, LinkedIn and others that allow users to share information with each other.

Often the term social networking is used interchangeably with social media. I tend to disagree with this usage. Social networking is something that is enabled by social media platforms. However, social networking is not the only use of social media.

Social media lends itself well to the marketing world and in fact social media marketing is what has led to the increase in use of social media. Social media has created is a new world of content creators. This content can come in the form of simple status updates, such as "I'm walking the dog", or via pictures, videos, blog posts, or even product reviews.

Social media has also created a new currency, often referred to as social capital. Social capital is the ability to perform tasks for others in the hope of some form of reciprocity. This might be introducing one person in your network to another person in your network to aid them in job hunting. You are expending social capital on behalf of the first person.

Alongside this is the concept of influence, which is the ability to get other people to perform tasks on your behalf. In its simplest form this is often the ability to get people to click on a link and go to a particular website. At its more complex, influence becomes part of a marketing campaign and the influencer is promoting a product, service or company to increase usage, adoption or awareness.

 Note

Want to learn more about social media marketing in particular? If so, I recommend that you pick up a copy of *Social Location Marketing: Strategies for Engaging in Facebook, Twitter and Other Social Media,* by Liana Evans (published by Que).

Who Is in Charge?

Social media is a part—or should be a part—of normal marketing communications operations. So what does that look like within a strategy? First, companies need to decide where social media resides. If PR is the normal channel for communicating with the outside world, then that is where social media sits. If the online marketing department handles communications, it should handle social media. The problem for most organizations is that communication can be and is often handled by differing parts of the company. PR handles the media and so seems a natural fit for social media. Marketing handles customer and prospect communication, so again that seems like a natural fit. When organizations divide marketing into offline and online activities, the online organization seems a natural fit. These types of turf wars are often resolved in a way that fits more with the internal politics of the organization than with a real understanding of the channels. One solution is to create a new organization made up of the differing disciplines. However, this can lead to even greater segmentation within an organization and also lead to the trap of social media being sidelined—or worse, being given an overly high profile within an organization. Although it is an important element in any organization's toolkit, social media is not a silver bullet. It should not be given a status that starves other marketing communication methods of attention or creativity. Rather, it should operate in unison with these channels.

Placing social media within the online marketing organization makes sense to a lot of companies because they see social media as another online channel through which to direct their customer acquisition activities. Certainly, online marketers will generally understand the behavior of people engaging in social media and are well placed to establish some of the metrics that can and should be used to measure social media activity. However, PR has an important role to play as well, especially in the more complex types of engagements that include elements such as blogger outreach. Leveraging the PR department's experience with mass media will certainly benefit any organization thinking through a social media plan.

It is important for organizations to realize, however, that social media is different from other forms of marketing communication in that it has a two-way flow to it. For example, sending an email blast might get the response you want, but most recipients won't reply via email to your original blast. In fact, most email blasts are set up so that the recipients can't reply directly. Social media isn't like that—users have the expectation that they are in fact invited to respond and to communicate with the organization that has a presence on a social media platform. This is where choosing where exactly social media will reside within an organization becomes critical.

For the most part, PR and online marketing departments are used to operating in a vacuum. They do not usually engage directly with customers or prospects, which leads some organizations to place social media in the customer support or even sales functions, because these have more direct customer contact experience. Although this meets the needs of the customer or prospect, it often fails to meet the operational and strategic needs of the organization, especially those who are trying to use social media to communicate brand messaging. In fact, by placing social media solely in the hands of your customer support department, social media is considered by some companies to be a "precious" resource—something that should never be abused or sullied with something as gauche as a marketing message. This "touchy feely" theme has gained ground among some proponents of social media as a method to "listen", "engage" and "get closer" to the customer. Although these certainly play a part of any good social media strategy, they have to be balanced with objectives that produce results. It is hard to convince the C-Suite that increases in "likes" on the company Facebook page is actually a measure of success if they see no corresponding bottom-line improvement. I know of no business that has achieved growth, increased market share, or improved revenue based on the number of "followers" or "likes" that they have received.

In addition, social media users do not care how your company is organized. This often comes as a shock to large organizations that have spent time, money, and resources on deciding exactly how to divide the operating expense, revenue, marketing budgets, and other costs into neat compartments that make tracking activity and results so much easier. For example, a customer might figure out that she can get a better deal from the Small Office/Home Office division of a company rather than buying as a consumer. If so, that customer isn't going to be concerned about what impact choosing one over the other has on the business metrics. The customer just wants the best deal.

Likewise in social media, if a company has an account that is specifically created to promote new offers, it is likely it can expect that account to receive customer support questions. If the company has a customer support account, it should expect that account to receive sales inquiries. Social media users are looking for information that is helpful to them; they don't want to do the extra work involved in accurately identifying what an account's internal purpose is. For evidence of this, take a look at the number of questions that are asked on Twitter that the user could easily have used a search engine to find the answer. Many users would rather type the question and wait for the answers to come to them. Understanding this type of approach to information gathering can ensure that organizations plan their use of social media accordingly. Look at it from the audience's perspective and the possibility exists that the company will achieve a lot more than looking at it from an internal perspective.

This means that whatever department is given the task of operating social media accounts must be aware of the other relevant divisions within the same organization. For a small business, this might be one or maybe two people who are also multitasking on other fronts. So the issue is never really a problem, or it shouldn't be. However, in larger organizations, this can be a real issue, especially where sales commission and other incentives attached to performance are affected.

This impact needs to be factored into a strategy that hopes to achieve widespread adoption across an organization. Does a marketer operating a Twitter account who answers a sales lead share in the commission for that sale? Does a salesperson who answers a customer service question get part of the customer service operator's bonus? Clearly, these things have to be thought through when defining a social media strategy. It is as much about internal alignment as it is about communicating with customers and potential customers. Often setting up a social media strategy will highlight internal communication friction points, and it is important to address these before launching a serious social media effort. A potential customer is unlikely to be very impressed by a response to a question on Facebook that says, "I don't know the answer to that, I only do marketing."

Although it would be impossible for any one person to know all the answers to questions for any particular large organization, what *is* important is the following:

- The person running your social media efforts knows where to find answers.

- The person running your social media efforts knows how to route customer inquiries to the right person or department.

- The person running your social media efforts must be empowered to conduct the necessary interdepartmental follow-ups to ensure that the customer is responded to in a timely fashion.

WHAT'S YOUR DEFINITION OF TIMELY?

What constitutes a timely fashion in social media is not what most large organizations are used to. On Twitter, a user expects a response in a few minutes. On Facebook, a user might allow 30 minutes for a company to respond. By contrast, a company can reasonably expect to have 24-48 hours to respond to an email. Social media is immediate, and the users of it expect immediate responses. Noticing two days later that someone reached out to one of the company's accounts to ask a sales question is too late. That person has already moved on, quite probably to a competitor. In addition, it is not enough to simply notice when someone is directly talking to one of the accounts; it is important to notice and take action when a user is talking about the organization or its brands.

Where Is Everyone?

All this has to be taken into consideration when creating a social media strategy. A strong awareness of where the target audience spends most of its time is very important to any organization. Before committing to a particular channel, any organization should confirm that the people they want to communicate with are actually using that channel. This is true of all organizations but especially so for the smaller business. For these, the choice of social media channels can seem bewildering. "Where will I find the time?" is the most often asked question by the small business sector when thinking of social media. For already time-constrained businesses, the prospect of spending hours on Twitter or Facebook or trying to create content for a blog seems just one more task that will go on the to-do list, never to be actually crossed off. Worse still is when businesses try a shotgun approach to social media and attempt to use all the channels at once in the hope that they will reach someone, anyone, just so that they can show that it works and that they are in fact "engaging" the audience.

Whereas an element of experimentation is always good and often attractive given the relative low cost of entry of social media, it's also true that it can produce results that had not been previously considered. All this should be undertaken with an element of caution. Blunders in social media can be very high profile, and the audience has become increasingly unforgiving in its response to campaigns it considers to be disingenuous to the medium. Audience identification does not necessarily require the use of sophisticated tools. There is no shortage of social media "listening" tools, many of which are worth considering as part of the broader strategy. However, utilizing free tools to establish a basic understanding of the platforms is usually all that is required. Using the search tools built into free social media tools will be effective. In fact, you can save a lot of wasted effort and false starts by taking the simple approach first. Regardless of whether the strategy is for small or large business, a strategy that starts small and builds as competency increases is much more likely to produce results than one that proposes multiple launches across multiple platforms.

After you have identified a starting place, it is not enough to set up a Twitter account, or a Facebook business page, or any other social media presence and then sit back and expect the people to arrive on their own. The strategy has to include the content that will attract the potential audience and the methodology for making that audience aware that the content is available. The belief that the audience will generate the content is sadly untrue. User-generated content has long been seen as the panacea to the issues of developing compelling content for organizations. Compelling content was seen as the solution to driving traffic to a website. Driving website traffic was seen as the solution to online brand awareness and brand elevation. This is the flaw that so many social media strategies are built on. User generated content is not like graffiti. Just because you build a wall, it doesn't mean someone will write on it.

Although conversations happen about brands, products, services, and organizations on social media platforms, they do not necessarily happen at the time and location of the organization's choosing. In fact, the majority don't. So the "build it and they will come" philosophy is flawed.

Instead of expecting users to generate your content, you need a strategy that places your company where the conversations are happening and positions it to listen and then respond. Early social media strategies focused a lot on the listening piece. In fact "listening" was the mantra of the social media world in 2009. Whenever a social media "guru" was heard to be giving advice, the word "listen" was always uttered. However, I disagree with this. If your social media policy stops at listening, you are neutering your organization. Responding to what is being said and preempting what might be said are the keys to a successful social media strategy. In the world of social media, actions do speak louder than words. Acting on what an organization is hearing is the key to executing a successful strategy. Many companies struggle in deciding what action to take. That is not to say listening is not a part of the strategy—it most definitely is. To reiterate, the listening isn't where it ends.

Keeping Your Ear to the Ground

So how does an organization listen to social media? The method can be as simple as using the search function built in to free social media monitoring tools. Certainly for the very small business or for those with a very narrow focus, this will usually suffice, at least early on. For the larger organization and especially those that intend to use social media for more than one purpose, the investment in a more robust social media monitoring tool or service is essential. There are many such tools to choose from, and ultimately budget and importance of social media to the organization will be deciding factors.

It is possible to build free listening tools fairly easily using RSS readers such as Google Reader and the output of the search function from platforms such as Twitter. What differentiates this approach and makes it unsuitable for most organizations of any size is the lack of filters and contextualization. Although the free option is appealing because of its free nature, it can prove quite costly in the amount of time that is required to weed through all the results—especially at first, when the terms being used in the search are not as focused as they might be or if the user doesn't understand how to utilize logic operators (AND, OR, NOT) in search terms.

This is where investing in a service or tool can pay big dividends. Also, most third-party services or tools provide some form of "sentiment" analysis, which allows for quick parsing of feedback into groups, such as good, bad, and indifferent. This sentiment analysis saves time, but does have a steeper learning curve than what you'll find with free monitoring tools. However, after you have mastered these more advanced tools, you'll be able to turn data into actionable information. A good strategic plan will include the use of one of these tools.

They Said *What?*

Rushing to defend a brand, product, or service just because it attracts a negative blog post is not necessarily the best course of action. Although no voice should go unheard, there are degrees of response. If the blogger's audience is limited to perhaps only a few readers a day, then should an organization mobilize the full weight of their PR department in reaching out to them? Obviously not. It is this contextual piece that is also important in the listening. Know who you are listening to and what is the person's angle? Who else is listening to him? Does he have a platform? Can he influence your audience? This is why the listening piece of social media is a lot more complex than many marketers realize. It is not enough to count how many times your product was mentioned or how many times your branded tweets were re-tweeted. Knowing the level of influence of those you are interacting with is crucial to being able to cope with the volume of interactions that many brands will receive.

By making these assessments, an organization can prioritize its outreach and its responses. In effect, you are carrying out social media triage. This helps to ensure that the resources you have, which might be limited, are directed where they are needed most and can achieve most. I have never encountered a marketing department that had unlimited resources. In fact, it's usually quite the opposite—they have too much to do with too few bodies to achieve it.

Trying to counter every criticism with a well-thought-out blog post, tweet, Facebook post, or video comment would burn out most marketing departments before they ever started achieving goals in social media. By targeting their responses, organizations can achieve the same effect. Responding to those who have a large influence will often reach the other commentators on the same topic. Many of the secondary or less influential content creators will have used the topic simply to generate traffic—they are the "me too" content creators who are adding to the overall noise because they see the potential for them of posting about a trending topic. By answering the most influential of the content creators—or if possible, the originator—the entire group of commentators are often answered. Instead of making 100 responses, a company can often quiet the crowd with one or two well-placed responses. This frees up the resources to focus on other activities and still allows the organization to be responsive.

For example, suppose an organization notices that they have some detractors in the blogosphere. If that organization takes the time to identify who they are, what their reach is, the number of visitors their blog gets, how many comments each post receives, the company can decide if it is worth doing some form of counter blog activity or outreach to the content creator. Often the creators are looking for a response from the organization, and when they get it they can turn out to be quite amenable to writing reasoned pieces.

TURNING NEGATIVES INTO POSITIVES

Recently, a large telecom company went through a takeover. During the takeover, a website dedicated to news about the company appeared. It focused on highlighting every piece of bad news it could find about the company. The company's PR team did some strategic outreach and even passed information early to the blogger so that the blogger was viewed as part of the press corps and could break news. By creating a special relationship with the blogger, whose posts were receiving considerable traffic, the team managed to turn a critic into a more measured observer. Although the team was never going to turn the content creator into a proponent, they did limit the damage that the blogger could and was doing.

This willingness to reach out to critics is an important part of any social media strategy and requires buy in from the very top of the organization. Marketing, PR, corporate communications, and customer support all require that a plan be in place before it's needed and not after the fact. After the C-Suite starts noticing bad news, it is too late to try to convince them that outreach will help. Likely, all they want to do is make it go away, often by stemming the flow of information rather than directing it.

Fear of bad news is often the reason that the C-Suite gives for not wanting to engage in social media. The reality is not that they fear the bad news itself, but they fear their organization's ability to deal with it adequately. This is where the social media strategy comes into its own. By having contingencies in place, a marketing department, or whichever department is tasked with the creation and operation of the strategy, can show its value and the value of social media.

What about positive comments? Contrary to what the C-Suite might think, it is not all doom and gloom in the world of social media. Often customers are only too pleased to finally have a channel through which they can express their appreciation of a job well done, a product that performs better than expected, or a service that made a difference to them. The hotel industry leaves comment cards in rooms, but no one fills them out when they have something positive to say. They are completed only when something went wrong. Social media is the place where the happy customers can leave their comments, to be seen not only by the staff but by other potential customers and, just as important, competitors. How amazing is that? Customers who want to say great things about the organization! Responding to these, even with a simple thank you is often enough to create an increased level of affinity, not only from customers making the observations but from their networks as well.

This simple act of "noticing" someone and acknowledging them is a well-documented social phenomenon. Doing so creates a pleasurable experience for the person receiving the recognition, the person doing the recognizing s and observers. This is a side-effect of the public nature of social media, but one that is extremely valuable in its application and in its ability for companies to build affinity through social media channels. Although this might sound very calculated and cold, it is no more so than any of the techniques used by mass media channels to create emotional responses to images, sounds, and situations. Commercials on television tell us stories of where and how products are used, to the point that sometimes the product becomes almost invisible. The story sometimes becomes more important than the product itself. This strategy is effective because viewers have a positive emotional response and therefore associates that feeling with the commercial and the product or service being advertised. Learning the techniques for doing this is a book unto itself and certainly not something we can dive into here. However, keeping this in mind will help your company not miss opportunities to have a positive effect on your customers and, in turn, increase your bottom line.

The Perfect Face for Social Media

Social media has been described as giving organizations the opportunity to "personalize" their brands, products, or services. When many brands first joined Twitter, they hid behind a corporate logo with no human face on the account. Although this protected them, it also created a barrier. How can you interact with a logo? For some types of accounts, this was a shrewd move—or at least a necessary one. For example, Dell's Twitter account tweets are primarily a stream of offers from its outlet store. Putting a face to this would have been unnecessary because the account isn't attempting to interact. Instead, it is there simply to stream information to those who are interested. By not humanizing the account, the company avoided the complications of the account being swamped with questions. However, the account does receive many inquiries, not all of which are associated with the outlet store. But the number of inquiries not associated with the outlet store is less than Dell would receive if the account had a face.

In contrast, many brands that are considered to be successful in their use of social media have a high-profile spokesperson who is the face of that brand's social media. Some have achieved almost celebrity status from this level of exposure, and not without cause. Some company members are celebrated for their innovative use of social media and for being extremely approachable, choosing not to hide behind their corporate logos. These people agree to face the public for the good and the bad that it brings.

PUTTING A FACE ON A COMPANY

Scott Monty at Ford, Chris Barger at General Motors, and Jeffrey Hayzlett previously of Kodak are well-known examples of people who are approachable and do not hide behind corporate logos. All three are key members of their respective company's social media efforts. The benefit of having a personality attached to a brand is that it can bring instant brand recognition in the real world. It can also help position the brand in ways it was not seen before. Who would have thought of Ford as a leading organization in the realm of social media before Scott Monty? Now Ford is cited constantly as an organization that really understands social media, and rightly so. However, if Ford had kept its team anonymous, would it have achieved the same level of affinity with the social media using public? Some would argue that it would not. However, downsides exist to having a personality as the social media face of an organizational brand—such as what happens when that person leaves the company?

When the social media "face" leaves the organization, does she take with her all the brand equity that she has built up? Does the brand start to lose credibility because the brand no longer has that well-known social media "face?" There is a definite risk involved in investing heavily in a single point of contact for social media. Whereas smaller organizations tend to lack the resources to do anything else, larger organizations can do well to develop multiple team members who are equally empowered to become "the" face as situations call for it. In effect, what a social media strategy needs is a strong succession plan for whoever is the organizational face in social media. Planning for the inevitable departure will alleviate many of the issues associated with this type of transition. In the same way as most organizations plan for succession in the C-Suite, so it should be in the social media team.

So how do all these elements come together in a cohesive social media plan? The key to a successful social media plan—as with any planning in business—is to know the objectives first. Understand what it is that you are hoping to achieve, what the organization is going to do with social media, and then form a plan around that goal or set of goals. To the extent possible, the goals should be very well defined. The clearer they are, the easier it becomes to define the plan that will lead to achieving those goals. Clearly defined plans also make for clearer metrics. Yes, metrics exist in social media just as they do in any other business activity. Not only is it possible to measure elements of a social media program, but they most definitely should be measured.

It is also essential to ensure that the organization has assessed its own capabilities to actually carry out the plan. A plan that requires more resources than are actually available is never going to work.

Measure Twice, Execute Once

What goals are appropriate in social media for a business to set? That is a broad question and in some cases only individual businesses can set them. However, some generic goals for social media activity can be set. The first and most obvious (but for some reason the most commonly missed) is revenue. Why would you engage in a business activity without having some way to tie it back to a revenue goal? That is just bad business practice. Anything you do should ultimately be tied to revenue. However, this is not the first measure that will be applied, nor is it the easiest. Simple metrics can be the number of page views of a specific web page, the number of clicks on a specific link, or the number of requests for information generated by a specific campaign. In fact, most companies are already measuring these same metrics in their other online marketing efforts. The complexity of these metrics can gradually be increased as the social media activity gains complexity (as it moves from simply having a presence through active conversations to running campaigns that are specific to social media).

It is essential that pre-social-media activity in terms of website visits, email addresses acquired, customer conversations, support queue times, free offers accepted, and so on are all base-lined before a social media effort is launched. It's hard to point to success if you don't know where you were as an organization before you started. After the effort is underway, it is likely that the resources won't be available to go back and capture the prior state data, so it is very important to ensure this happens before committing to the social media presence.

One reason that I often hear for "doing" social media is "our competitors are doing it." This is not a reason, unless you have real visibility into your competitors' cost structure, resourcing, and goal setting. It's very easy to confuse real success with what appears to be success. Sometimes this pressure will come from the C-Suite. They will point to the number of "fans" or "likes" a competitor's page has on Facebook, or the number of followers a competitor's Twitter account has and use these as indicators that the competitor has gained a serious advantage. But these numbers can be very misleading. These types of numbers can be "gamed" in many ways, and this is why they are unreliable as indicators of social media success and why they should not be included in the metric set for assessing the efficacy of a social media program.

Words such as "engagement, listening, and conversation" are used a lot in social media, but what do they really mean for a business? Where do they fit into a social media strategy? How do they impact goals?

The answer to these questions is that without them as a basis, it is hard to define a social media strategy that isn't just advertising on Twitter, Facebook, YouTube and so on. What these phrases—which have recently become hackneyed and diminished in value because of overuse—mean for any organization is that they have to be prepared for their messaging to be interacted with in a way that has not happened previously. This knowledge will aid the organization in creating a strategy that really demonstrates an understanding of social media. This knowledge also helps better prepare those who are charged with managing a company's social media efforts. It becomes especially valuable as companies start to create content that will ultimately be interacted with by customers, potential customers, competitors, and others in ways that they had not imagined when they created the content. Remember that ownership of content is something that becomes a very gray area in social media. Even though an organization might delete a tweet after someone else has retweeted it, ownership has transferred. The company that made the original tweet no longer owns that content and cannot delete it.

Realizing that this type of activity is measurable will impact the types of goals that an organization decides to measure. For example, a social media strategy might focus on the reduction of phone calls to a support line. The focus might be to empower customers with information that already exists on the Web, and provide that information in a more manageable, accessible, and digestible way.

Knowing that customers will interact with an account or page that has a clearly stated objective—to assist, for example—will allow an organization to measure success very clearly and very quickly. Did the number of phone calls go down? Do customer satisfaction surveys show improvement? Has the number of customer contacts via social media increased? Ultimately, these metrics can be tied back to cost savings, operating expense reduction, and therefore bottom-line improvement.

Future Proofing

Although direct selling through social media has yet to be achieved in any real sense (and for the most part the attempts at it remain in the domain of spam and hard sell), new technologies are appearing that will increasingly make this possible.

Shopping cart and payment systems are already being rolled out for Facebook, so that companies with business pages (formerly known as "Fan" pages) are now able to offer items for sale directly from Facebook, replicating their existing website-based catalog or creating specific offers available only to "fans" of their page.

Creating a unique, Facebook-only shopping experience will definitely be a way for many retailers to create increased affinity for their fans and to differentiate themselves from their competitors. Given the already low cost of entry to this space and the equally low cost of implementing these systems, it will also make it possible for smaller organizations to take advantage of this type of storefront. This is yet another example of how some social media platforms are enabling smaller outlets to compete with their larger competitors.

Also, systems are being established that will eventually enable payments to be made via Twitter in the same way that they can be made via SMS (text messaging). The recent rise in charity fundraising via SMS (for example, the HAITI campaign) has brought this opportunity to the forefront for mobile marketers and developers of mobile systems who want to leverage platforms such as Twitter for direct revenue generation. The capability to send a tweet to a specific account and make a payment has a lot of attractions for many, and it may be that the charity fundraising path will be the first to realize real success in that field. It is likely, as with the SMS-based systems, that these will focus around micropayments ($10 or less) and be of a fixed-price nature, just as with donations made via SMS.

Because of their low cost of entry nature, these systems are likely to lend themselves to adoption by organizations of all sizes, which in turn will increase their adoption rate among users. It is not unimaginable that the microblog of the near future will include the capability to place orders with a post. For example, a pizza company might set up an orders account that can be messaged to place a delivery order, a pre-agreed price being a part of the data that is transmitted via the message. Another use of these systems might lead to a microblog version of eBay, allowing real-time auction bidding via a messaging system that would allow all parties to see the bids as they happen. Using the current Twitter terminology, building a stream around certain hashtags to allow for ease of monitoring would make this type of auction environment not only possible but very engaging. Combine it with a payment system and you have a very compelling environment for both sellers and buyers.

At the time of this writing, these systems are purely speculation. However, anyone putting together a social media strategy needs, at the very least, to be aware of the potential uses of social media platforms that might exist in the near future and the directions that some of the existing platforms might take so that they can build their organizations responses into the strategy. This type of "future proofing" is what separates the agile companies from those who appear to be social media observers who move with the speed of a glacier.

To all this strategy for the overall use of social media, we add social location marketing as a specific use within it. As if Twitter, Facebook, YouTube, Flickr, and so on weren't enough to cope with, social location marketing has arrived with the importance of any zeitgeist movement and demands attention like a screaming four-year old. So just where in this grand plan is a marketer to fit this in?

The bulk of this book is dedicated to leveraging each of the key social location sharing platforms. However, working without a plan for how to use each of these platforms as part of a larger social media strategy would be pointless.

The Plan

Before you try to insert social location marketing into your overall online marketing strategy, it's helpful to map out your strategy. Following is a sample plan that shows how social location sharing fits into the bigger picture. An effective social media plan is going to include all the following elements we have been discussing:

- Organizational fit
  - Decide which department or departments are going to control the channel.
  - How integrated is each department and how will they pass information between them?
  - What resources already exist in house to use social media?
  - What resources will require training/need hiring?
- Goals and objectives
  - What is the vision for social media use?
  - What does the organization want to achieve and when?
- Team structure or Individual personality
  - Will there be an individual face or a group that customers relate to?
- Location of the intended audience
  - Where is the target audience now?
  - Where are they likely to be?
- Metrics
  - What results are important to the organization?
  - How will they be measured?
  - How is success defined?
- Financial return
  - How much will it cost to achieve the goals?
  - How much will they return if they are achieved?
  - Tools and services
  - Free versus paid
  - In-house or consultancy

- Future proofing
  - Where will potential customers go next?
  - What changes to existing platforms will impact the plan?

Location, Location, Location

So where in this plan is there room for social location marketing? How much effort will it take? The answer to these questions can be summed up in the usually vague response favored by consultants: "It depends." However, I am going to avoid the usual vague responses in this book and try my best to give tangible answers.

As Mary Kay Ash is quoted as saying, "Life is short, order dessert first." So I am going to provide the good news first. Of all the social media channels, social location marketing is perhaps the easiest point of entry for any business. At the very basic level there is little to do in the way of setup, there is little content to be created, and at this stage only a small amount of moderation to be done. All this sounds too good to be true, right? Well, as I said, this is at the basic entry level. Get your venue set up correctly, claim it (at least with Foursquare), and you are good to go.

So if it's so simple, why isn't everyone already doing it—and why would an organization or an individual marketer need a book to show them how to do it? The truth is, as with the other elements of social media, none of it is rocket science. However, there are easy ways to achieve things and there are hard ways. So when you are figuring out where this fits into a social media strategy, it is important to understand what can be done at the various levels of competency and then make an honest assessment of where the organization is on the scale of social media knowledge.

As discussed at the most basic level, social location marketing can be a straightforward process of ensuring that your location exists in the databases of the various tools, and then sitting back and waiting for people to interact with it on those platforms (Foursquare or Gowalla, for example). This is a very passive method of using it, which is at the zero point on the scale of interaction. The next step up is to actively engage in the various platforms by signing up for them and learning what each offers the users. Having discovered, for example, that Foursquare focuses on location check ins and awards "mayorships" for frequent check ins, a business might want to offer rewards based on that. Meanwhile, it won't take long to find that Gowalla focuses more on "trips" and so a successful strategy might be to partner with other nearby locations to create fun and rewarding trips for users that result in some type of reward that the businesses have contributed to. MyTown, on the other hand, is more like a game of monopoly based in the real world, with the buying and selling of properties. So tying rewards into that theme might fit the business better.

As with all social media channels, finding the correct audience and matching that with the organizational business objectives is key. Simply picking Foursquare because it is most popular (or at least seems that way this week) is not a good strategy. Find out how the platform is used most often and how it fits with the organization's existing communications strategy. For example, businesses that already have a customer loyalty program are going to find integrating with Foursquare straightforward because they are already rewarding customers based on the frequency and number of visits to a location or set of locations, which is exactly how Foursquare works.

However, a business that has one-time locations (a real estate company selling homes, for example) is more likely to find Gowalla a good fit because of their trip-based game play, which encourages users to visit more than one location (perhaps open houses) in a given time frame before being rewarded.

As you can see, fit and function is the key to discovering which of the platforms will work best and therefore fit within a social media strategy. This might imply that an organization can't use more than one platform, which isn't the case. However, as with other social media platforms, I recommend becoming at least competent with one platform before adding others. Discover what the organization can achieve with the first platform before deciding to attempt a different platform. It is worth noting that users tend to fall into two distinct camps: those who have already decided which platform best meets their needs and those who remain undecided and use more than one service at a time (or use one of the services that allows them to check in on multiple platforms simultaneously).

The reasoning behind whether a company knows which platform is right for it can be as simple as a phone preference. For example, currently Gowalla does not provide good support for Blackberry, but it has great support for iPhone and Android. Foursquare and BrightKite are available on all phones. MyTown is available only on iPhoneGowalla has a much higher loyalty based on the design of the user interface and in game graphics than the other platforms and so tends to appeal to those users who are looking for that in a tool. Knowing even these basics about the user base can help an organization establish which platform is most likely to have users who will be likely customers for the location. Table 2.1 outlines support offered for each social location tool by the major players in the smartphone market.

Table 2.1   Support for Social Location Sharing Tools

Platform/OS	iPhone	Android	Blackberry	WebOS	Add Comments	Add Photos	Collect Rewards
Foursquare	Y	Y	Y	Y	Y	N	Y
Gowalla	Y	Y	Y	N	Y	Y	Y
SCVNGR	Y	Y	N	N	Y	Y	Y
MyTown	Y	N	N	N	N	N	Y

continues

Table 2.1   Support for Social Location Sharing Tools (Continued)

Platform/OS	iPhone	Android	Blackberry	WebOS	Add Comments	Add Photos	Collect Rewards
BrightKite	Y	Y	Y	N	Y	N	Y
Whrrl	Y	Y	N	N	Y	Y	Y

Having established the basics of a strategy by determining which platform to use, it becomes easier to flesh out that strategy with the type of interactions that the organization wants to utilize on that platform. For the smaller business, this is probably going to be limited to "free" offers for completing something within the tool, such as a number of check ins, a trip, purchasing the property, and so on. Without the benefit of a large marketing budget, it is hard to buy into the more elaborate offers that these platforms have. However, that shouldn't stop smaller businesses from taking part in those types of offers. Some very effective affinity programs have been put together for these platforms by small, single location businesses, which have led to incredible returns and increased revenues.

Larger businesses with the budget to become involved at a higher level will want to explore the custom offers that all the platforms are now offering. From sponsored badges in Foursquare, to hidden game objects in Gowalla, to redeemable game tokens in MyTown, each of the platforms has found a way to partner with large organizations and events to deliver value-added promotions through their channel to users.

When tied to other social media activities, these can be relatively low-cost methods of achieving awareness for products, services, or brands, especially when compared to the mass media alternatives. A budget of $40,000–$60,000 will buy a Foursquare dedicated badge for two quarters, tying that to a coupon redemption campaign, or free trial offer and social media promotion of the badge, and an organization can save tens of thousands of dollars compared to a mass media campaign that might last only weeks.

Numbers like this start to make a compelling case for businesses to utilize these tools at all levels. Small, medium, and large organizations can create, with some planning, campaigns that capture the imagination of users, who are, after all, customers and potential customers.

The capability of social location marketing to fit into all elements of the social media purchase cycle—and to do so in a low-cost, ease-of-entry manner—makes its use compelling. As more organizations come to this realization and the user base increases in size, the tools will adapt to the ways in which both the users, seeking rewards, and the organizations wishing to offer them are utilizing their platforms.

3

Games
People Play

It is important for marketers to understand the influence of game theory on social location marketing. Although I have no intention of providing a complete psychology lesson in game theory, I do believe that without a chapter on the topic, this book would be lacking in its completeness.

Game theory is a subset of economic theory that attempts to offer explanations of interactions between human beings and between human beings and inanimate objects that surround them. Specifically, game theory attempts to use math to predict an individual's behavior in strategic situations, or games, in which an individual's success in making choices depends on the choices of others. These explanations are used across multiple disciplines, including economics, psychology, sociology, marketing, and market research.

As animals, human beings are inherently social. We like to group together for a number of reasons, including security, collaboration, and for the element of "fun" that human interaction affords us. We are, in fact, not alone in the enjoyment of fun; many other animals have been found to laugh and play games with each other. However, in this chapter and for the purposes of the book, I am going to confine myself to the role of game play and social interaction among human beings.

The point here is that game play is not something that has recently happened because of sites like Facebook or because of the advent of social location sharing. Human beings have always been social. Technology, however, has enabled us to play games with people who live across town, in another state, or even in another country. Whether it is with family members, friends, or work colleagues, proximity is no longer a requirement for the game to occur or for it to be enjoyed.

Although it is true that some games—chess for example—have been played remotely for years (I used to play with an Uncle via mail when I was growing up), technology has expanded the type of games being played, the appeal of those games to a broader audience, and has increased the instant gratification nature of the games being played.

So who actually plays games? In particular, who plays Internet-based, social networking games? A study by PopCap found that 55% of players in the United States and almost 60% of players in the UK are women. Of these women, the average age in the U.S. was 48 and in the UK 36. Interestingly, only 6% of all social gamers are aged 21 or younger.

Women are more likely (68% vs. 56%) than men to play online games with their real-world friends and twice as likely to play with family members as their male counterparts. So are these people just sitting at home all day playing games? Actually, far from it. The truth is 41% of online gamers work full time and a total of 42% of those surveyed earn $50,000 per year or more. 95% of online gamers play multiple times per week, and 60% of them play for at least 30 minutes each time. Quite obviously, playing games is an important part of social networking for a significant portion of people who use social networking apps. Whether they are using iPhones to play Words With Friends or Facebook to play Farmville, playing games with others is an important part of the social networking world and something that should not be ignored by marketers.

However, there is more to it than simply seeing these game platforms as another media buying opportunity (though undeniably they present that opportunity). It's important that you learn why people play games and how those games appeal to different genders and ages. This will allow you to build game play into your social location marketing campaigns and capture the true spirit of the apps that your customers are using to communicate.

For example, if the average online social gamer is a 38-year-old woman, earning $50k a year or more, does that mean this is your most lucrative marketing opportunity? What if your target audience is men aged 24–39; wouldn't it make more sense to find a way to reach that audience instead?

Ultimately, knowing your audience—a theme I will return to many times in this book—is what determines whether using social location marketing is the appropriate channel for your organization. However, just because your audience isn't the average user doesn't mean that this form of communication isn't relevant to them. In fact the Pew Internet and American Life Report recently revealed that men use social location sharing apps twice as often as women do. However, this statistic might have more to do with the fact that typically, men adopt new technology earlier than their female counterparts do. Also, early incarnations of the social location sharing apps focused more on competitive behavior than they did on collaborative behavior. As you might guess, competitive behavior is typically more appealing to men, whereas collaborative behavior is more appealing to women.

Suffice it to say that with the introduction of Facebook Places, we can expect to see the number of women using social location sharing apps change over time—in fact, a very short period of time.

 Note

Facebook is known for its strong appeal to women (see Brian Solis's report, "In the World of Social Media, Women Rule," where he highlights that Facebook has 57% female users vs. 43% male users). Given that more women use Facebook and that Facebook Places allows users to share their locations and more, it's clear that we will see an increase in the number of women using social location sharing apps.

More than any other social network, Facebook has the capability to bring social location sharing into mainstream use by social network members. Even though Foursquare, Gowalla, and other social location sharing apps have huge user bases, we can expect the social location sharing concept to become more mainstream now that Facebook is a player. As social location sharing becomes more commonplace, marketers will have to be ever more aware of what elements make for good game play and what makes a campaign attractive to people using each of the social location sharing apps.

If we take a more detailed look at the Pew Internet and American Life Survey results, the current state of usage of social location sharing apps is quite surprising (see Figure 3.1).

The survey shows that the primary users of apps such as Foursquare and Gowalla are young Hispanic males earning at or just above the average U.S. wage. This is probably not the target audience that a lot of marketers running social location marketing campaigns are targeting, and yet this survey tells us that is who is using these apps.

 Note

This survey is the result of a 3,000-person population being interviewed in both English and Spanish.

All internet users	4%
Men	6*
Women	3
Race/ethnicity	
White, Non-Hispanic	3
Black, Non-Hispanic	5
Hispanic (English- and Spanish-speaking)	10*
Age	
18-29	8*
30-49	4
50-64	2
65+	1
Household income	
Less than $30,000/yr	3
$30,000-$49,999	6
$50,000-$74,999	6
$75,000+	4
Educational attainment	
Less than High School	5
High School	3
Some College	4
College +	5

Figure 3.1   *Indicates a statistically significant difference. Zickuhr, Kathryn & Smith, Aaron. 4% of online Americans use location-based services. P3, Pew Internet & American Life Project, 11/4/2010, http://pewinternet.org/Reports/2010/Location-based-services.aspx, accessed on 11/15/2010.

Again this reinforces the point that knowing your audience is extremely important, and knowing the user base of the latest social communication channels is also crucial.

Anatomy of a Game Player

Game players are often described as falling into two main typologies: Classic and Romantic. Gamers have two very different approaches to how they take part in games and how they derive pleasure from game play. It is important to understand these two typologies and think about how they fit with your intended audience, campaign, and your goals for the campaign.

Classic—These players are driven by the need to minimize risk while maximizing their gains. They typically look for strategies that allow them to make advances in the game at every turn, even though those advances might appear minimal. Their primary goal is to advance their positions ahead of their original positions. Chess players are often considered to be part of the Classic typology. They study potential outcomes and seek to learn all possible resultant moves based on the move that they make. In this way, they have a sense of "knowing" in advance what their potential gains are based on their opponent's response—whether that opponent is human or machine. They enjoy rule-based game play because this allows them to "learn" the potential moves as part of learning the game. They view this as essential to the game. They do not get the same from "emerging" games—where the outcomes are determined by what actions the user takes and what events unfold based on the actions of the user.

Romantic—The Romantic game player typology is most associated with high-risk takers. They seek to find the one decisive blow that will ensure their victory over their opponent. They are also likely to seek ways to intimidate their opponents and convince them psychologically that they have already lost, even if this is not the case. They are more drawn to emerging games than purely rule-based games. Poker players often fall into this typology because the "all in" mentality of risking everything for the ultimate payoff is a well-known display of the romantic game play.

Overachievers and the Easily Bored

The reasons people play games are as multitudinous as the people playing the games. These reasons range from boredom, escapism, killing time, socializing, competition, entertainment, status, and peer pressure—the list is almost endless. However, there are a few main categories that all these reasons can be bracketed by, and these tend to be divided by the driving force behind the gamer.

Serious Gamer

These are the gamers that spend hours on end locked in darkened basements, who have over developed thumb muscles, live on pizza and Red Bull, and wear headsets to talk to their gamer buddies (all of whom have extremely awkward sounding "in game" names). At least that is how the media would have you view them. Actually, many of these hard-core game players are professionals who use the game play as a form of steam valve. However, whether they hold to the media stereotype, they have one thing in common: hard work—or at least an expectation of hard work.

They expect to work hard, whether slaying ever more difficult monsters or solving increasingly complex puzzles, to advance to the next level. Their expectation is that they will be challenged and feel a sense of achievement at the end of each challenge. This is how they place value on the game that they are playing. If the game is too easy, they feel that they have wasted their money or time. If the game is too hard, they may move on to something else.

Casual Gamer

This is the type of gamer who plays when they remember to play. They aren't particularly bothered by the challenges, though they like to have a sense of achieving something when the challenge is met. They are likely to either be noncompetitive players or be competitive only at the time of play (for example, they play to win, but do not remember the score the next day). They are more social in their game play and when playing with friends are more likely to be playing for the sense of bonding than for any sense of "beating" their fellow players.

Games that are easily picked up and dropped are ideal for this type of player. The smartphone game Angry Birds is popular for this very reason. Players can sit with it for hours and try and beat their own scores or those of other players. Or they can simply dip in to the game for a few minutes while they are waiting in a line. These are not game traits that would appeal to the serious gamer. However, they fit the casual gamer extremely well. Games designed for the smartphone user tend to fall into this category, and certainly campaigns focused on social location marketing would fit into this category as well.

Masters of the Universe

These are the gamers that, usually, fall into a younger age group. For them, mastery in the game world replaces the lack of control that they experience in their real lives. In the real world, they have to abide by rules set by parents, schools, and other authority figures. In the virtual worlds they can often rise to a level where they set the rules. They become "legends" among other gamers and garner a level of respect that eludes them in the real world.

This desire to have mastery over a game system also leads to the creation of cheats, because this type of gamer is likely to want to find ways—by any means possible—to beat the system. Foursquare experienced this early on when people were checking into places that they had not been in order to gain the "Mayor" status. The need to have the status without actually earning it drove this behavior.

Foursquare and the other app developers have gone to great lengths to ensure that this behavior is as limited as possible. In fact, Foursquare recently introduced a mechanism whereby venue owners can remove a user as Mayor if they believe that the user earned it in a way that was not legitimate. It is important that the campaign you create for a social location sharing app have some form of real-world validation—whether it is uploading a picture, performing a task, or interacting with staff. You should never rely solely on the game to validate a user's participation.

Young Guns and Old Codgers

There is, rather unsurprisingly, a difference in the expectations of gamers of varying ages. Older gamers tend to want a journey on the way to the goal. They want to be a part of a story that unfolds through the game play, that draws them along, and that is something they can actually enjoy and feel connected to as they play the game.

Younger players tend to want to get to the destination—the "are we there yet" mentality that any parent who has ever undertaken a journey of longer than 10 minutes with a small child is all too familiar with. They are less interested in a detailed story, though context is important. They need to know why they are doing something, but they don't necessarily need to be involved in an unfolding story. They want to know why the characters are there but they don't want to be involved in their story unless it makes getting to the destination easier.

Interestingly enough, this same dynamic tends to generally divide the genders, with men being goal focused and desirous of an ending and with women being more story focused, enjoying the journey and less focused on the final outcome. Women also tend to want the opportunity to be collaborative in their game play. That means games that have stories that weave interaction with others into them are very attractive to them.

Again this is important to note when considering a social location marketing campaign. If the target audience is going to be women, what are you doing to ensure that they are going to get some of these needs met? If your audience is men, how are you going to ensure that they get to the goal in a fashion that provides a challenge but doesn't consume a lot of their time?

Are We Having Fun Yet?

Nicole Lazzaro, founder of gaming design company XEODesign, has written extensively on the components of good game design, and I recommend that anyone who has a deeper interest in how video games are thought through read some of her work. Also Roger Caillois covers game categories in his book, *Man, Play & Game.* I also recommend this book as further reading on this topic.

Caillois and Lazzaro both define four distinct game types, and they have many similarities. Lazzaro defines four elements of fun and the emotions that they generate.

- **Hard Fun**—Generates emotions of frustration. The focus in this type of fun is on problem solving and strategy. This fits with our earlier description of the Serious Gamer who wants games to be difficult and who wants increasingly harder problems to solve. An example of this would be the online game World of Warcraft.

- **Easy Fun**—Here the focus is on curiosity. This type of game fun generates emotions of awe, wonder, and mystery. This fits with our description of the casual gamer, in particular the older and female gamer. They are looking for rich story environment, something that they can become immersed in but something that they can also leave at any point when other priorities take precedence. Trivia games, such as the Facebook game QRANK, fit into this category.

- **Altered States**—This is the sense of mastery that we referred to earlier: the escape from reality and the sense of excitement at that escape. This group wants the opportunity to exercise an increased sense of control over outcomes and to feel powerful among a peer group. Games such as Grand Theft Auto fit this typology.

- **People Factor**—Here the focus is on competition, sometimes with the help of others, such as working in teams to defeat others. The range of emotions in this type of fun includes schadenfreude (amusement at the misfortune of others), social bonding, and personal recognition. This applies quite well to Foursquare as a gaming app: the knowledge of "ousting" someone as Mayor of a location, the broadcasting of that message across personal social networks for others to see, knowing that in some cases members of that network will find it amusing to see the Mayor replaced.

Caillois defines his four types of game play in the following manner:

- **Competition**—In these types of games the pleasure is derived from overcoming the challenge of an opponent, of defeating an enemy, whether real or virtual. In addition, the development of skills necessary to win creates pleasure. Games involving strategy and those that include teamwork often provide this element, such as chess or physical team sports. SCVNGR certainly provides the infrastructure into which a marketer could create challenges that would meet this type of game play.

- **Chance**—Games that include the element of chance inspire the players to try to find strategies and methods of play that minimize the element of chance and to look for potential outcomes dependent on the inclusion of chance. In its most extreme form, players are in fact using an adaption of probability theory. Think of the movie *21*, which was based on the story of the MIT Blackjack team, whose story was told in the book *Bringing Down the House*. Here, real math geniuses used probability theory to try to overcome the element of chance by counting cards.

- **Vertigo**—This corresponds to Lazzaro's Altered States concept. These are gaming elements that provide a sense of disorientation or disconnection with the real world. Whereas Caillois cites activities such as skydiving or riding roller coasters as examples, virtual worlds, online games, and console-based games have been recognized for providing this type of sensation. Certainly games where the normal rules of life—those of physics, biology, and chemistry, for instance—are suspended, altered, or rewritten fall into this category.

- **Make Believe**—This is the sense of using one's imagination. The ability to create scenarios and to control the environment are important in this type of game element. The player requires a strong element of control over how things will end. In addition, not everything should be shown to the players; they require the ability to think through a situation and discover, sometimes through trial and error, how to find the appropriate solution.

None of these elements are exclusive. Any game might consist of several of these elements at different stages. In fact it is important for certain types of games that they include several of these elements to ensure some form of longevity. For example, linear games tend to have a limited shelf life. Once a player has played through all the levels, killed the very last monster and solved the very last puzzle, then that game is put away and the next one is rolled out. Now compare that to something like chess.

A chess board, at face value, presents itself as being much less complex to master than a video game of multiple levels. But the chessboard is not put away to be forgotten after a game has been played. Quite the opposite occurs—games are replayed, and new challenges are issued. Players want the opportunity to face new opponents. The game pieces themselves are not the game, the players are the game. Each time the pieces are laid out, they hold the potential for a new outcome that is dependent solely on the players who control them.

This level of what marketers term "stickiness"—the desire for a user to continually return to the board—is what makes game play so important to social location marketing. It is important that you find the right elements for the campaign that fit the intended audience, that mesh well with the app that is being used, and that meet the needs of the campaign message. These are the key features of a well thought out social location marketing campaign that effectively leverages the spirit of game play.

Remember, each individual derives different levels of pleasure from different games, although this will depend on the type of gamer the user is. However, it is also true that different games offer different levels of pleasure. The psychologist Mihály Csíkszentmihály (pronounced MEE-hye CHEEK-sent-mə-HYE-ee) outlined what he refers to as the "Flow"—a state in which game players become so involved with the game that all other considerations fall away. Users are involved in the activity simply for the sake of the activity. In this state, players use their skills to the utmost to remain inside the game.

Csíkszentmihály outlined eight elements that contribute to this state of "Flow":

- **Activity**—Players want to feel the activity they are engaged in is one that requires skill. However, the level of skill is variable. It must be something that is at a level that the gamer already has or can see a clear path to achieving the skill in a reasonable amount of time. Also, the game must provide for some type of leveling. That is, if the player competes against the game system, it should start out as an even balance and become progressively harder. Imagine beginner chess players playing their first game of chess against a grand master. The result would be demoralizing for the beginners and they would likely give up on the game. Equally for the grand master, there is no challenge and so the game itself becomes pointless. A good example of this was the Jimmy Choo campaign "catchachoo" described in Chapter 5. It was relatively easy for users to take part, but people who were familiar with the area had a distinct advantage over newcomers.

- **Concentration**—The need to concentrate on what we are doing and therefore make progress in the game is something that has to be carefully controlled, especially with regard to social location marketing. Given that the apps run on smartphones and the environment in which a smartphone is used is usually one full of distractions, the amount of concentration required to succeed needs to be relatively minimal—especially if all the game play takes place on the phone. For example, players should not miss out on a reward simply because they were distracted by wait staff taking their order. This would engender animosity toward the brand, rather than loyalty. This is why extending the gameplay beyond the device and into the environment is particularly important for social location marketing campaigns. Using the device as the gateway to the game rather than the gaming environment itself increases the possibilities for the marketer.

- **Goals**—Player must understand, from the outset, the point of the activity. Vague promises of a reward are not enticing. Concrete goals (for example, get to this level and win this) are much more motivational. Also, the goals have to be commensurate with the effort. As I will discuss in later chapters, if a user spends hours of time completing your challenges only to find that the reward is a free coffee, your campaign is likely to be met with derision, not praise. Think this through carefully when putting together the game play elements of your campaign. For example, the progressively harder challenges that are possible in SCVNGR allow the user to choose how much time she will devote to your campaign and therefore how much of a reward she is likely to receive.

- **Feedback**—Everyone likes to know how he or she is doing. Think about the workplace. If you never get feedback after a big presentation at your annual meeting, think of the angst that creates for you. The same applies to games. Players need to know how far they have progressed and how much further they have to go. In game theory, this is known as the progressive dynamic. Often the simplest method for showing this is a progress bar.

Figure 3.2 shows a user how complete her profile is on a social networking site. It also shows her what actions she needs to take to reach the next level of completeness. This is a simple graphic, yet it is also surprisingly motivational.

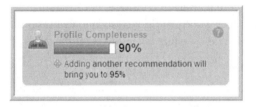

Figure 3.2   *LinkedIn Progress Bar*

- **Involvement**—Being engrossed in the game frees the user from his other worries. The sense of escapism is an important element for many game players. It provides them the opportunity to focus their attention on something else and get away from the daily grind. The amount of time spent with a game will determine the level to which this is achieved. However, even the simplest of games—if they are absorbing enough—will provide this escapism.

- **Control**—The ability to control the environment in which we find ourselves is an overwhelming human need. Games—especially those of an electronic nature—often provide worlds in which the player can bring absolute control to the environment. Early examples of this were known as management simulators, which ranged from sports management games to city creation games such as Sim City. These games are still hugely popular and the strong element of control is a major factor in this enduring popularity for the genre. Farmville is also a game of this type. Farmville is played exclusively within the Facebook platform, and at the time of this writing, it has more than 85 million players—all of whom are competing to grow crops, sell them, and make a profit while fighting off the challenges of the environment and other elements outside of their normal control. The fact that the game requires work is overshadowed by the fact that it allows for the player to control other major elements within the game.

- **Self-Absorption**—The ability for a game to reduce the amount of self-absorption a player exhibits is another major factor in the success of a game. Players who are able to step away from themselves and concentrate on acquiring a new skill or develop an existing one find the game more rewarding than those who are not given this opportunity.

- **Time Perception**—Time flies when you are having fun, so the adage goes. This is especially true of a good game. The ability of the game to become so engrossing that the amount of time spent playing it is no longer of importance to the player is key to ensuring that the player will want to return to play again. This does not mean that the game has to take up hours for game play. In fact, a game that takes only a few minutes to play can become just as engrossing if the game play meets many of the other requirements.

Now that we've looked at several viewpoints on effective game design, it's important that you are able to apply what you've learned here to your own social location marketing campaigns.

It is important to remember that any good social location marketing campaign will extend beyond the app itself. Simply relying on the game play contained within the app will not provide a sufficient enough reason for the savvy social consumer that uses these apps to want to engage with your campaign.

That means offering a free coffee to the mayor of your coffee shop no longer cuts it (even though this might have been an enticing offering 18 months ago when social location sharing apps were in their infancy). You must offer more—not just in the sense of the reward but in the game play that leads to the customer getting the reward. Even though this technology is still nascent, marketers are already fighting what is being termed "check-in fatigue." Social consumers are asking "why bother?" They need a reason to take part. They need something more engrossing and that extends the experience of the location beyond their phones.

After all, your location, whatever it is, is more (or at least should be more) interesting than your customer's phone. The idea is not to make your customers fans of Foursquare, Gowalla, Yelp, SCVNGR, or any of the other apps. The idea is to make them fans of your business and build loyalty with your location(s).

So building game play into your campaign that entices them and absorbs them while they are in your location is what will get them talking about your brand. Ultimately, this is what you are trying to achieve. Don't lose sight of that.

From the elements I have identified in the previous section of this chapter, which elements fit best with a social location marketing campaign in terms of game play?

The Ingredients

Like any good recipe, the quality and quantity of the ingredients make all the difference. So it is for social location marketing campaigns. The following ingredients are all essential for your campaign to leave the right taste in the mouths of your audience.

- **Skill**—So far, we've clearly shown that an element of skill—whether the use and development of an existing skill or the acquisition of a new skill—is important to game players. They want to feel like they have gained something from playing and that they are better at something than other players. This could be a demonstration of their knowledge—for example, in a trivia-based game—or their ability to compose a photograph in a funny pictures competition. Whatever the competition, the inclusion of an element of skill is very important.

- **Competition**—Even though the research suggests that males respond more to games that have a strong focus on competition, that does not mean females are not competitive. They most certainly are; however, the degree to which this is important to the player is what varies between the genders, and so whether the target audience is male or female, your social location marketing campaign game play must include some form of competition and some form of showing how well a player has done against the competition.

- **Concentration**—The game should require attention. The player needs time to focus on the game. This is where extending your campaign to the real world and removing it from being solely based on the user's phone allows you to remove some of the distractions that platform suffers from. In addition, by giving players the opportunity to focus on the game, you are also meeting the need that the experts identified—that is, the players entering an altered state of mind that allows them to escape from their normal world activities and thoughts and become less self-absorbed. You are connecting with their need for excitement and removal from their current existence.

- **Fun**—All the elements I have previously described have emphasized the need for fun; in fact, Lazzaro defines all the elements of game play in terms of fun. I would also add that fun should be the goal of the game in social location marketing. A reward of some kind at the end of the game is a great bonus, but early experience shows us that many players do not actually collect their rewards, especially if the reward has a low financial value. Instead, they play for the sake of playing, simply for the opportunity to have fun and share that fun with others.

- **Progress**—Players need to feel that they are moving toward a goal, the reward, the end of the level, or even the end of the game. They need to know how they are progressing both overall and against other players. Whether this is the use of a progress bar, a leader board, a league table, or some other device, players want to see that their efforts are in fact leading to them being credited for that effort.

The Execution

All this theory is great, and no doubt you have followed intently along with every element discussed here and are now at the point of saying to yourself, "Okay, but what the heck does a game like this actually look like? Our company makes widgets; we aren't a games company, we don't build things for spotty teens to play on their X-Boxes, we aren't going to spend millions on trying to develop the next World of Warcraft or even the next exercise craze for the Wii.

That's actually a good thing. You don't want to be in the games industry, unless that is the industry you are in already. The point is that although the theory might seem to make all of this very complex and demand that you understand how complex multiplayer online games are designed and coded, none of that is actually true.

I recently attended a conference in Las Vegas, and at the Sony booth I encountered a game being used as a marketing device that meets everything I have discussed in this chapter so far. Now, given that this is Sony, the technology company behind the PlayStation, I am sure you are expecting me to describe an amazing 3D virtual world populated with fantastical characters with which I was able to interact and that I lost a day in this alternate universe, in some experience that mirrored James Cameron's movie *Avatar*.

Instead, what I am going to describe to you is a game that involved plastic cups. Yes, just a collection of 30 plastic drinking cups, the kind you can find in the party aisle of any grocery store. Of these cups, 29 were blue in color, and 1 of them was red. The object of the game was to transfer all the blue cups so that the red cup moved from the bottom of the stack to the top of the stack.

The player had to keep both hands in contact with the cups at all times, and each cup had to be moved individually (see Figure 7.3). In addition, Sony required that you compete against a minimum of two other players when you took part, and your time was entered onto a score board to see how you measured up against all the other players who took part during the conference.

The prize was entry to a drawing for a video camera. So the immediate payoff for a player was nothing more than the ability to find out where you ranked against other conference attendees who played the game. This game had all the things we have described. It was fun, it took concentration, and in doing so made the players less self-absorbed as they focused on the task in hand. Players could immediately see what progress they were making because they were able to note the position of the red cup as it made its way up the column of blue cups. In addition, the time-keeper called out the amount of time they had used so far.

The game required a certain amount of manual dexterity, not so significant that it was impossible to master but significant enough that times varied greatly from player to player.

Figure 3.3 *A set of plastic cups makes for a great game.*

For example, when I played the game I managed it in a time of 1 minute and 6 seconds. The young lady in the picture beat everyone with a time of just 48 seconds! People lined up at the Sony booth to play this and other games that they had arranged, all of which were being played with the same set of plastic cups.

This is a great example of how a game can be all the things that a player expects and yet be surprisingly simple in its nature and very low cost to execute. There is no reason something like this couldn't be replicated at a café, bar, restaurant, or a retail outlet utilizing the social location sharing app as the method of entry to the competition. Get the players to check in at your location first, and then they get to play the game.

In doing this, you have managed to not only get them to spread the word about your brand, location, and so on, but you have managed to extend the engagement beyond their phone and into the physical space that you are occupying. This works equally well for businesses without physical premises or locations that are not normally open to their customers (in the business-to-business arena, for example). I will discuss this in Chapter 8, but it is more than possible for these types of games to be played at public locations—why not at the local park, marina, landmark, and so on?

Hopefully, you have seen that although game theory is a fairly complex subject and we have only touched on it in this chapter, it is possible to incorporate these concepts into simple and executable games that your business can afford and that will generate positive word of mouth about you as well.

4

Introduction to Location Sharing Tools

Before we get too involved in "how" social location market-ing works, we are going to look at the "what" and learn what started all this in the first place. It is no accident that phones have become smarter and as they have, the market-ing opportunities in the mobile platform have increased. What might surprise some readers is the reason behind this growth in the market place and how interwoven the U.S. Military, U.S. Government, and public safety were to the changes that made all the social location sharing, geo-tagging of pictures, and other various uses of GPS in our phones possible.

What Is and Isn't Social Location Sharing?

Many terms describe tools that share a person's location. Geo-location services, location based services (LBS), and social location sharing (SLS) to name a few. These are not all the same thing and in fact have a hierarchy that it is useful to understand before discussing how to use them for marketing.

Geo-Location Services

Geo-location services is the top-level term that covers all types of services that provide the location of a device anywhere on the planet. These devices include personal GPS devices found in many vehicles and boats (both fixed units that are a permanent part of the vehicle and portable devices). Also included in this category are the handheld GPS units used by hikers, bikers, hunters, anglers, and runners. All use some form of geo-location service that presents GPS data in a format that is useful to the particular application that the user has selected. For example, runners overlay a route on their locations and save that route for later repetition. Some runners also add additional information, such as time of day, temperature, heart rate, average speed, and so on. Someone using a GPS in an automobile might overlay location with traffic information, road construction notes, points of interest, and so on.

Personal Locator Beacons (PLBs) used by hikers, light aircraft, and marine craft are also good examples of geo-location devices. PLBs share the user's location only in situations where the user has turned the device on. PLBs are generally activated only when the user has an emergency (a capsized boat, for example) and are intended to direct rescuers to the user's location. Although PLBs aren't social devices, I include them in the geo-location services category because they are not tied to cell phone service, as are other social location services.

Services such as OnStar (the in-car assistance from GM) or Lo-Jac (a company that helps locate stolen vehicles, motorcycles, and even laptop computers) are also geo-location services. These devices utilize GPS data and overlay it with their own data.

Location-Based Services

Location based services are the next level down in the hierarchy. LBSs are services that disclose the location of a user via (in most cases) a cell phone or other device that is connected to the cellular network. This term is often used when referring to social location sharing. However, I maintain that this is an incorrect usage. Location based services include social location sharing tools; however, they are much broader and include what are best described as passive location sharing tools. These include things such as the family locator services from cellular companies Sprint and Verizon in the United States. This type of service is passive in nature in that the end user (the family member) is not actively sharing his or her location. Instead, the

GPS chip in that person's phone is actively tracked via a service that ties numbers to one account. This service is primarily aimed at parents wanting to check on the location of their mobile-phone-carrying children, although it could also be used by small businesses to track delivery or service vehicles.

This technology has been extended to non-cell-phone devices that look like watches, or can be embedded in shoes for young children to enable parents to find their child if they lose sight of them. Some versions fit onto the collars of the family dog so that if it strays, its owners can locate it. These are all passive in nature—only the very smartest of dogs would be able to be trained to use a cell phone!

Vehicle tracking is a popular commercial use of passive location based services. Domestic uses include OnStar, which can provide turn-by-turn navigation instructions that are sent right to the user's vehicle. Commercial applications include cell phones that transmit the user's exact location, allowing, for instance, shipping companies to pinpoint the location of commercial drivers without asking them to check in.

Given that the U.S. federal government banned the use of cell phones for everything except hands-free calling for commercial drivers, and breaking that law can result not only in hefty fines but loss of their license, these services are invaluable to shipping companies in answering their most popular question: "Where is my stuff?" One such service is WaveMarket's Veriplace Location. Aimed specifically at carriers and based on a family locator service that already had developed this service is a good example of how the B2B space can utilize location based services in a way that benefits them.

Social Location Sharing

And so we come to the crux of this book and the services that we are going to focus on. Social location sharing is the term I use to describe the various services that require a user to actively share his or her location with a network. This network is a group of people and companies with whom the user has agreed to share that information, as well as a broader network via connected social media platforms. It is the active nature of these services that sets them apart from the other services, which are passive in their nature. This active participation makes them so intriguing and so compelling for marketers. Why would someone want to broadcast their location to their own friends, let alone groups of individuals that they have, in all probability, never met in real life? We have looked at the behavioral explanations in Chapter 3, "Games People Play," so we won't recount those here. If you skipped that chapter, I'd encourage you to go back and read it for a fuller explanation of why people want to be involved.

Later in this chapter, we look at where the individual platforms came from, what each of their offerings are, and what differentiates them from each other. Before that, let's consider them as a whole. Although no clear winner has been declared at the time this book was written, Foursquare seems to be a strong favorite. However, most of the marketing industry is still holding its breath, waiting to see what the behemoth that is Facebook will do with its entry into social location sharing. While not strictly a social location sharing platform, Facebook cannot be dismissed as becoming a major player in the space. Its initial entry is to attach location to status updates in a very Twitter-esque manner. However, in parallel, its team has already started to do outreach to physical locations and offer them window stickers that remind patrons to update their status with their current location and mention the venue that they are visiting. Although this is hardly likely to deal a death blow to any of the existing platforms, the fact that they are taking these services seriously enough to invest in them shows that they have a role to play in social media marketing.

In addition, Facebook's location deal with the McDonald's chain gives rise to the suspicion that they chose McDonald's because of their worldwide locations more than any other reason. If Facebook decides to get aggressive with social location marketing, having a worldwide partner such as McDonald's is a very quick way to establish a beachhead.

MCFACEBOOK?

In May 2010 it was reported that McDonalds was developing a Facebook application that would allow Facebook users to check-in at its locations in the U.S. and then post various coupons to their Facebook pages. This was seen as the first real step by Facebook into the social location sharing space. It was also reported that Facebook was not charging McDonalds to create this application and that their actual play is more likely to encourage all users of social location sharing services to utilize those services through Facebook and then for Facebook to make a revenue sharing deal with those services.

Balancing against this is the large scale media deals already secured by Foursquare and Gowalla—not the least of which is the one between Foursquare and Starbucks. However, no media partner is likely to turn down the opportunity to secure a partnership deal with Facebook should the opportunity rise. This potential means Facebook has to be considered in the social location sharing tools mix. At the time this book was written, Facebook still needed to adapt its mobile platform for true location sharing. Facebook's current mobile platform extended to all mobile phone platforms, but trailed other social location sharing tools in general functionality, usability, and design. It currently has no social location sharing specific functionality, so the user is left to do all the work, which is unlikely to yield a high adoption rate.

Unlike the other social location sharing platforms, Facebook's initial entry to the market does not offer the user any form of platform-specific rewards program or game play. Again, the lack of these features could be remedied and will certainly need to be if Facebook is going to make a serious attempt to capture market share in this space. However, given its sizable user base and that it already has a reputation for—at the very least—hosting games, such as Farmville and Mafia Wars, it is not too much of a stretch to see Facebook making inroads here. In fact, it's not too much of a stretch to see Facebook creating an environment in which a third party could tie into Facebook's location extension and utilize this to make a location-aware game that users could share with their network of friends.

Because Facebook mixes both personal and business environments so effectively already, a tool that could capitalize on that environment and combine it with social location sharing would be very attractive to marketers looking to leverage the enormous reach that Facebook provides with its membership numbers. Whether that would be enough to make the other platforms redundant is doubtful, but it would certainly hasten the consolidation of the space and perhaps spell the end of the minor platforms that are currently appearing and vying for market share with today's leaders in the space.

Where Did All This Social Location Sharing Start?

Social location sharing traces its roots to 2000. That was the year the American government decided to abandon Selective Availability (SA)—a method used to scramble Global Position System (GPS) signals. Selective Availability was the U.S. government's method for deliberately degrading the GPS signals available to civilian users, primarily on the grounds of national security. It was thought that allowing civilians to utilize the service at times when it was a priority for the U.S. military would endanger military operations. Under the Bush administration in the mid-2000's there was talk that the President should be able to order the shutting down of parts of the service, again in the name of national security. This was discussed as a way of ensuring terrorists could not make use of the service to coordinate attacks. In addition, it was proposed that the U.S. government retain the capability to shut down other countries' access to the GPS satellite network if that were to endanger U.S. national security. These measures have not been enacted, and given the reliance on the service by both commercial shipping and aviation, it is unlikely that any attempt to pass a bill of this nature would be successful.

Prior to the abandonment of SA, civilian use of GPS was very unreliable and did not allow for the level of accuracy that we take almost for granted today. In fact, prior to the abandonment of SA, the most accurate GPS fix was limited to about 100 yards. After these controls were released, the fun began.

Dave Ulmer is credited with creating the geo-game concept in May 2000, and by the end of the same month Matt Stum had coined the phrase "geo-caching." The concept was simple. Take a container of some kind to a remote location, note the coordinates given by a GPS device and publish them—usually in those days to the Usenet lists. Others were then tasked with finding the container and recording their details in a log, or they would take an item from the "cache" and replace it with one of their own. In effect, it was the geek version of a scavenger hunt, using the latest technology. The use of the Internet had become fairly widespread at this time and was a communication tool of choice for many. Combining this with the now more reliable GPS system made for a great game environment. Literally, the world became the game board. The game is still popular in both urban and rural environments among those with an interest in the outdoors and in sharing little-known, out-of-the-way spots. That these geo-caching games lent themselves to both game play and technology has already been exploited by some of the newer social location sharing platforms. We will look at this later in this chapter when we take an in-depth look at each of these platforms and how they work.

In 2002, the removal of SA benefited the cell phone industry. As the rise in use of cell phones became evident—even replacing the use of landlines—the emergency services found that 911 operators were not able to clearly identify a caller's location. Also, callers requesting assistance from 911 had difficulty identifying their exact locations. In an attempt to reduce this problem, the government mandated that all new cell phones be GPS enabled so that they work with the new Enhanced 911 (E911) system which displays the caller's ID information as well as their latitude and longitude when dialing from a cell phone. After the technology was in place, the potential for additional services was quickly realized by other providers. However, it would be another few years before the appearance of tools that enabled this vision. Let's look at those services as they appeared and how they differentiate themselves.

Loopt

One of the earliest of social location sharing services—and one that is still in existence—is Loopt (see Figure 4.1). Founded in 2005, Loopt has faced many challenges

Figure 4.1   *Loopt isn't the player that some other social location sharing tools are, but it is available on all cell phone platforms—something its competitors cannot boast.*

and has been somewhat overshadowed by the more game-oriented platforms such as Foursquare, Gowalla, and MyTown. However, it does have the benefit of being available on all cell phone platforms, something that some of the newer platforms struggle with providing. Loopt also was the first service available from all U.S. cell phone providers since the advent of Short Message Service (SMS).

Loopt has faced adoption issues because of its method of recruiting new users via SMS. This method received a lot of attention when it was discovered that by signing up, users were in fact authorizing Loopt to send invites to everyone in the user's address book via SMS. Further, the Loopt system did not respect the STOP message agreement, whereby the recipient could reply with the word STOP and no longer receive messages from Loopt. Loopt later addressed this issue, but in the interim new services had appeared and despite their early attempts to integrate rich content into their platform, Loopt currently trails the newcomers in acquiring a broad user base. It is, however, worth noting that the rich content model on which the newer platforms have decided to build was in fact created by Loopt, who signed deals with content providers, including CBS, as early as 2008. Later in the book we will look at the impact rich content makes as a differentiator for these platforms and how marketers can leverage it.

BrightKite

BrightKite appeared in 2007 and by 2008 had become somewhat of a darling favored by social media influencers, who touted its features and hypothesized on where BrightKite might go and how it could become even better (see Figure 4.2). Interestingly, a lot of the thoughts around where BrightKite might go were in the same direction that Loopt had started to travel and where subsequent services have gone (more on that later). For many reasons, BrightKite never fulfilled this potential, even with recognized social media influencers promoting it. BrightKite was acquired in 2009 by mobile social network Limbo—an unfortunate name because that is a fair description of where BrightKite has remained. Having lost momentum, it has been relegated to the "also ran" category. But it is still worthy of mention as

Figure 4.2   *BrightKite had its moment in the sun, but is now relegated to the "also ran" category.*

being one of the first, and certainly during its heyday of 2008, the most popular, of the iPhone-based social location sharing applications.

Quite possibly, the advent of a broader Smartphone user base and the multiple platforms has proven too difficult to keep up with. Indeed the "native" application for BrightKite on other Smartphones comes from third-party developers. An example of this is MyKite for the Blackberry. This was enabled because BrightKite took the first step in this arena of creating and releasing an application programming interface (API) for its platform, which allowed third-party developers to produce tools based on, and that interacted with, the data that BrightKite held. This, too, is a model that subsequent platforms have chosen to follow and one that allows the platform to grow without the original developers doing all the work.

Yelp

Although Yelp has existed since 2004, it is a more recent player in the mobile social location sharing marketplace (see Figure 4.3). It started as a venue and service review site, and as such quickly rose to become one of the top 150 sites in the United States. Yelp content was integrated into the early platforms, such as BrightKite, and continues to be integrated into newer platforms such as Foursquare. Yelp's entry into the market came with a distinct advantage—thousands of loyal reviewers known as "Yelpers" who were already using the website to place reviews of venues and services. A number of these Yelpers are rewarded with Elite status. These Elite reviewers hold real-world events to recruit new Yelpers and promote Yelp, as well as receive recognition from Yelp.

Figure 4.3   *Although its been around since 2004, Yelp is a more recent—and successful—player in the social location sharing space.*

The concept of Elite reviewers is an attempt by Yelp to indicate that the person writes well enough, produces enough content, and has sufficient following to be trusted as a reviewer. There are various thoughts on how well this works. Yelpers are in fact secret shoppers of the information age. Armed with iPhone apps, they are able to make their reviews while still onsite. This makes the reviews much more immediate and, in some cases, much more punishing. With no time for reflection, a dissatisfied Yelper can slam a business onsite. However, not all has gone well for Yelp. With accusations of unfair editing, and bully tactics by sales representatives contacting small businesses and offering to have bad reviews removed in return for ad revenue, Yelp is now facing a class-action lawsuit.

The outcome of that lawsuit will be watched closely by all in the review space, not just the social location sharing space. The implications could bring a lot of extra administrative work for the newer platforms as they include Tips, To-Do's, and other user-generated content fields.

Foursquare

Foursquare is a revised version of an earlier attempt by the same team to create a game-based social location sharing tool (see Figure 4.4). The original was called Dodgeball, an SMS-based service that was acquired by Google in 2005. It was shut down as a service in 2010. In 2007, the original founders of Dodgeball left Google to found Foursquare. Foursquare was the first of the services to introduce the element of game play to the space of social location sharing and venue review. Participants are rewarded for "checking in" at locations. Rewards are based on the location type, the number of times they check in, and whether the location already existed in the Foursquare database. Game rewards include a basic leader board, which is run weekly and ranks participants in a particular location by the number of points they have acquired. Points are achieved by checking in, adding new locations, and for multiple check-ins in a given time frame. This element provides a great deal of competition among participants.

In addition, a series of badges can be acquired by participants. Some of the badges are generic, such as the Newbie badge awarded to everyone for a first check in on Foursquare. Some were originally city specific. When Foursquare first launched, it contained only certain cities in its database, and therefore game play was limited to those cities. However, this limitation was removed in early 2010 and replaced with latitude/longitude information, expanding the game play globally.

Badges are now a part of the sponsorship/advertising package that is offered by Foursquare, although many venues have found ways to create marketing opportunities around the preexisting and, more importantly, free badges. (I'll discuss this in more detail later in the book.) Foursquare took the smart step of releasing an API

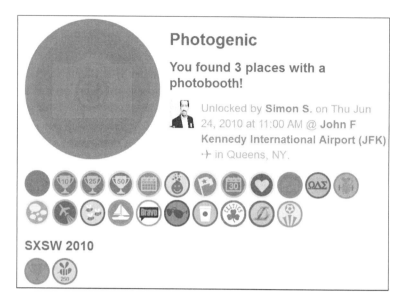

Figure 4.4   *Foursquare rewards users with Badges.*

early on. This has led to new applications based on their platform, which has also enhanced adoption. The API was released with not only a good set of documentation, but also a developer forum that acts as a strong community for developers. Foursquare technical team members contribute regularly to the forum, answering technical questions about the platform and making suggestions for how the API can best be used.

In 2010, Foursquare signed a number of high-profile media deals that have accelerated its rich content growth. This is certainly a good model to follow and one that was started by its predecessors in the space, such as Loopt.

Gowalla

Gowalla is produced by Alamofire (see Figure 4.5), an Austin, Texas-based software company. It launched in March 2009. Alamofire previously had success with the Facebook game PackRat. They took that gaming experience and a strong focus on design and brought it to the social location sharing space. This design focus sets it apart from other platforms. Most users of both Foursquare and Gowalla state a clear preference for the look and feel of Gowalla—the interface and the digital objects that the platform rewards users with.

At the end of 2009, Gowalla received $8.29 million in Series B funding. Gowalla focused on the iPhone platform for much of its growth, not releasing a variant for Android or Palm until 2010. As of June 2010, a Blackberry application was still awaited.

Figure 4.5   *Gowalla has a strong focus on attractive design.*

In February 2010, Gowalla followed in the footsteps of its main rival Foursquare and released an API for developers to work with. This has certainly aided its adoption and is leading to new applications being built for Gowalla. However, without the strong community focus that other API's enjoy, this is likely to be a harder win. Gowalla has also followed Foursquare into the rich content space by signing a deal with the Travel Channel and other media outlets.

The Travel Channel deal is a great fit for Gowalla because one of Gowalla's unique features is "Trips." This allows users to complete check ins at groups of locations, and as they do so work toward completing a Trip; having completed a Trip, the user earns a new reward. Gowalla added to this rich content mix in May 2010 by signing deals with both National Geographic and the Washington Post. The Washington Post deal creates trips that are based on content in the "Going Out Guide," whereas the National Geographic deal sees the creation of 15 unique walking tours of cities across the United States, Canada, and Europe. These types of deals help to differentiate the Gowalla platform from its competitors. Though many of their deals have focused on travel, that is not all they are restricted to, and marketers looking to utilize this platform should think beyond trips and travel information. At its core, Gowalla is definitely a social location sharing platform capable of offering real opportunities to organizations looking to make it work for their customers and potential customers.

Gowalla's game play mirrors PackRat by focusing on the trading of digital objects. This concept is core to Gowalla, with users being able to acquire new digital objects at various locations as they check in there and leave other objects behind for other users to collect.

What Gowalla lacks at present is a clear path for users to be rewarded by venues, unlike the "Mayor" route in Foursquare. However, with the much greater funding that Gowalla enjoys, it is only a matter of time before it unveils a method of integrating with the venue owners who are looking for a way to reach Gowalla's growing audience. That is not to say that marketers can't and shouldn't leverage Gowalla right now. It would be a huge mistake to ignore the Gowalla platform and its user base. You'll learn more on how that can be done in later chapters.

MyTown

As the popularity of social location sharing grows, so does the number of platforms vying for a share of the marketplace. Each tries to bring something unique to the space or to take a variant of some other platform in a new direction.

MyTown (see Figure 4.6) is one such platform. MyTown incorporates Monopoly-style game play into the social location sharing space, enabling participants to buy and sell their favorite venues. Players are rewarded with increased ability to buy new locations the more frequently they check in. Players can also leave comments on a venue when they check in and receive rewards for doing so. MyTown has taken the venue promotion in a different direction after signing a deal with the clothing store H&M. Rather than simply making the rewards dependent on the local venue, MyTown users who are near an H&M store are alerted to discounts in the store by finding that H&M merchandise is available in the game. Checking in at the H&M store then unlocks discounts available in the store. This builds both loyalty to the game and to the venue. This is the first of this type of deal to incorporate a form of "push" notification, but we can expect to see more of this type of marketing as the social location sharing space grows.

Figure 4.6   *Booyah's MyTown brings Monopoly to the iPhone.*

Other Social Location Sharing Tools

The social location sharing space continues to add new services all the time; PlacePop, BlockChalk, Bump, FoodSpotting, and Graffiti are all trying to be the next big thing. All have something to offer, but given the lead held by Foursquare, Gowalla, MyTown, and Yelp, it will be a hard struggle for any newcomer to grab real market share. Focusing on niche users might be the way we see the space develop, though undoubtedly we will see some shake out in late 2010 or early 2011 as platforms merge or disappear.

Picking the right platform to align with is definitely an important part of developing a social location sharing marketing plan. The rest of this book focuses on just that. It is important to bear in mind that although this book covers the existing technology and to some extent presents visions of the near future, all this social location sharing is happening in the real world, and that is ultimately where the audience that any organization is trying to reach exists. The technology will get you only so far. After that, the organization must work out how to close the final gap between technology and the real world.

Real World Uses for Social Location Marketing

Marketing communications have always been about delivering a message to a receptive audience. Social location marketing falls into this category. However, the twist that social media has brought to marketing communications is the expectation of the audience that they will, at some point and in some way, "meet" the brand in the real world. Exactly what that means varies from brand to brand and from audience member to audience member.

In some cases the "meet" is conducted through blogger/influencer outreach. In others, it is competitions. Whichever direction an organization chooses, it has to realize that this is part of the deal in using social location marketing as a channel. The advantage that social location sharing offers a marketer is that identifying those they want to "meet" is extremely easy. After all, those people are already broadcasting their use of the location. So the real world outreach is made that much easier. In addition, after the outreach is conducted, it is easier to promote both as an organization and through the audience member. People who are broadcasting their location are unlikely to be wallflowers, so if they are treated well by a location, organization, or brand, they are going to share that experience on other social media platforms. The connectivity that is presented by social location sharing platforms is another compelling reason why choosing social location marketing as an entry point into the broader social media world makes a lot of sense to organizations of various sizes. Instead of trying to understand what content they should be producing and where it fits, they can rely more on providing an outstanding customer experience and let the customer share that for them.

As we have already discussed, a total reliance on customer-generated content would be a very flawed strategy. However, given that the majority of the content on social location sharing platforms is customer generated, this does give an increased opportunity to use social location marketing as the point of entry for organizations that are looking for low-cost, low-risk methods of entry to social media. Companies gain the benefits of social location marketing while doing what they should be doing anyway, which is providing a compelling reason for customers and potential customers to build an affinity relationship with them.

Passion brands have long had an easier time of building affinity than the rather more mundane brands. For example, it's easy to understand why Disney has little problem building affinity, whereas an accounting company might not attract the same level of enthusiasm. However, great customer service, no matter where it is provided, will always produce increased levels of affinity. Social location sharing tools allow organizations to focus those efforts into tangible communications that not only provide an improved customer experience but also acknowledge that the consumer has a choice and that the consumer chose that particular organization to do business with.

Saying thank you, which is all a customer loyalty/rewards program is, has always been key to any small business. Larger brands have relied on volume rather than individual touch points. Social location marketing offers the opportunity for larger brands to not only continue with their usual method of operation but to incorporate the types of outreach that are usually more familiar to customers of smaller, more local, operations. As with any of this type of activity, scalability is always the challenge, and operational integration is key to this. Whether that is technology, staff training, a mix of both, or more involved cross-functional integration, it is essential if these tools are to provide value to the larger organization and ultimately value to the customer.

Case Study

Venue: Capital Hotel—Little Rock, Arkansas

Participant: Amy Bradley-Hole, Marketing director

Background: The Capital Hotel is a boutique hotel in Little Rock, Arkansas. With 94 rooms, it has long been perceived as an upmarket location, out of the price range of the younger local residents of the city. The hotel has two eateries—a fine dining restaurant and a bar and grill. The latter has a more relaxed atmosphere and would be very suitable for the younger crowd if only they knew of it. The hotel underwent a massive renovation over a two-year period, reopening in late 2007. The marketing manager wanted to change the perception of the bar and grill and reach out to the local community of freelancers, social media enthusiasts, and those who were more "plugged in." The first step toward this was to host the Little Rock Tweetup. This immediately positioned the bar and grill as being part of that community.

The Move to Foursquare

Amy was already a user of Foursquare and decided that incorporating Foursquare into the marketing communications plan made sense. She had noted that customers had already created the venue in Foursquare and were checking in. She reached out to Tristan Walker, VP of Business Development at Foursquare, to register specials and got a rapid response. She also talked through the concept of having a sponsored badge, but at a starting price of $10,000 this was out of her budget range.

Having decided that the Capital Hotel would be a venue, the next step was deciding how to promote that fact. The Capital prides itself on its boutique feel. That guests feel more like they are staying with friends at their home than at a hotel is central to the mission of the hotel. Putting up signs to tell guests and visitors to "Check in on Foursquare" would run counter to this core principle.

Instead, the wait staff in the bar and grill were trained on Foursquare use and were encouraged to ask people who they saw with cell phones if they had checked in. If the guest or visitor didn't know about Foursquare, the staff were trained to show them how to find it on their phone and how to use it.

The team is quick to congratulate Mayors on Twitter. In fact, one Mayor started a buzz all of his own. When the team reached out to congratulate him, a group of women who were also in the bar started a conversation on Twitter about how cute the Mayor was!

Amy made a conscious decision to keep the rewards for Foursquare lower priced but still attractive. New Mayors receive a free Capital Hotel T-shirt; those checking in for the tenth time get a free dessert. There are some smart thoughts behind these prizes. If someone does game the system to become Mayor, what they get, the T-shirt, is in fact free advertising for the hotel. If someone gets a free dessert, chances are that they are going to buy an entrée and drinks to go with it. By pegging the prizes at a lower cost to the hotel, the risk of someone gaming the system is reduced. As Amy points out, "Higher value prizes attract scammers."

These rewards have to be created in association with Foursquare directly by completing a form on their website and at the time of writing cannot be created directly through the Foursquare interface, which might become a barrier to adoption as the space increases.

What was the result? The hotel experienced a 20% increase in visits from the target audience crowd in just six weeks. The first Mayor was "crowned" in two weeks and ousted just one week later!

So what would Amy like to see as new features in Foursquare? Not surprisingly, better stats. Because while all this game play is great, if you can't tie it back to the rest of your marketing efforts, it becomes rather meaningless. In addition, a better way to communicate with those that check in, on a permission basis, would definitely enhance the ability to build community.

Let's see if Foursquare rolls these features out in the near future.

You can find the Capital Hotel on Twitter at @CAPITALHOTEL, @ASHLEYSLR, and @CAPITALBARGRILL.

5

Industries Making It Work

Most industries can make use of social location market-ing as an effective communications channel; certainly, none should dismiss it without first clearly exploring the idea. Some industries in particular have made an early start and have blazed a trail that others in similar or asso-ciated fields can follow.

It is important to note that for some industries social loca-tion marketing is a difficult option, and for some it is sim-ply not an option. This is true of social media marketing in general. If the industry has a customer base that is unlikely to want to share their purchases, their considera-tions or their locations, trying to force the use of social technologies on them is unlikely to work.

For example, I think it unlikely that the bail bond industry is going to find much use for social location marketing as a communication tool; it might be hard to explain to your network just how you became the Mayor of Jonnies Quick Bail Bonds, unless there is a really funny story behind it. Even then, sharing it on an app that your employer or future employer can access is probably not the smartest of personal branding moves. Equally, I'm not sure I'd want to get a Facebook communication letting me know that they have good rates on bonds this week. It doesn't fit with the medium, and it doesn't fit with the nature of sharing information, which is at the core of social media.

It is that core that differentiates social media from other forms of marketing communication. It might seem strange to be pointing that out in Chapter 5 of a book, but I think it is always a good reminder. The end purpose of social media is not to simply push out a message through yet another channel, but to deliver a message in a way that is both compelling and shareable, and that the recipients will want to share with their network.

As we have already learned, this is true for social location sharing. The nature of any campaign conducted via social location sharing is that it will be both compelling and shareable and will have an inducement/reason for being shared.

Regardless of the industry or whether the organization has a physical location, the fastest spreading campaigns will be those that both provide compelling and shareable content, and easy ways to share that content. For example, Foursquare has a more competitive feel to it and is focused on the status of mayorships and obtaining badges. Mayorships and badges tend to appeal more to male users. Gowalla is more focused on the acquiring of digital objects and the posting of pictures, which appeals more to women. SCVNGR is very focused on game play and the completion of challenges, therefore appealing to younger users who typically become bored with games that provide no challenge and are quickly completed.

It is important to think about the target audience when selecting an app. For example, Victoria's Secret might want to target the male customer base by building a campaign on Foursquare. There, becoming Mayor has additional rewards that increase his standing within the game and that provide him with something that is appealing to his female partner other than the usual lingerie that the man might purchase. Thereby he can increase his real-world standing. For example, through the use of the tips feature, Victoria's Secret might easily provide male buyers with tips of what women really want provided by the Victoria's Secrets models themselves. This type of interaction is likely to increase usage of Foursquare at Victoria's Secret (also increasing appeal to women users who see their male partners using Foursquare in a way that benefits both of them).

Equally, a clothing store such as American Apparel, which typically caters to the younger customer, might use SCVNGR to set up challenges at their stores that encourage their target audience to snap pictures of themselves in the same outfits as the mannequins in the store, maybe even with the mannequins in the picture. The sense of silliness, challenge completion, and the uploading of pictures all fit with the existing lifestyle of American Apparel's audience. The addition of social location sharing and game play enhances the experience for this particular portion of its customer base.

A little creativity goes a long way in social media, and especially so in social location marketing. Encouraging interaction beyond the check in is essential. Campaigns that focus only on the check in will be very short lived and are unlikely to reach the level of social sharing that would be a part of any real measure of success. If you treat your company's physical location as a real-world extension of the game environment that the social location sharing apps provide virtually, the players are much more likely to reward you with the level of sharing that you are seeking.

The following sections discuss how different industries are putting social location marketing to work.

Fashion

Traditionally, the fashion industry was not known for embracing social media. In fact, the fashion industry was quite scornful of bringing customers closer to the fashion houses for fear of trade secrets or the details of new collections being leaked.

Wesley R. Card, CEO of the Jones Apparel Group was quoted as saying:

"Even though I know we need to embrace it as a corporation, I am a little apprehensive."

This is not all that unusual. In fact, it is more common than not for the C-Suite to be nervous about social media. Given that fashion is a highly talked about subject, embracing social media was not something that the industry could avoid for long. Whether they liked it or not, bloggers, tweeters, and social media participants were talking about them. The advantage that the fashion industry has is that it is constantly reinventing itself (they call it seasons). So after they decided that social media might actually have a place in their world, it was quickly embraced.

Suddenly, bloggers were being invited to shows during fashion events; they were given front row seats and provided with Wi-Fi to enable them to write and post at the event. Given that previously this was the realm of print journalism—which is still struggling with social media—it was clear that the fashion industry had woken up to the reality that people want instant information.

What the fashion audience didn't want anymore was a magazine that showed them the New York fashion week two months after the event. The social media savvy audience wanted the fashions from the catwalk, preferably as they happened but at least the same day as the show. Magazines couldn't deliver that in their traditional

Figure 5.1 *The fashion industry is now a power player in social media.*

formats. Social media could meet the need. For their part, the fashion houses recognized this as well and realized that social media was a good thing for their industry.

Facebook, Twitter, and other social media apps have now become a staple of the fashion industry's communication method. Some of the best looking Facebook business pages belong to fashion brands. Diane Von Furstenburg, a long-time advocate of transparency in the fashion industry, is a power user of Twitter, regularly sharing updates with the almost 100,000 fashion forward followers that want the inside scoop on what is happening at DVF (see Figure 5.1).

The fashion industry has had several successes with social location marketing in recent months, ranging from big brand stores to individual label events. Fashion is not an industry that you might immediately associate with social media. This, however, would be a mistake. The team at Coach, for example, uses social media extremely well in its efforts to bring the brand closer to its customer base by posting pictures and videos from Coach events, which of course always feature their products.

Jean brand Levi's also utilizes social media as a central part of its marketing communications. It hosts events during popular gatherings, such as South by South West, mixing offline and online word-of-mouth marketing to create buzz about their products and brand.

These brands can achieve success because they know their customer profile extremely well. Coach knows that they are an aspirational brand for many young women, so the pictures they post show women who are similar to its target audience. It is also likely that Coach's target audience carries smart phones. If that is true, it's not too much of a stretch to assume that they are engaged in social media via mobile applications, which would include social location sharing apps.

In April 2010, Jimmy Choo organized a treasure hunt in London called the "CatchaChoo" campaign (see Figure 5.2). The concept was that a Jimmy Choo representative would place a pair of Jimmy Choo sneakers at a location, snap a picture, post it to the CatchaChoo Twitter account, and finally check in with

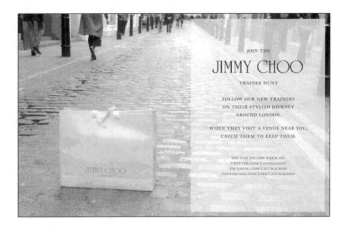

Figure 5.2 *Jimmy Choo, I've been following you...*

Foursquare to share the location of the sneakers. The person who found both the sneakers and the Jimmy Choo representative, and approached that representative with the phrase "I've been following you," won a pair of the sneakers.

Although it was a simple concept, it played to the users' sense of fun, gaming, and achievement. Best of all, it rewarded them with something of high value (for the non-fashion conscious, a pair of Jimmy Choo sneakers retails for around $500) that was worth putting in the effort to follow both the Twitter and Foursquare accounts of the brand.

By including the element of the verbal confirmation as well as the location tracking, Jimmy Choo's was able to counter the issues of GPS unreliability and the system being gamed, which are especially important considerations when you are handing out high-value prizes.

By adding in this safeguard it provided the brand with the opportunity to ensure the campaign worked properly and provided them with photo opportunities that could be shared on other social media outlets, such the brand's Facebook page, which encouraged others to take part in the campaign. After all, it's one thing to hear about an offer, but quite another to see people actually win. By melding several social media sites into one campaign, the brand was able to bring to play each of the site's strongest attractions for the users.

During the New York Fashion week, Fashion house Marc Jacobs partnered with Foursquare to create the "Fashion Victim" badge. The badge was awarded to those attending Fashion Week who checked in at any Marc by Marc Jacobs stores in New York and elsewhere in the United States. The reward was extended by randomly selecting four people who had unlocked the badge in New York to receive tickets to the Marc Jacobs show. See Figure 5.3.

These types of partnerships recognize the needs of the customer to feel recognized by their favorite brands, to be rewarded for their ongoing loyalty, and to feel that

Figure 5.3 *If you were lucky enough to unlock the badge in New York, you were awarded a Fashion Victim badge.*

they are a part of a brand community that receives "insider" information that other casual customers are not getting. Campaigns that have two reward levels—one that is an intrinsic part of the app and one that is part of the real world—have a strong appeal to users of social location sharing tools. Status, badges, and recognition within the community of users is a motivator, but the addition of something more tangible to a campaign has a much higher chance of being talked about, shared, and commented on than simply the awarding of a badge within the game.

This is a valuable lesson for marketers to bear in mind when thinking through the construction of social location marketing campaigns. There must be a real-world element for maximum effect. Users will not talk about your campaign if their only rewards are points, badges, status upgrades, or other game objects. For them to share with their network in a personal way, the reward has to be something that evokes a response at the personal level, preferably an emotion such as excitement.

Retail

Retail is an area in which you might expect to see social location marketing being leveraged early and often. Retailers—especially those with brick and mortar stores—are acutely aware of the need to provide their visitors with a great experience to ensure that their visitors become customers. More important, retailers want those visitors turned customers to become repeat customers.

The retail market has long explored reward programs. One of the earliest was the very simple clip card type that was marked, stamped, or punched each time a customer made a purchase. Eventually, these became electronic cards that are tied to point-of-sale systems and direct mail campaigns that include offers, specials, and discount coupons.

The advent of online retailing did not see a decline in this type of reward program. Shoppers still want to be rewarded and engaged, even if they are not interacting directly with a store representative. Understanding this behavior pattern of "I will buy something from you, but what's in it for me?" is key to understanding why rewards programs are key to the progress of social location marketing campaigns. Although some retailers might view this as almost a sense of entitlement on the part of the shopper, it can become a differentiator in the way a consumer makes a purchasing decision.

The key is to make the rewards attainable, have a tangible benefit to the consumer, and not be something that can either be cheated or acquired in a way that doesn't also benefit the retailer. Although this sounds ridiculously straightforward, too often retailers fail to recognize these basics and make the rewards worthless to the consumer because they are too generic or so valuable that it is almost impossible to offer the reward to the majority of customers. Neither situation is ideal.

Given the amount of customer data that most loyalty systems are capable of capturing, rewards that are generic are almost inexcusable. Although it is impossible to do individual print runs when sending thousands of discount coupons out to customers, it is feasible to group them.

For example, sending a discount voucher to a children's electronics store customer when that customer's buying pattern and visits to the store shows no indication of buying that type of product is counterproductive. Not only is it going to land in the trash can quickly, but it might leave the customer wondering why the voucher was sent or why he or she wasted time opening it. This leads to a decline in open rates of future communications, whether electronic or direct mail. Therefore, the closer to personalized experiences retailers get, whether online or offline, the better.

For example, a chain of electronics goods stores will be divided into different departments, such as computers, telecommunications, home theater, appliances, and so on. By learning the customer's buying behavior, it is possible to group coupons and offers by customer persona. Those who have bought computers and accessories might be interested in offers for additional computer accessories and possibly home theater. Those same customers are less likely to want to receive offers about children's bicycles.

However, cross-sell and up-sell opportunities can't and shouldn't be ignored. Just because a customer has never bought an appliance, it doesn't mean they aren't in the market for one. If you miss the opportunity to let them know you have an offer for them, you are leaving money on the table—money that your competitors will happily collect. However, most of the offers I receive seem to have no relevance to me whatsoever and don't relate to purchases I have made with a particular retailer.

So what relevance does this have to social location marketing? Social location marketing is the perfect means for learning what each customer is interested in purchasing and then marketing directly to that customer. Campaigns that are untethered from appropriate customer data—as is the case in the majority of social location marketing campaigns—are much harder to make relevant. However, with a little thought and creativity, retailers can create compelling campaigns that provide the right level of relevance and incentive.

Creating relevant campaigns that incentivize your customers can range from seasonal offers/rewards that tie into existing in-store promos to category-specific rewards based on store performance. Although most businesses enter their venues in social location sharing apps as a single location, if they have multi-departments they could enter each of the departments separately. For example, electronics, appliances, music, phones, and home theater could all be sublocations of the main location, such as "Electronics@Joe's Gadgets." Customers could then check in specifically where they are shopping within the store.

Rewards and offers can be segmented across the store by department, which allows relevance to be built in. Using segmented offers also allows you to tie rewards to in-store promotions—especially those offered by third-party suppliers. Tying rewards to in-store promotions can be a powerful marketing tool that is both low cost and can be leveraged through a social location marketing campaign. Setting up rewards and incentives such as those discussed here isn't difficult. Doing so simply requires a little thought about what would appeal most to your customers and what is likely to be most successful.

Partnering with a specific social location sharing tool, such as Gowalla, can also lead to a more integrated and rewarding experience for the end user. Partnering also allows the retailer to offer more compelling ways to involve its customers, which leads to more sales. For example, why simply have a generic pin for your chain of stores? Why not partner with Gowalla to have a custom one created (such as the custom Levis pin shown in Figure 5.4)? You could create something that stands out on the customer's profile page and attracts the attention of his or her network. This is a simple, low cost, and effective method of branding within Gowalla.

Figure 5.4   *Creating a custom pin is a low cost branding method within Gowalla.*

Build a reward around the earning of the pin, or better yet create a tour within the store so that the customer checks in at various departments and is therefore exposed to all your in-store merchandising, and then claims her reward. In a space that small, it is easier for users to game the system by simply standing in one place and checking in at all the locations created within the store, so giving away a 50" flat screen TV to everyone who completes it is probably not a good idea. However, giving away something small or something that is an inducement to further purchases would be worthwhile.

Another idea is to use SCVNGR to set up a treasure hunt through the store, inviting people to interact with, rate, and snap pictures of themselves at various locations. For example, Best Buy is currently running a lot of promotions of their new line of electric bikes. Why not host a challenge in store that perhaps involves trying out the latest 3D TVs, followed by a computer department experience that leads to the audio department and ends in a test drive of an electric bike? This becomes a simple way of driving traffic through an in-store set pattern, which is something that traffic flow analysts in larger stores already try to establish. Social location sharing tools can be leveraged to achieve the same effect that previously required changing the entire layout of the store to direct traffic in a specific pattern.

Customer expectations are rising constantly with the release of new technology. Customers are looking for the environment around them to integrate ever more with their technology adoptions. It is no longer enough for a store to post a window cling or put a sign by the checkout that reminds users to check in at their location. This only leads to check-in fatigue. Rather, retailers and other marketers using social location marketing must look at ways in which they can provide an interactive experience in-store that leverages the technology in the pocket of their visitors—an experience that will convert them from browsers to buyers and from one-time customers to loyal fans who act as advocates in both the real and virtual worlds.

Integration is fast becoming a key to extending the social location sharing applications (see the Tasti D-Lite case study at the end of this chapter for a good example). Some social location sharing apps are being rolled out that serve no purpose other than to integrate with loyalty programs and to make it easier for both consumer and store to use the systems. Rather than emphasize the social networking or gaming aspects of the previous generation of apps, these apps exist solely to make interacting with social location sharing programs easier.

One such app is Shopkick (www.shopkick.com). Shopkick is currently being rolled out on a trial basis by stores such as Best Buy, American Eagle, Sports Authority, and Macy's. At the time of this writing, it was available only for the iPhone. Shopkick is an app that the customer runs prior to entering the store. After the customer enters a store, in-store technology picks up the presence of the user's app and registers the user at the store. This is not a social location sharing application in the way we currently understand them, because it does not rely on GPS. Rather, Shopkick is a hardware/software combination. Instead of relying on the phone's GPS, the in-store hardware seeks a signal from the app running on the phone. The signal tells the in-store hardware that a user running Shopkick is nearby, allowing a connection to be made. It is, however, a potential direction that social location sharing might go in, and it is interesting to see it being explored by retailers first.

This concept of moving away from the manual check-in service and to an automated service that requires only that the customer be running an application has a lot of potential. The customer is "pushed" relevant coupons and offers that are usable in the store when they are there or on future visits. This technology is even more emergent than the others in the social location sharing space (it launched early September 2010), but it will definitely be interesting to see both the customer and merchant adoption rate for this. Certainly it requires less effort by both the customers and the stores, which is always a good indicator of adoption.

The concept requires less training for the store, and because the customers do nothing other than install and run an application, they don't forget to check in; therefore, they don't miss out on reward opportunities. The retail space, in particular, is especially attractive for Shopkick. In what is already a fiercely competitive space, additional costs for training on social location marketing tools are hard to justify. Although it is very early in the adoption cycle to show real numbers, this type of engagement can only increase conversion (from browser to buyer) in the longer term, especially if the offers that are pushed are kept relevant and useful.

Given the amount of innovation, it will be interesting to watch the retail industry closely for ideas on how to leverage social location marketing for all other markets. This is true because many ideas that are born in retail transfer readily to other customer-focused segments.

Food and Beverages

This was one of the first areas to embrace the concept of social location marketing. Indeed, the earliest rewards offered by venues on Foursquare were the now ubiquitous free cup of coffee for the Mayor (see Figure 5.5).

Figure 5.5 *Mayors get a free cup o' Joe.*

Since then, the concept has grown in popularity across the board with these types of venues, venues are becoming more adventurous in their use of social location sharing apps and the way in which they offer rewards (see AJ Bombers case study in Chapter 6).

This desire to become more adventurous is a great benefit for the users. When marketers either choose (or are forced) to be more creative, the result is often an increased benefit to consumers. Certainly, marketers are being constantly challenged to improve their offerings, if only from a creative perspective when it comes to social media marketing and in particular with social location marketing.

Some critics of social location sharing have observed what they refer to as "check-in fatigue" and that users, having been avid members of the social location sharing community, become jaded with the process of checking in at every venue they visit.

Part of that fatigue is caused by the lack of incentive to participate in social location marketing. If marketers want consumers to use apps such as Foursquare and Gowalla so that they can market to them, it's up to the marketers to give consumers a reason to do so. The days of a free cup of coffee have passed. With the increasing sophistication of the apps, coming up with compelling reasons for consumers to allow themselves to be marketed to will become easier. For example, the savvy marketer can use SCVNGR (see Chapter 6 for more details) to get beyond the check in and encourage the visitor to become engaged with the venue in a way that a simple check in does not allow.

However, this level of creativity is not restricted to SCVNGR. All the social location apps offer opportunities to take the engagement beyond the check in if the marketer has a good vision of who their target audience is and how they are currently using the app. This is why I think it is essential for any marketers who want to seriously fold social location marketing into their social media marketing plan to be actively involved in social location sharing and to use as many of the applications as possible. Only then can you truly understand which apps best fit your particular customer profile and create campaigns that best meet the needs of those customers.

Beyond the usual suspects that form the top tier of social location sharing tools (Foursquare and Gowalla, for example) are the tools that integrate with more than one service and then offer marketers (particularly in the retail space) the opportunity to build reward programs of their own design on top of the location data.

One such service is WeReward, which offers a cash-based incentive program for marketers to leverage (see Figure 5.6). WeReward is integrated with Facebook, Twitter, Yelp, Google, CitySearch, and Foursquare and is available on iPhone, Android, and Blackberry operating systems. WeReward provides users with the capability to check in using their usual apps and participate in reward programs that can lead to cash rewards.

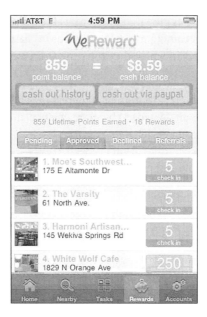

Figure 5.6 *WeReward is a cash-based incentive-based app for iPhone, Android, and BlackBerry.*

For example, both Domino's Pizza and Jones Soda Company operated programs using WeReward in which customers were tasked with checking in and uploading a photo of their purchases. For Domino's, it was a picture of the pizza box, including their receipts; for Jones customers, it was pictures of the bottles that had been purchased.

By requiring customers to upload pictures, the brands were able to verify the purchase and then offer a monetary reward per point earned. The brand sets the value of the points and controls the budget of each campaign. WeReward only charges the brand (such as Domino's) for those customers who actually take action (such as taking a picture of a pizza box), so the brand is paying on a per action basis, not on a per view, per click, or other model that is so common in online or mobile advertising.

In effect, if the campaign does not drive actual customers, then the brand pays nothing because there are no setup costs or minimum commitments. This makes for a very compelling case to use this type of service. While similar in nature to SCVNGR, the added level of financial rewards makes this a service that should strongly be considered by marketers with the intent of actually engaging their customers beyond the check in. In my opinion, this service is a must for all campaigns of the future in social location marketing.

McDonald's tried Foursquare as part of the national (in the U.S.) "Foursquare Day" on April 16 (4/16 is four squared). They offered a total of 100 gift cards valued at either $5 or $10 to Foursquare users who checked in at their venues on that day. The external sell was not the only obstacle to this campaign. Internally, many members of the marketing team had never heard of social location sharing and Foursquare. So, as with many social media campaigns, there was an element of internal education and convincing before the campaign could be launched.

By selecting a day that was already receiving media attention, McDonald's was able to piggyback on the attention and increase the publicity for its own campaign. This is where the creative thinking part comes in. Don't just think about your own campaign, but think about how that fits with broader campaigns that are capturing the media and the attention of your potential customers. McDonald's saw an increase in the number of visitors to its restaurants, which rose by 33% on that one day. They also saw a much broader raising of social media awareness—some 600,000 social media users choosing to follow, fan, or otherwise engage with the brand on other social media sites. Also, McDonalds garnered more than 50 articles in the traditional press covering its campaign. A regular campaign would struggle to receive one tenth of that coverage.

For a one-day campaign, those results are hard to beat. Traditional media would be extremely costly to even attempt to replicate that type of result. Although they don't disclose the sales effect, with a 33% increase in foot traffic through the doors, one can safely assume that McDonald's saw a corresponding increase in sales.

What is really interesting here is the cost of the investment for McDonald's—a company that spends millions of dollars every year on advertising and marketing. The total cost of this campaign was $1,000. Yes, you read that correctly: $1,000. This type of success is very achievable for marketers using social location marketing provided that you use it in ways that appeal to the user base. The gift cards as rewards appealed to McDonald's customer base because they are likely to be repeat customers. So by visiting the store and checking in, customers had the opportunity to win what was, in effect, a free meal. This was a simple inducement, but because McDonald's knows its customers, it was an effective one.

It is not just restaurants that are leveraging social location marketing campaigns. Domino's pizza partnered with Foursquare in the UK to offer customers a free side dish valued at approximately $14 when they checked in. What is unusual about this is that Domino's has no dine-in restaurants in the UK. They are take-out or delivery venues only. This means that customers checking in are not staying at the venue but ordering take-away food. This clearly illustrates that a venue, even in the food and beverage space, does not need to be limited to those that offer the "sense of community" that is associated with bars and restaurants that actively promote coming with friends.

Similarly in Australia, Coca-Cola partnered with Foursquare to run the Coke Machine Fairy campaign. Coca-Cola did this by creating an account in the name of the Fairy on Foursquare. The fairy would then visit locations around Sydney,

Australia, and leave a "magic" can (see Figure 5.7). The Fairy would then check in at the location of the can.

Today's prize: a $300 @GeneralPants_
voucher. Watch this space!

19 PM Sep 9th via foursquare
Retweeted by 3 people

Reply   Retweet

COKEmachFairy
Coke Machine Fairy

Figure 5.7   *Coke drinkers in Australia were rewarded for finding the "magic" can.*

Foursquare users who had become "friends" with the Coke Machine Fairy would then be able to see where the latest check in was and know where to look for the "magic" can. The first person to actually find the can was then rewarded with a real-world prize—something along the lines of a gift certificate to a clothing store, for example. Although this type of campaign has been run before and on other apps (Gowalla, for example, used this type of promotion to launch its own app), what makes this stand out is that Coca-Cola has no physical retail locations of its own.

There isn't a store that you can go to that is specific to the brand. Even the vending machines are owned and operated by other companies. So for Coca-Cola to leverage social location marketing, it had to co-opt other locations to promote Coca-Cola.

By offering prizes that weren't specifically connected to Coca-Cola, it provided a fun element—tracking down the Fairy—and perceived value to the customer/user. Prizes weren't just more Coke (which the person had already purchased), but clothing and other items.

The Coca Cola example proves that companies that might have thought there were no social location marketing opportunities available to them need to think again. Finding something that will induce people to come to your venue has always been the challenge for any food and beverage outlet. Social location marketing doesn't solve that issue. However, what it *does* do is provide you with a low cost/no cost channel to promote the offering. Understanding this distinction is the key to understanding how to use social location marketing.

You will no doubt have noticed in this chapter that I continue to press home the need to know your customers. The use of social location marketing only reinforces that need. Thinking through the offerings that are likely to be most appealing to your audience and then those that will appeal to the users of this type of technology is key to having an effective campaign.

When designing your first campaign, you should review what's already been successful for your company and then marry that with social location marketing. Obviously this is not the first time Domino's has offered free food as an inducement to get potential and repeat customers to come to their venues and place orders. However, adding the requirement that the customer has to check in on Foursquare not only limits the uptake of the offer but provides Domino's with a unique snapshot of its customer base. They now have an idea of how many are early adopters/smart phone users who like to share socially.

Gathering this data helps them build future campaigns that are slanted specifically toward this audience. This trial and adapt methodology is frequently used when implementing social location marketing strategies. Because the entry cost is low when it comes to social location marketing, organizations large and small can afford this approach. In contrast, using a trial and adapt approach with traditional forms of marketing would be cost prohibitive because errors or missteps can be costly—both in terms of brand reputation and financially.

Hotels and Travel

Perhaps more than any other industry, the hotel and travel industry understands the value of good customer service. They understand that word of mouth can be both a blessing and a disaster, depending on the experience the customer chooses to spread. They also know that customers are much more likely to talk about a bad experience than they are about a good one.

Intercontinental Hotels partnered with Gowalla as a method of leveraging social location sharing as part of its marketing communications. When guests checked in at either the Holiday Inn or Crowne Plaza, they received targeted promotional information through Gowalla about Intercontinental's "Hit it Big" rewards campaign through which guests could receive either double points or up to $500 in gift cards during the summer months. The point of using Gowalla is that Intercontinental knew that the customer was actually on property when they received the promotion and were therefore more likely to respond to the call to action than if the customer received the information through a more traditional means, such as via email.

Similarly the Wynn Hotel in Las Vegas claimed its venue on Foursquare and set up a special for users. Having completed this process, the hotel was rewarded by guests who not only checked in but left valuable tips for other guests. These tips included such information as which rooms have the best views, drink recommendations, restaurant recommendations and more (see Figure 5.8).

Figure 5.8 *Wynn Hotel in Las Vegas offers specials to customers on Foursquare; customers, in turn, offer valuable tips for other guests.*

This type of user-generated content adds to the experience of the user checking in at a location and is especially important for the hotel industry. Although a guest might well have read a review or two before arriving, being given tips by other guests as they check in on Foursquare or another app is quite another matter. These onsite tips immediately remind customers that they are part of a community experience and prompts them to leave their own advice and tips for other guests. This sharing of information occurs without the hotel having to expend resources creating the content.

Hotels continue to put out feedback forms in their rooms, but those forms go largely ignored until a guest has a bad experience. With the advent of customer ratings on booking sites such as Expedia, Hotels.com, and others, guests are free to share their feedback at anytime, whether it is good or bad. Many of these systems—because they are independently run—show both the good and the bad and sometimes the downright scathing.

The hotels on the receiving end of these reviews have no opportunity to edit the comments before they are seen by the buying public, which adds validity and credibility to the site, but does little for the hotel being reviewed. If your hotel business gets enough bad ratings, you could find yourself with a PR nightmare on the very websites from which you are hoping to have bookings made.

Given that the hotel lobby and the reception desk are the first point of contact in the real world for a guest, a bad impression here is very likely to be shared with the guest's network before the hotel staff even get the opportunity to offer an explanation or greet the guest. Travel is, by its very nature, a tiring and sometimes trying process. Travelers often arrive at their destinations in a less-than-optimum frame of mind. They are looking for a painless and swift experience at a minimum. The more they have paid, the more they are looking for in terms of a frictionless experience.

It is often the minor friction points that at the moment of occurrence seem to create so much annoyance that they are shared with a user's network. I recently saw a tweet that described the check-in line for a car rental service at an airport in the following way:

"I swear I have given birth to children in less time than it is taking to get a car."

Not the best recommendation for a car rental service by a customer who had just gotten off a plane, written and shared with a large network before the company representative could even greet the user. This is the power of a smart phone and the simple act of adding a comment to a location check in.

This type of comment is not only viewable at the time it is written; it is now permanently attached to the location. Other potential customers, arriving from flights and about to check in at the airport, can view this comment. Are they likely to choose this service, with this type of comment?

In all likelihood, the customer service representative never saw that comment; most organizations do not use these services as methods of feedback or to follow up with customers who have a bad experience—at least not yet. These services are poised to replace the comment card, the customer survey, and the myriad other methods that have been deployed by organizations to garner customer feedback in the past.

Why go through the process of designing expensive surveys when you can simply review the comments that your customers are leaving when they check in?

Why not build a reward system around the check-in process that asks customers to not only check in but rate the experience at the same time? This would provide a company the reassurance that the feedback was relevant to the experience since the feedback was given at the time of action.

By making the customer participation in the feedback process as painless as possible and by reducing the disruptive nature of the feedback process, the customer is more likely to participate. Given that the feedback is likely to be given during the stay, the hotel or destination also has an increased opportunity to rectify any issues, perhaps even turning the situation from a loss into a win.

These positive situations are often followed by an equal amount of social sharing because people rarely like to be the sharers of only bad news. Everyone likes a story with a happy ending, and when an organization shows that it is responsive to the bad experiences of its guests and takes steps to put things right, people share those stories, too. Often the expectation is not that the organization won't make mistakes but that they will own the mistake and make amends as swiftly as possible.

Had the car rental company I mentioned earlier in this section been using the same social location sharing app that the comment was left on, they could have reached out to the customer and offered to make amends—a free upgrade or something that might equal a happier customer experience.

Some hotel chains and travel companies are already adopting social location sharing tools to tie in with their preexisting customer loyalty programs. Utilizing services, such as Top Guest, that offer the ability to integrate social location sharing check ins with a hotel chain guest loyalty program makes it easier for the customer to earn rewards and easier for the hotel chain to promote its locations.

The premise is very simple. When guests check in at a hotel, they are either encouraged to utilize a social location sharing tool, such as Foursquare, Gowalla, or Yelp, to share their locations, or they are automatically checked in by producing their loyalty cards.

Either way, the check in is shared to their networks. This immediately provides the location with credibility among the users' network. Why? Because for the most part, what we think of as word–of-mouth marketing is really referral business. Referral business is something that the hotel and travel industry has long been acutely aware of as a driver of business.

If I am looking for a hotel in a specific location or even just a particular brand of hotel, I am more likely to pay attention to a requested or even unsolicited recommendation from my network then I am to pay attention to a branded marketing message via traditional mediums.

By unsolicited, I refer to the stream of sharing via status updates to which the users of social media are constantly exposed, such as Facebook posts, Twitter updates, LinkedIn updates, and Tripit plans. All of these form the backbone of the social media connected individual.

Still, timing is everything and timing will not always prove to be serendipitous for the brand. The network has to be large enough that the status update has the potential to reach others who are in the process of considering airlines or hotels for their travel plans.

However, given the large volume of customers all sharing their locations with their networks, gathering and using this data becomes an area of increasing returns. Brands are starting to leverage an increasing amount of social data as part of their customer relationship management process and are identifying customers who have networks of sufficient size that they can actually affect the brand's efforts. Influence is the new black. Just as a maitre d' will still snap to attention when presented with a black American Express card, soon brands will find ways of identifying their most influential customers and treat and reward them accordingly.

Social currency has the potential to become as much a factor in how a brand does business with a customer as the credit score is today. A user's ability to gather a large following and, by virtue of his or her perceived social media status, wield purchasing influence on that following is already a valuable asset. Following on the coattails of social media, these influencers will become primary targets of marketing campaigns. Brands that are investing in how to identify influence and what exactly that influence means to them will be best placed to leverage this change. As social media and social location marketing gain ground and acceptance by both users and brands, brands that have built these key influencers into their marketing campaigns will be well ahead of the curve.

As you can see from these examples, integration is definitely the path that social location is taking for the hotel and travel industry (if not all others). This involves investment beyond the normal marketing campaign and starts to involve IT and infrastructure changes that affect the business as a whole—certainly at the enterprise level of adoption. For the smaller business, integration comes at a lower cost and at a lower technology point, but at a higher resource cost in the form of staff training and so on.

If you read the case study of the Capital Hotel at the end of Chapter 2, you will see how they tackled the integration issue by training their staff on how to utilize social location sharing tools and how to pass that information on to customers. This illustrates how smaller hotels can still compete with the larger players in their space, even when the larger players can afford to provide technology solutions by integrating the tools into how they do business.

Integration doesn't always mean expensive technology solutions. Integration can—and often should—be more about how these services become a part of the normal method of doing business.

By encouraging staff members to become advocates of the new business methodologies outside of work, a business becomes its own word of mouth hub and activates customer interest in what it is doing that is different. Differentiation, not just at the product or service level but at the delivery point, is something that attracts attention and encourages customer exploration.

Think back to the McDonald's example earlier in this chapter. This offer didn't draw lots of people to its restaurants simply for a chance to win a $5 gift card. People came to the restaurants because McDonald's was embracing something that very few people had actually heard of—Foursquare Day. This implied that McDonalds was plugged into the cutting edge of popular culture and that by association, its customers could also be a part of that experience. In other words, it wasn't something that they perhaps had previously associated with buying a Happy Meal. By exposing its customers to Foursquare, McDonald's was creating an audience for future campaigns. People new to Foursquare learned how to use it and joined existing Foursquare users as an audience for future social location marketing campaigns. This is a very important consideration when determining how your existing customers and potential customer use the technology.

If you believe your customers or potential customers are not early adopters, as AJ Bombers did at a local level and McDonald's did at a national level, provide an experience that introduces the technology to them and encourages them to use it. Become the source of information, not just rewards. The marketing process can be both educational and informative, as well as a vehicle to drive sales. By providing customers and potential customers with an insight into the future, they have another reason to regard your brand as an object of loyalty.

Think of the way Apple markets its products. Much of the loyalty is driven by the fact that Apple customers believe they are on the inside track of new technology. You don't have to be a technology company to achieve the same cachet. Simply partnering with the right technology as part of your marketing can do that.

Summary

After studying how social location marketing can be used in various industries, several common themes should have emerged. First, it's important to know your audience, which is important with any form of marketing. Second, it's important that you understand how your customers use social location apps, such as Foursquare and Gowalla, so that you can tailor your marketing efforts accordingly. Last, and perhaps most important, you need to add some imagination to the mix.

Assuming that you have determined that social media marketing in general and social location marketing in particular is a good match for your customers, keeping these three basics in mind will go a long way toward ensuring that your campaigns are successful. What cannot be overstated is that with social location marketing, it's okay to try something and adjust as necessary on-the-fly. Given the low cost of entry for most social location marketing campaigns, you can use a trial and adapt approach that would be cost prohibitive in other forms of marketing.

In addition, keeping a careful eye on how social location sharing is evolving is very important. The examples given in this chapter revolve mainly around Foursquare and Gowalla because, as the early leaders in the field, they are currently the ones with the most compelling case studies. However, as discussed in Chapter 4, they are not the only apps available. Other apps are being designed to compete with Foursquare and Gowalla, while still others are being designed to put an entirely new spin on social location sharing. You also shouldn't ignore Facebook and Facebook Places. While Facebook Places has yet to prove itself commercially useful (at the time of this writing, anyway), it is only a matter of time before it starts to produce results. I would expect to see case studies starting to appear from companies that have already found ways to leverage Places as it currently exists.

You might remember that Foursquare started out as a game. Before Foursquare offered business metrics and the plethora of other partnerships, businesses found ways to incorporate it into their marketing mixes, so you can be sure that businesses are already finding ways to incorporate Facebook Places into their marketing mixes, too. As the existing apps recognize the need to move beyond the check in, watch for new feature sets. I think we'll see features added that allow for better integration with existing corporate infrastructures. I also think we'll see features such as those found in WeReward that allow smaller organizations to create compelling reward programs around their customer loyalty programs.

Today, there are services available that will construct marketing programs using social location sharing apps in a method that requires very little involvement from the marketer.

The appearance of these services is not necessarily an indication of the stability of social location sharing. However, their existence does imply that a significant number of companies are investing in the concept and that means it is here to stay. This in turn means that more organizations and more verticals will start to incorporate it in their marketing mixes. Just as micro-blogging started with numerous apps that gradually mutated into the market leader, Twitter, so it is likely that the social location space will devolve. However, where I see a big difference in social location sharing is that there is unlikely to be a one-size-fits-all solution that works for all verticals. That means we will see more diversity remain in this space than we saw in previous shake ups of the social media tool set.

Facebook, while bringing with it the largest audience of any single social media app, is still not the right place for every business to carry out its social media communications. The same holds true with Foursquare, Gowalla, Yelp, and any of the other social location sharing options currently available. I strongly believe we are at least another year from seeing the rising curve of innovation in this space start to plateau to such an extent that it will become obvious which app best fits which vertical. Even the apps themselves have shifted focus over the past six months. For a while it seemed that Gowalla was going to focus almost exclusively on the travel industry, which seemed a logical choice given its "Trips" feature.

Gowalla pursued and secured partnerships with the Travel Channel and National Geographic. However, in recent months, that seems to have been downplayed as Gowalla pursued other industries and broadened its offerings.

What *is* certain is that every app is starting to include metrics capabilities, which is something that the more established apps already offer and is demanded by business users. For example, Yelp has had a business dashboard for quite a while. Foursquare now offers some business metrics. Gowalla and SCVNGR promise these are in the near future. If the rest of the apps are to continue to secure partnerships and be taken seriously by businesses, they will have to incorporate these metrics. Marketers demand these metrics capabilities so that they can provide the kind of performance feedback the C-Suite requires. When these metrics capabilities are not available, an app can quickly fall out of favor with business users.

Andrew Koven, who leads e-commerce for Steve Madden, has been critical of the experience his brand has had with these services. He said results from its partnerships with Foursquare and Loopt haven't been very compelling to date, and he didn't see much reason why Steven Madden would sign up with Shopkick.

Although part of that negativity can be attributed to setting unreasonable expectations for an emerging service, it also has a lot to do with being able to provide accurate resultsets to partners. If these apps are to meet their true potential—and I truly believe that they have the potential to affect the way brands of all sizes do business in the future—then the apps themselves have to start to develop more robust reporting systems. These reporting systems must be able to clearly show those compelling results for their users and allow for more streamlined communications between the brands and their customers and potential customers.

Brands want to be a part of the community. Simply knowing that they had X number of visitors check in at one of their locations on a given day won't cut it in the longer term. They want to and need to be able to reach out to those visitors. They want be able to tie those visits to sales or abandoned carts in much the same way as the detailed metrics provided by online shopping allows them to see customer behavior.

Ultimately, social location sharing tools—at least from a marketer perspective—should allow behavior to be modeled in the same way as web store analytics do for the online shopper. Where did the customer come from? Which competitors have they visited? What did they view in my store? What did they purchase? Where did they go after they left the store? Of course this will sound like a privacy nightmare to most people outside of the marketing sphere and even to some within it. However, given that this type of data is readily available to the online marketer, the expectation that social location marketing will marry online/mobile marketing to the real world, it is not unreasonable to think that marketers will want to match as closely as possible the type of data that they capture in the purely online world.

Case Study: Integration and the Seamless Check In

Venue: Tasti D-Lite, East Coast United States

Participant: B.J. Emerson

Background:

Tasti D-Lite is a chain of ice cream stores originally founded in New York in 1987 and now headquartered in Tennessee. They made the decision to enter the social media realm and were experimenting with Twitter and Facebook. In doing so, they caught the attention of their point-of-sale supplier, PC America, who had been experimenting with the Twitter and Facebook APIs.

PC America offered to integrate the Tasti D-Lite social media effort into their POS system, and after some brainstorming it was decided that Foursquare would also be integrated into the system.

Tasti D-Lite wanted to provide a process for their customers that was as seamless as possible, that encouraged adoption, and that increased customer data. In the end, their concept was surprisingly simple, at least from the outside.

They would integrate their social media efforts with their customer loyalty program, allowing customers to update their Twitter status, post to Facebook, and check in on Foursquare at the same time by using their Tasti-Treat Card. Further, they would allow the customer to preselect the messages that the system sent out for them or create their own. If no messages are selected or created, a default message would be sent.

For example:

"I just earned 5 TastiRewards points at Tasti D-Lite Columbus Circle, NYC! http://myTasti.com."

A simple enough message, but one that contains both the brand name and an inducement to the customer's network to also use the service—after all, who doesn't want rewards? The customers are given an additional 1 point for each social network that they connect their account to for each purchase that they make. Adding Facebook, Twitter, and Foursquare gives them three additional points for every purchase, which accelerates the point at which they receive free items in store.

In addition to earning points, customers also receive updates on when their favorite flavors are back in store. This is a great way for Tasti D-Lite to promo limited time flavors, such as Pumpkin during Halloween.

Tasti D-Lite had some very good results with this program. More than 27% of the customers who had a loyalty card opted to connect it to their social networks (see Figure 5.9). The average number of connections each customer had was 91.

Figure 5.9 *Tasti D-Lite saw nearly 30% of its customers who had a loyalty card connect it to their social networks.*

As Figure 5.8 shows, a predefined tweet can still elicit responses from a customer's network. Multiply that by the number of customers that were willing to connect their loyalty card to their social network accounts and you have more than enough content to drive real sales.

Part of this success is undoubtedly the fact that Tasti D-Lite, by opting to integrate their social media campaign with their loyalty program, made it frictionless for their customers to take part. If the customer has no additional steps to take, then why would they not want to take part?

6

Know Your Apps

Having explored the background to social location sharing and the various reasons why people might use it as a method of social networking, it is time to get your feet wet with the various apps. This chapter assumes two things:

- *First, I assume that you have a smart phone (an iPhone, an Android-based phone, a Blackberry or Windows Mobile phone).*

- *Second, I assume that you either don't already have an account on Foursquare, Gowalla, or the other apps, or that you have only recently set one up—and you're still learning how to use it.*

The second half of this chapter focuses on social location sharing venues and getting your business listed, as well as the best ways to leverage the different apps. Finally, we will look at the different offerings from each of the apps (Foursquare, Gowalla, Yelp, and so on) that can be utilized as part of your company's marketing plan. In Chapter 7, "Marketing to Social Location Sharers," we will explore the types of social location marketing campaigns that you could create.

As a marketer, you should be a regular user of social location sharing apps if you hope to be able to leverage them effectively as part of a SLM campaign. Why is this so? There are several reasons:

- Because each of the apps are still developing, it is not possible to be successful by simply reading blogs, Twitter posts, or even books to stay on top of the new features that are being rolled out. By using the apps your customers use, you stand a much better chance of being able to see the new changes and how those might affect your marketing plans.

- By using the same apps your customers use, you put yourself in the shoes of your audience, which gives you an insight that might otherwise be missing from your marketing campaigns.

- Last—but not least of all—as a user of these apps, you will become subject to other marketers' offers and campaigns. That means you will be exposed to new creative ideas for how to leverage the apps you and your customers are using. You will gain a sense of what appeals to your customer while gaining very useful insight into how your own campaigns affect the user community. You will also see what works, doesn't work and what has limited appeal, which will help you avoid making costly mistakes. Although using all these apps can seem burdensome, it is truly the only real way to learn about social location sharing quickly and effectively.

Foursquare

URL: www.foursquare.com

The Foursquare home page (see Figure 6.1) presents some useful information about the app for the new user, including an animated video that answers the question "What is Foursquare?" The home page also features a scrolling list of the latest badges that have been unlocked and tips that have been left by users. This is entertaining, especially when people you know appear on the list. Even without being logged into or registered with the site, it is possible to make use of the search engine to locate people and places (either by name or by tags). This can be useful to get a sense of what an organization's venue looks like in the general search and indeed if it is correctly tagged. It's also useful for finding friends to see if they are in fact registered with Foursquare.

Click Join Now and you will be presented with the sign-up screen (see Figure 6.2).

Knowing the latest badges that are available and how they are awarded can lead to some very simple campaign wins that will produce quick results for little or no investment. We will discuss these opportunities later in this chapter.

Completing and submitting the sign-up form will take you to the next stage, which allows you to connect with people you are already networking with on Facebook

Figure 6.1   *Foursquare's home page.*

Figure 6.2   *Foursquare's sign-up page.*

and Twitter (see Figure 6.3). Again the issue of privacy raises its head here. Do you want to share your location with the people that you are connected to on Twitter or on Facebook? How much of an issue is that for you? The answer to this question varies from individual to individual. Some are very comfortable sharing their location with their entire network. Others are comfortable sharing only with select individuals.

Figure 6.3 *Foursquare offers to connect you with your Facebook and Twitter friends.*

The next step, shown in Figure 6.4 allows you to select up to six Facebook friends and send them a direct invite to join you on Foursquare.

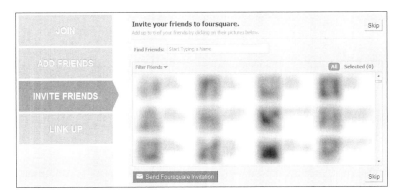

Figure 6.4 *Choose your favorite six Facebook friends and send them a direct invite.*

The final step, shown in Figure 6.5, allows you to connect your Foursquare account to your Facebook and Twitter accounts so that your account activity is shared with your network automatically. This activity sharing includes the awarding of Mayorships and badges along with check ins. Although selecting this option might seem like a logical thing to do, it is worth noting that if you are a regular user of Foursquare, your network might get annoyed at seeing a constant stream of check ins and begin to resent your connection. I caution against allowing the service to push notifications unmonitored to your network.

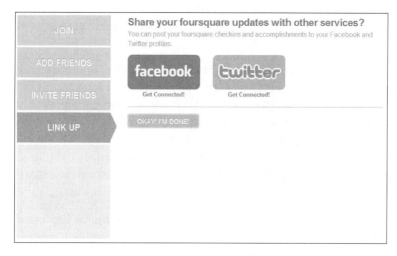

Figure 6.5 *Use caution when linking your Foursquare activity with Facebook and Twitter—your friends might not be amused.*

Connect the services but select to share check ins with your network only when they are worthwhile and add something to the network, such as at a particularly good restaurant. When doing this, you are providing interesting content for your network, and that makes you more valuable.

The next screens tell you about using Foursquare on various mobile phones, including being able to utilize text messaging for those people without a smart phone. Yes, at the beginning of the chapter I mentioned that you would need a smart phone. Although you can "play" via text, it lacks much of the interface and the sharing. For example, you can't see your friends in the near real-time environment that smart phone users can, and so Foursquare loses most of its appeal when used with a text interface.

The Foursquare Fine Print

Before you dash off with your new Foursquare account, it's worth mentioning some of the links at the bottom of the home page that prove very useful, especially to marketers.

Privacy on Foursquare

As with many social sharing networks such as Facebook and Twitter, privacy is a primary concern for users. For some, it is such an overwhelming issue that they choose not to join these types of social networks. For others, it is an "after the fact" concern. They claim that they had no idea how much information they were signing up to share. Foursquare's privacy statement makes it very clear what information they will share about its users, who they will share it with, and under what circumstances they will share it. It is important to understand this statement, especially as a marketer.

Knowing what information will be shared with particular organizations gives a marketer a better understanding of the type of data they can expect to obtain from Foursquare and how they will be able to obtain it. At present, most organizations are limiting themselves to using the publicly available data. However, it is only a matter of time before we start seeing marketing-based applications appear that utilize the Foursquare Application Programming Interface (API) to obtain richer data about users in the same way that marketers can now leverage the Facebook API.

Knowing that the use of the data is likely to change over time is important to the individual user and the marketer. The media storm that Facebook created when it announced its intention to change the way in which it made users' data available to third parties was in part caused by the fact that users did not foresee how powerful and valuable their data would become. Also, as the value of that data increased, the ways in which it would be used would change. Fortunately, users are becoming increasingly more aware of these issues as more of these sharing tools are leveraged by marketers. This is fortunate for both sides because users are more careful about the data they share with the apps (Foursquare, Gowalla, and so forth) and therefore with marketers. Marketers benefit because their leveraging of the data is less and less likely to cause the types of PR nightmares we saw in early 2010.

Almost all marketers contemplating leveraging SLM will or at least should consider building an application that provides them with richer data. There are several reasons for this:

- An abundance of applications for SLS data that the marketer can leverage
- Relatively cheap cost of entry to build these applications
- Availability of developers to do the work

The other concern for users of Foursquare when entering their information into the sign-up page is what data will be revealed to their "Friends"—that is, their network of Foursquare users. The settings page allows users to control what others can see about them.

As you can see in Figure 6.6, you can make selections that reveal your phone number, email address, Twitter account, and Facebook account (if you have connected those at the initial setup). Users are often surprised to suddenly get text messages, phone calls, or email from people who were sharing in their Foursquare experience.

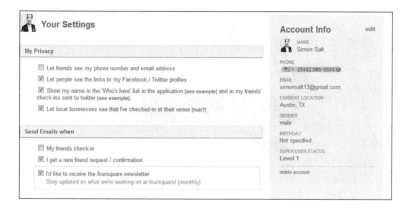

Figure 6.6   *Use caution when choosing Foursquare's security settings.*

If you do not carefully manage these settings, the mobile version of Foursquare will share this data with anyone you are connected with. This is not such a great experience when you suddenly get a phone call from that creepy guy you just connected with at a Happy Hour, only to find that he now has your phone number and can text you whenever he wants. The message here is to manage your data carefully on Foursquare just as you would on any other app and share it only with those people you are most comfortable with having it.

As you can see in Figure 6.7, when the check boxes are all selected, it is possible to access all of a person's data by looking at his or her profile page from the friends list. Clicking Text or Call will give you that person's phone number. Clicking Twitter will link you to his or her Twitter page; clicking Facebook links you to that person's Facebook profile. The Email option is self-explanatory. This can be very bad for the individual and very good for the unscrupulous marketer who wants to build a database of contact information from visitors to his company's locations by adding those visitors as friends and then harvesting contact information. I'm not suggesting that as a methodology, but I would not be terribly surprised to see it going on, especially within certain industries.

Figure 6.7   *If you aren't vigilant, your private contact information can easily fall into the hands of an unscrupulous web marketer. Note that this user's name, photo, and email address have been intentionally hidden to protect the user's privacy.*

Foursquare's Blog

This is where Foursquare makes announcements about new developments and partnerships that they have formed. Also, Foursquare posts success stories from partners that have leveraged the Foursquare app for business success. This is another very useful information source for how Foursquare is being used by marketers. You can see what has been tried, what has worked, and how the campaigns were organized. Although they do not provide all the details, the details they do give provide a starting point for a marketer new to SLM and who is looking for models that are repeatable or at the very least adaptable. Certainly, it gives you something to work with that is more imaginative than "free coffee for becoming Mayor," which was so popular when rewards first came to the minds of marketers using SLM. Leveraging ideas from others' campaigns is a logical step because your customers are expecting your campaigns to be more engaging.

The Foursquare blog is definitely worth adding to your blog reading list or your RSS feed if you have one. Getting the information directly from Foursquare is usually better than reading it secondhand from any of the other news sources (although they provide insight into what the announcements mean). Keep in mind that when a marketer chooses to set up a campaign utilizing a social location sharing app, with the exception of special cases we will consider later in this chapter, there is no vendor/client relationship. So the type of information flow that some larger organizations have come to expect doesn't necessarily exist. That means it is important to know where to go for the breaking news and information that could affect the campaign you're running or the ones that you are planning to invest in.

The Foursquare Profile Page

The next page to look at is your profile page. This is where you will be able to see your progress within the app. This is also where you can see what others will see about you. What they see about you is how they decide whether to share their locations with you, just as you view their information to make the same decision.

Initially, your profile page will look rather empty and uninteresting, just as it did on other social networks before you had started to engage and produce content that others could interact with (see Figure 6.8). Yes, you are going to produce content. All social networks are really social publishing platforms—whether it is pictures on Facebook, status updates on Twitter, blog posts, videos of your cat on YouTube, or your location on Foursquare—it is all content.

Figure 6.8   *At first your Foursquare profile page is pretty spartan.*

The first thing you will probably notice is the Also on Foursquare link at the bottom of the page. These are Foursquare partner companies that provide content to Foursquare that make the process of checking in at certain locations more interesting and that also lead, in some cases, to the awarding of limited edition badges.

Clicking these links will add them as "Follows" rather than "Friends" on your profile, so you won't be bombarded with messaging by these brands. However, you can check their pages by clicking the "Following" link to see what they are offering in the way of tips, deals, and so on. For larger brands, using Following links this is a great way to connect with social location sharing app users and certainly worth considering as part of an SLM budget. More on these pages later.

What is appealing to many users about the way Foursquare has constructed the profile page is that it displays your activity information in one easy-to-read dashboard. You'll see Tips you have added about venues, items you've marked as To Do, badges you have earned, and the places you have become Mayor of. All this information is supplemented with your most recent check-in activity and the list of your Foursquare friends (the network you are sharing your location with).

When a user searches for other users by name, if that name results in a profile page and the person is not already a friend, the searcher is shown a limited version of the profile page. What the searcher sees is the current city/state location for that person, any tips left by that person in the city that the searcher is in, any To Do's in the searcher's city, badges, and friend list. What the searcher does not see is any Mayorships or the recent check-in history. This affords a certain level of privacy to users.

What a user cannot do from this web interface is actually check in at a location. That must be done from a mobile device. This prevents the problems that were experienced early on with Foursquare where users were able to check in at any location without actually being there. This was a big barrier to adoption by marketers because it was too easy for users to "game" the system.

The Foursquare Mobile Application

It is worth noting that the Foursquare mobile application interface varies on each phone operating system. The longest standing and most developed variant is on the iPhone. I'll mention any significant differences between versions of Foursquare for different smart phones, especially if they affect the user experience. The most common difference in the interface is the location of features, rather than a difference in features.

Most of what you do with Foursquare will be done via the mobile app on your smart phone. The most common screen that you will use is the Places screen. There you select your location to check in. This screen is divided into two sections: My Favorites and Nearby. The first section is populated by checking in at certain locations on a frequent basis. This first section also can be populated with those locations that are most often checked into by friends near you.

The Nearby section lists those locations within a certain radius of your current location. In cities, this radius will normally be 500 meters. Yes, Foursquare uses metric distances as the unit of measure, so if you are not familiar with it, now is a good time to learn. Although the majority of the locations you want to check in to will be in the list, some will not appear immediately.

Selecting Search enables you to enter the name of the venue and have that venue returned as a place at which you can check in. In the rare instance that a venue is neither listed in the Nearby section nor returned in the search results, you are given the option to add this as a new location. Although this might seem onerous, there is a small reward for doing so: extra points, which we cover later in this chapter.

 Note

> It is also worth noting that searching is another way to check whether your own venue is listed in the Nearby section and to think through the user experience when another user wants to check in at your location. How many steps do users have to go through? What is in it for them? We discuss listing venues in a later section of this chapter.

As you can see in Figure 6.9, the results shown in the Nearby list have no discernable pattern. It is not ordered by distance, alphabetically, or by type of venue. This means that users must scroll through the list to find the location they are looking for. Again, it is worth considering this when entering your own venue. Make sure that it is properly entered, without typos in the name or the address. These can easily become barriers to the user with a short attention span looking for immediate results. Given the device and the timing of use, this pretty much describes most social location sharers.

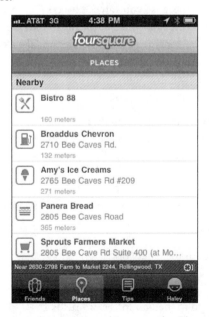

Figure 6.9 *Foursquare results are returned in a ramshackle order.*

Selecting a venue from the list takes the user to the check-in screen. This screen shows the user who the current Mayor is, if there is one, and who is currently or most recently checked in at the location, if applicable (see Figure 6.10). It is also possible to see the current Tips for this location. You may also add your own Tips. The Details tab (Map tab on the Android) shows the location on a Google map. The Details tab on the iPhone and Blackberry shows recent tweets from the location. The map might be a little puzzling to new users, but it is actually a good visual way of verifying that the location is correct.

Figure 6.10   *The Foursquare check-in screen shows the Mayor of your current location as well as people currently checked in.*

Recent tweets are useful because you can see tweets from users at that location and from the vicinity. This is especially useful for those who are new to an area—for example, visiting on a business trip. It is possible to make a connection with these Twitter users and ask questions about the venue or broader questions about the area. In this way, Foursquare becomes more than just a check-in tool and fulfills its role as a social networking tool.

It is important to remember that this is after all "social" location sharing, and as such is as much about the social element of what users experience as it is about the location sharing. Users of social media/social networking want to meet certain needs:

- Increase their own knowledge by asking questions of "friends"
- Display their own knowledge by answering questions
- Grow their network
- Add Influencers to their network
- Be seen as an influencer
- Be seen as the "go to" person in certain fields

Social media/social networking tools allow the user to achieve all of these in varying degrees.

Not all users have all these needs, but all of them have some of these needs. So when using social location sharing apps, it is important to remember that the aim is to be social. The question is, however, do you or don't you share your check ins on other apps or share your check ins with your Foursquare network? Choosing not to share might seem counterintuitive, but it is an option worth considering. The Tell My Friends option is, by default, always selected. However, deselecting it will still check you in at the venue and gain you whatever rewards are applicable. It will not, however, add the check in to the list of venues you have visited. Instead, your network will see Off the Grid as your location. This is useful for those locations that you want to tag but don't want to share. Personally, I don't bother checking in at those locations. For example, I don't think my network needs to know when I visit the doctor or dentist. Some users will check in Off the Grid at these locations. Others will use the Off the Grid option when they are visiting clients so as not to reveal their precise location but still gain points or mayorship, which works well for a venue that you might be prepared to reveal at a later date.

My personal advice and practice is to share only those check ins that are notable. I don't share the fact that I'm at the gas station, but I do share that I'm watching a new release movie or that I'm at a well-known destination such as Graceland in Memphis. The reason for doing that is because it encourages conversation. People seeing that check in on Twitter or Facebook often will leave a comment or post a response. This opens up new conversations, sometimes with people that I have had very little interaction with. Those people are now interested in what content I am sharing, and sometimes that has much broader implications than simply sharing my location. It can and does lead to new readers of my blog, and even new clients. Of course this is more applicable to the smaller business than to the large enterprise, but the ability to influence and grow a network is a major concern for most marketers whether they are independent or part of a much larger team.

Not all users agree with this and specifically cross-post to all platforms all the time. I have polled a few of them and they in turn state that they actually saw an increase in the level of interactions that they received after adopting this practice. What this reveals is that it is important to know your own network and what it expects of you.

Make sure that you do the research, even if it is anecdotal. Doing so is always worth the effort because it can help you not lose significant members of your network simply because they are bored with seeing posts of you grabbing a foot-long sandwich at Subway for lunch. The flipside is that perhaps you live somewhere that provides you with the opportunity to share lots of interesting locations on a consistent basis, or your network finds the comments you add to your check ins interesting or humorous and so they want to see more of that type of content.

Gowalla

www.gowalla.com

The difference between Gowalla and other social location apps is immediately apparent from the home page (see Figure 6.11). The cartoon images of people—all of whom are more "trendy" looking, hanging out at a coffee shop—immediately tells you the type of audience that the service is geared toward. As mentioned previously, design is a big part of the Gowalla philosophy and they seem to want the visual experience of using their app to be a major part of the attraction for the user. Given their design company background, that is hardly surprising.

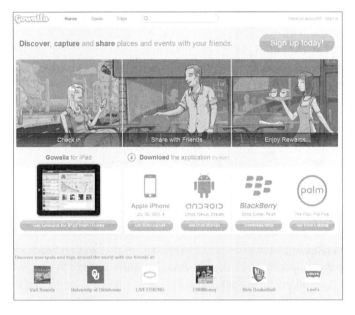

Figure 6.11 *Gowalla's trendy graphics immediately tell you this app is aimed at the urban, cool user.*

As does Foursquare, Gowalla places its partnerships at the bottom of the home screen, giving prime importance to them and using them to encourage users to see what these partnerships have to offer to them as users. Placed centrally is the availability of the app on various mobile phones, again displaying that the platform is for every type of phone user.

The menu at the top of the screen shows Spots, Trips, and a search bar. These are available whether you are logged in or not. They're available even if you don't have an account.

Spots

Spots (see Figure 6.12) are basically venues. However, not all Spots are retail locations. A spot can be any notable point that other users can visit.

Figure 6.12   *Spots are venues, but not necessarily retail locations.*

As you can see, selecting Spots will give you both Featured spots and New spots. The Featured spots give you a clear indication that Spots are less about retail locations and more about experiential locations. One doesn't exclude the other, but this does make the world of Gowalla more like the real world.

New spots are, of course precisely that, as the world of Gowalla has expanded far beyond the USA. As shown in Figure 6.13, spots have recently been added in Estonia, Saudi Arabia, England, and of course the USA. We'll look at Spots in detail later in the chapter.

Figure 6.13   *New spots are, well, new...*

Trips

This is the way that Gowalla allows users to group spots to form interesting ways to explore an area, a city, a state, or places around the world. By visiting all the locations in the trip, a user is awarded a pin for completing the trip. Each time a user checks in at one of the locations, they are notified that they are on a particular trip. Some of the trips have been created in association with Gowalla's partners, whereas others have been created by users. As a user, you can create 10 trips for your network and other users to complete. We'll talk about how this integrates into using Gowalla as a marketing tool later.

The trips feature certainly is Gowalla's main differentiator in terms of use. None of the other apps have this type of option, and it certainly made them an obvious choice for the travel industry, including The Travel Channel. The trips are an excellent way for users to experience their surroundings in ways that they might not have found on their own. Gowalla is, in fact, a user-generated travel guide for different locations.

Again, this plays directly into the social element of social location sharing: giving and getting information that might otherwise have been beyond the user's ability, knowledge, experience, or budget. By providing rich content, the Gowalla user becomes recognized among other users and is therefore considered a valuable resource. By acting as the conduit for this rich content, Gowalla becomes the social location sharing app of choice for those seeking both the information and the recognition.

Figure 6.14 shows only a small selection of the trips that are currently on Gowalla. A user first visiting the site sees many of these trips that can be completed. However, as with all user generated content, you are somewhat at the mercy of the users who created these trips. Some will be very useful, others perhaps less so. This is why completing trips generated by your network is sometimes a better choice than launching on a trip created by a random stranger. But, if your taste is for adventure, why not do a trip created by a stranger?

Search

The search bar works regardless of whether you are signed in or whether you have an account. Again this is useful for the casual browser and for those determining whether their venue or a favorite location is listed before trying out the app. Try searching for anything familiar to you, such as "Coffee Shop" and Gowalla will return a list of coffee shops starting with the ones that are nearest to you (see Figure 6.15). How do they do that? The Internet Protocol (IP) address assigned to your computer or phone tells Gowalla approximately where in the world you are and therefore allows Gowalla to return relevant results, because Location isn't all about mobile devices.

Figure 6.14 *Let Gowalla be your user-generated travel guide.*

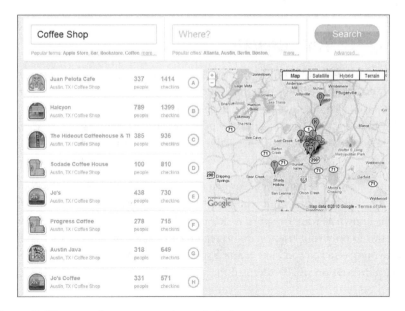

Figure 6.15 *Gowalla isn't magic, but it feels that way sometimes.*

This search is particularly useful if you want to find new places to explore or you are in a new town. Notice that the results are ordered by the number of check ins, a measure, at least in the Gowalla world, of popularity. This is worth noting if you are marketing a venue, given that the results are also shown on a map. The higher up the results table you are, the more likely it is that users will visit your venue if they are unfamiliar with it. The ranking acts as a blind recommendation table. The other functionality of the Gowalla search is that you can also search for venues in other places, not just where you are currently located, which is not true on other social location apps. So you can plan trips ahead of time.

For example, if you want to know what recommended museums are in Tallinn, Estonia, try it as a search. Now when you go on that trip to Estonia, you will have at least three places you can visit that you know other Gowalla users have visited and have bothered to check in. Click the name of the venue and you can view pictures that have been uploaded by other users as well. This way you can do research on your destination before you even arrive.

Again this sharing is the strength of the social element of SLS. The information that is available is not necessarily of the curated type. It isn't sanitized or edited, nor is it from a glossy, overproduced photo shoot, but from the camera phones of other users just like you. That doesn't necessarily make it any more reliable than if it were from a brochure, but the likelihood of you knowing one of the content creators is vastly increased; therefore, your ability to assess the content based on that relationship is also increased.

Setting Up Your Gowalla Account

Much as with any other online service, the Gowalla setup is fairly straightforward. Supply an email address, a password, and upload an avatar image and you are done. However, as with all other services, it is worth a couple of minutes to review the terms and conditions and the privacy policy. Again, the information provided here is from both a personal user perspective and from that of a marketer using these services.

Like its peers and competitors, Gowalla offers some privacy settings that will hide your location or at least limit who it is shared with. Gowalla's record of your locations is known as your Passport, which is by default visible to all. However, you can limit this to only your friends. If you read the privacy policy, you'll see that if you do anything else at a spot, like create a spot, take a photo and post it or drop an item, your location will be revealed to those beyond your friends. Worth noting.

Digital Objects

Another differentiator for Gowalla is the collection of digital objects (see Figure 6.16). As previously mentioned, this is a historical carryover from the Alamofire Facebook game RatPack. In Gowalla however, not only are these objects collectible, but they have been utilized and are likely to continue to be leveraged by marketers as opportunities to interact with Gowalla users.

Figure 6.16   *Ever try to fit a longhorn into a backpack? In Gowalla, you can!*

Currently, the number of digital objects is approximately 150. However, this number varies because unofficial objects have crept into the game and specific marketing objects have also been used. Some of these objects still exist in the Gowalla world and wait to be discovered even though the campaign they were associated with has long since ended. More on objects and marketing later.

So what is the point of these objects? Nothing really—they are there to add a little game play to the Gowalla environment. They don't "do" anything. However, there are some tips to collecting them. When you start with Gowalla you receive three objects that you carry with you in a "backpack." To pick up a new object, you must drop an object at the same location. So if you were carrying the Basketball, the Teddy Bear, and the Keep Austin Weird T-shirt and wanted to collect the Longhorn, you would have to drop one of the first three objects. You can also "vault" an object, which adds it permanently to your collection. However, once it is in the vault it cannot be removed. Yes, "permanently" means exactly that.

So avoid the newbie mistake of either vaulting all your objects or dropping them all where there is nothing to pick up. If you run out of objects in your backpack, you will have to wait until you check in at a location that has a bonus item. These bonus items are added to your backpack without requiring you to drop anything. The maximum number of items you can carry in your backpack is 10. Keeping about six to eight seems to be ideal, because it always gives you a selection of things to drop and some that you can decide to vault. Some users collect specific digital objects rather than try to collect them all—for example, food items or sports items.

At the time of writing (August 2010) the Gowalla API did not allow for "writing" to Gowalla, only "reading" from it. This prevented the obvious application of a trading site that would allow the direct swapping or trading of the Gowalla objects.

However, I expect this to be opened up in the near future. When it does it will certainly change the way these objects are viewed and has the potential to open things up even more for marketers with Gowalla or a third-party developer having the opportunity to produce an in-game currency or barter system in much the same way as online gaming environments World of Warcraft and even Second Life did.

Passport

As previously mentioned, the Passport tab is the history of your travels with Gowalla. The Passport page is visible to your Gowalla friends. This shows them your recent check ins, your top 10 check ins in order of the locations that you check-in at most often.. It also shows how many Pins and Stamps you have earned. Each of these are clickable, allowing you to view the actual locations that awarded them. In other words, anyone in your network can access your full Gowalla history, which, gives some users reason to pause before they check-in at certain locations.

The Passport also shows your friends by avatar, which means that each of your network members is able to connect with every other member of your network (see Figure 6.17). This may or may not be a good thing for your network and is still another reason to be proactive about who you add to your SLS networks. You will be known by the company you keep.

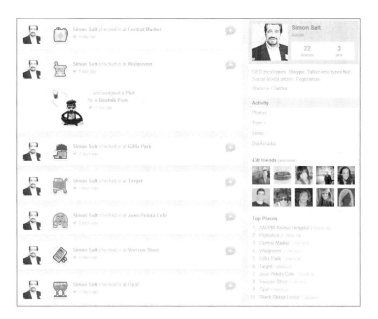

Figure 6.17 *Be aware of the company you keep!*

Adding friends is the last tab on the website. There's nothing particularly different here from any of the other social location sharing services. It offers to find your

Facebook friends, Twitter followers, and Gmail and other webmail contacts who are already using Gowalla. You can send them friend requests or you can send an invite to join to those not currently using Gowalla. Again from the privacy perspective, it is worth noting that if you provide Gowalla with your friends' email addresses, Gowalla reserves the right to store those addresses to see if your friends join the site. Of course, they will also use it for any other marketing purposes that they reserve the right to use it for.

As with the other social location sharing apps, you will spend most of your time on the mobile application rather than the website. It is at least worth knowing your way around the site for the few things you need to do there. At the time of writing, Gowalla is available on all phone operating systems in at least a beta form (Blackberry). The functionality varies among the phones, with iPhone and Android being the most fully developed and offering the most features. Blackberry and Palm are still very usable and should improve over time as more features are ported from the other operating systems.

Gowalla Mobile Application

The mobile application is divided into four tabs: Activity, Spots, Trips, and Passport (see Figure 6.18). Passport reflects the same information that is contained in the web version of the app, so I don't cover it in detail here.

Figure 6.18   *Click the tabs along the bottom of the screen.*

- **Activity Tab**—The Activity tab shows recent check ins by people in your Gowalla network, with the most recent check ins listed first. It provides the user's name, the location, and any "comment" the user added at the time of check in. Selecting the user's name gives you a detail page for that particular check in and allows you to add a comment to the check in that the user can then see. This is great for communication between members of the Gowalla network, but it also provides marketers with an opportunity to communicate directly with customers on an individual basis. The barrier here is the "opt-in." That means the individual user must be connected to the location through Gowalla. However, this is a good thing for both the marketer and the customer. It becomes a permission-based marketing communication, which is always preferable and always more powerful and much more likely to lead to a response to a call to action.

- **Spots Tab**—The Spots tab shows the locations in your vicinity. There has been much criticism of all the social location apps over how accurate they read the GPS chip in various phones. This is a hard thing for the developers to get exactly right. Bearing in mind that they are trying to provide both a reasonable list and accuracy, and that they are tackling different phones with the same operating system, they do an acceptable job most of the time. Different users will have different results—I have seen the Gowalla app place me several kilometers away from my actual location. This becomes problematic because of the way Gowalla handles check ins, which are performed from the Spots screen. You must be within reasonable proximity of the location you are trying to check in to for the check in option to appear. If the software doesn't read your location exactly, you will not be able to check in. Sometimes this has more to do with the hardware and can often be solved by turning off and then reactivating the GPS service on the phone. It is worth bearing this in mind when using any of the tools in this book. It is also worth noting when thinking of how your potential customers might be using the tools to check in at your location. What are the alternatives for them, in terms of your outreach through marketing?

- **Trips Tab**—The Trips tab shows trips that you can complete that are near you. It also shows you how many of the stops on the trip you have already completed. As previously mentioned, Trips provide an interesting entry point for marketers to social location sharing. They are also a good point of entry for those without a physical location or a location at which general users would not check in. As a marketing agency, my company does not have a location at which people would normally check in. So I put together a few trips around the Austin, Texas, area for people to complete. One is a coffee house tour, because I spend a lot of time meeting people in coffee shops. The other is a vegetarian restaurant tour. Why would I put these together? It would seem that they have nothing to do with my business. However, whenever people check in at one of the locations on one of my trips, they are informed that they have just checked in at a spot on the IncSlinger Coffee House Tour or the IncSlinger Veggie Austin Tour. Instant brand awareness! When they complete the trip, if they have connected their account with Twitter, Gowalla posts the message shown in Figure 6.19. This provides you, as a marketer, with the opportunity to reach out to a potential customer and talk to them, congratulating them on completing the trip.

Figure 6.19   *People who complete one of my trips receive this message.*

SCVNGR

www.scvngr.com

SCVNGR (scavenger, for those of you who prefer not to try to work out the texting friendly name) is a very different app from its competitors. Launched to the public in 2010, it had been an underground "business only" app for a year prior to this. Rather than having a focus on the end user, the team at SCVNGR chose to focus instead on the businesses that would be providing the experience for the users.

They also focused on the game play aspect of social location sharing; their stated aim is to be the game app of social location sharing rather than the social network of social location sharing. That does not mean, however, that they are taking social location sharing lightly. Rather they are utilizing more game dynamics than the other apps do and therefore want to be considered that way.

Much of the SCVNGR app looks vaguely familiar to its two main rivals—Foursquare and Gowalla—in that it requires you to set up an account in the usual way. Enter your name and your email address and find friends on other networks that are or could become SCVNGR users.

After you create a profile, you'll need to download the mobile application to modify your profile, at least as far as overall personalization is concerned. Your profile picture is added from your mobile device and will then be reflected in the web version of your profile. Also, in the mobile app you make the privacy settings choice that the other apps have you make on the website.

At this point, SCVNGR has a privacy setting; you can share your location with everyone or share it with friends. The selection you make is a personal choice, but sharing only with friends seems to make most sense for most users. The settings screen on the mobile version also allows you to change your preference for having your account connected to Facebook and/or Twitter.

This is a slightly different way from how the other apps operate but is no great inconvenience; to join in on the fun you are going to need the mobile app anyway.

The Profile page shows you the number of places you have been, the number of treks you have completed, the number of challenges you have completed, and the number of points you have gained (see Figure 6.20). In addition, it shows your recent activity and the badges you have gained. Your friends are also displayed on your profile page.

Figure 6.20 *A typical SCVNGR profile.*

Places is the list of locations where you have checked in. Treks are similar in nature to Gowalla's Trips and allow a series of locations to be linked together to make for an interesting set of check ins. Badges are awarded for meeting certain challenges or for certain numbers of check ins. Beyond the sense of achievement, at this stage SCVNGR badges do not have a real-world function.

Challenges are where SCVNGR departs from the competition. Challenges are, as far as SCVNGR is concerned, the core mechanism of social location sharing. Challenges are the method by which businesses using SCVNGR as well as other users can incentivize players to interact with the environment in which they find themselves.

Challenges range from the most elementary, such as "check in" or "snap a photo" through to the very creative. A pizza restaurant I came across had two challenges that were a lot of fun. The first was to use the food on your plate to create a picture of the person sitting opposite you. The other was to take a picture of the food you were eating but from an unflattering angle. Why would you do these? Some people quite obviously wouldn't, but the point is for those who want to do something fun and get involved with the game play of SCVNGR, these types of challenges not only get them to use the application on their phone more often and more times at each location but also provide the location owners with the opportunity to have customers interact with their venue in tangible ways.

It would not be too hard for a restaurant to run a competition based around the challenge of creating a picture in food of the person sitting opposite you. Judging is straightforward matter of looking at the pictures and deciding who the winner is. The prize? Maybe a free pizza on the next visit. This type of reward has much more appeal for the game player than simply trying to check in most often over a set period of time or finding digital objects that (at present at least) can't be traded.

The additional differentiator for SCVNGR over the other apps is the capability to build custom rewards directly into the game without having to fund an expensive partnership or develop custom content. The tool (www.scvngr.com/rewards/new) allows you as a user to develop a reward by filling out a very simple form (shown in Figure 6.21).

As you can see from Figure 6.21, very little information is required to generate a reward. All you need to include are

- Where the reward can be awarded
- The title of the reward
- The description of the reward
- How many points are needed to receive the reward
- The limit to how many people can win
- The expiration date if applicable

SCVNGR uses a lot of game theory in the interactions that it creates with its players. One of these, dynamic progression, is leveraged through the rewards section, but applies to the points section. A user gains points at a location by completing challenges.

- A check in gains a user 1 point
- Taking a picture gains them 2 points

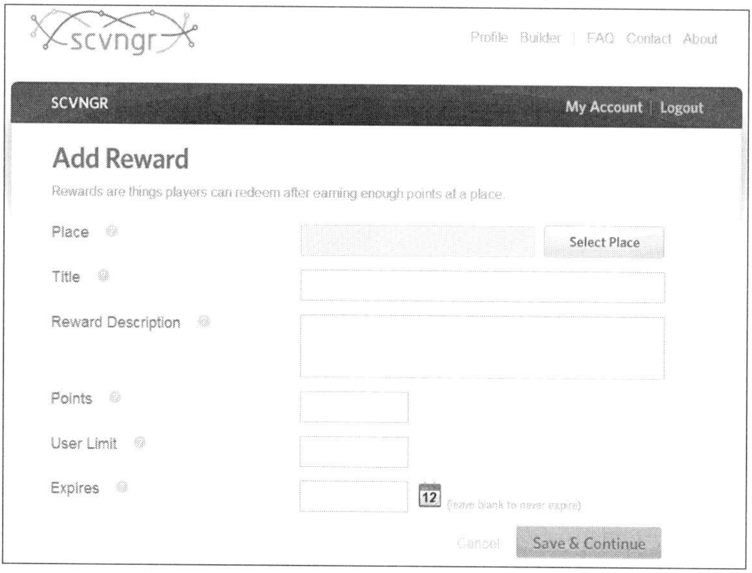

Figure 6.21 *Building custom rewards directly into the game is easy using this tool.*

- Other challenges might gain them as many as 3 points

By telling the player how many points they need to achieve a reward, SCVNGR provides the player with an incentive to keep returning to the location and keep completing challenges, including the more difficult challenges in order to receive the reward. When we see a progress bar, we want—in fact, we are driven to—move that bar toward the goal at the end. This is the element of dynamic progression that SCVNGR clearly understood and leveraged in the rewards function of its app.

Social Check In

This feature is unique to SCVNGR. SCVNGR has leveraged the "bump" style technology and built a proprietary system that allows more than two people to complete the check in at the same time and be awarded points based on the number of people completing the check in. For example, if you check in with eight other people and you all do so using the Social Check-in feature of bumping your phones together, then each player will receive 18 points (2 points x 9).

Beyond just being a nice implementation of technology, this provides a very interesting data point. This shows a venue how many people actually check in with friends. It also shows which users are more likely to check in with friends. This, in SCVNGR's words, provides a social coefficient that gives a level of "socialness" of a particular venue.

Why would you want to know this information? If you owned a bar, and if you knew that the average socialness score of all bars in town was 0.38 and your score was 0.29, you would immediately know that your bar scored lower than the average. This could be a function of two things:

1. Your customers don't use SCVNGR very much (perhaps because you don't incentivize them to).

2. Your bar doesn't encourage people to arrive in groups.

Now if you are looking to attract nontech customers who like to drink alone, this is probably a good thing. However, if you are trying to be the newest, greatest Happy Hour spot, this is probably a bad thing. You can now work on improving this score as part of your broader marketing efforts. However, this would not be the only measure you would apply, but by adding real data points to the marketing equation, you can make decisions that are more tangible to those outside the marketing department—for example, the COO or CFO.

Another example is a retail chain that had multiple outlets around the country. They would be able to compare different stores for socialness and add that data point into their analytics about various store performance. If the average for all stores was 0.35 and particular regions had variations that were below or above that, adjustments could be made to the stores. Equally regional averages would also be measurable, and therefore individual stores could make adjustments based on those.

Although it's not a definitive measure, it certainly goes a long way to answering the criticism so often leveled at social media, one of a lack of credible metrics that actually help with bottom line impact. We will have to wait to see how this implemented on a larger scale as SCVNGR increases its user base both in terms of players and businesses offering rewards.

The SCVNGR Mobile App

As with the other apps, the real interaction takes place on the mobile version. The main screen is the Places screen, which shows you the places near your current location (see Figure 6.22). Also shown are places that are currently offering a reward to those players that complete challenges, which is an immediate attraction and a differentiator for customers. Why go to a coffee shop that isn't offering a reward? Why not try the one that is?

For the marketer looking for a reason to use SCVNGR, this highlighting of venues with rewards is an immediately compelling reason to choose this app over some of the others. As previously mentioned, the use of game theory (see Chapter 3, "Games People Play") is a must have for any successful social location marketing campaign.

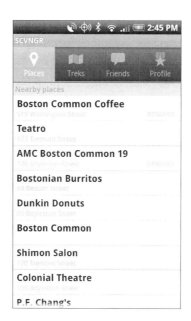

Figure 6.22   *The SCVNGR mobile app home screen.*

With SCVNGR some of that thought is already built in to the app; the use of dynamic progression bars as users collect points at the location means that the urgency is built in to the challenge.

By showing players how many points they have accumulated toward a reward and how many more they need, a venue can entice customers to keep returning. However, the reward has to be compelling enough and the points achievable within a reasonable number of visits, but it also has to be difficult enough that the venue gets repeat business.

For example, to ensure that players keep coming back, it should not be possible to obtain the reward by simply completing three challenges at the same time in the same visit. A better way to dole out rewards is to require that multiple challenges be completed even if the same challenge is repeated. This allows the customer to gradually accumulate points instead of earning them all at once in a single visit. Also, challenges that create content, such as uploading pictures add a better experience for other users and thereby encourage them to complete the challenges, too.

SCVNGR provides some useful tips on creating challenges on their website and includes the obvious caution: Nothing Illegal. This might seem ridiculously obvious but what seems funny in a creative meeting can have a nasty way of backfiring. For example removing a road sign seems funny to college students but is not a great marketing play.

Don't become *that* case study! When thinking through a challenge that is going to be repeated, make sure that it is as fun to do the second and third time as it was the first time. Nothing screams boredom more than something that was only mildly fun the first time and is definitely not a repeatable experience. It's like being a person at the party with only one joke. It gets a polite smile the first time, it gets a blank look the second time, and the final time it simply paints the teller as annoying.

Figure 6.23 shows how different challenges can be valued with increasing points: The check in gains the player only one point, whereas actually interacting with the location garners more points. The Info tab shows the player what the rewards are for completing the challenges; this is why it is important as a marketer to make the reward compelling enough for the player to want to complete the challenges.

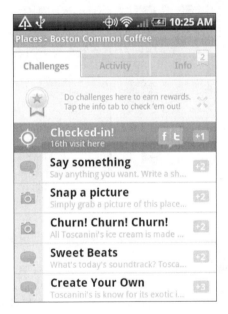

Figure 6.23 *SCVNGR values each challenge differently.*

The trade that is occurring here is time. The venue is offering something of value to the player. The player is offering her time and to increase the amount of time that she spends at the venue and interacting with the venue. The reward should therefore be attractive enough for the player to feel that she is being rewarded for her time but should also have an intrinsic value that ties into both the location and the sense of challenge that the players of this game feel. So going with the easy option of a free entrée or a coffee might not be appropriate. I have seen many food outlets that also have a line of T-shirts for sale. Offering something like this that also promotes the venue is something that the player can feel they achieved, has a distinct monetary value, and is attractive to the marketer.

The advantage of challenges being rewarded is that it overcomes one of the earliest criticisms of these services by marketers—that the system can be gamed. Certainly this was originally true, when it was possible for users of other systems to check in at locations where they were not. Challenges, however, are not reliant only on the GPS to be accurate, as is the case for check ins. Challenges are also reliant on inter- action with the location—something that is difficult, if not impossible, to fake. This allows marketers to offer high-value rewards for higher value interactions, and it means they can also leverage game theory by offering progressively more valuable rewards as a player racks up points. So perhaps a free coffee is only 20 points, but that free T-shirt is 100 points; this makes for a more fun and repeatable experience for the player (see Figure 6.24).

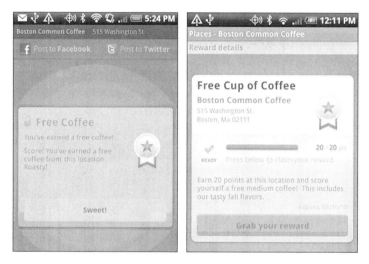

Figure 6.24   *Thirsty? You've just earned a free cup of coffee!*

Certainly SCVNGR gives an indication of where we are likely to see social location sharing and marketing develop. Although it is still reliant on the check in as an action, it does encourage both users and marketers to think beyond that and to see how sharing location can be beneficial and worthwhile to both.

Facebook Places

www.facebook.com/places/

No mention of social location sharing would be complete without the mention of Facebook Places. At the time of writing (August 2010), Facebook Places is only a few weeks old and has had mixed reviews in terms of both its appeal to users and its fit for use as a marketing platform.

While the app itself is vanilla in its implementation, and some observers have argued that this was the right thing to do given the potential user base, Places offers at ini- tial rollout nothing that would appeal to either the avid early adopter of social loca- tion sharing or the marketer looking for an additional way to leverage Facebook.

At time of this writing, the mobile application is available only on the iPhone; however, other phone platforms are supported via touch.facebook.com, which includes the Places tab and allows check ins this way. In tests against the other social location sharing apps, Places performs well in identifying the user's location and providing a list of the appropriate nearby venues.

However, Facebook has acquired social location sharing app Hot Potato, and that certainly has the potential to make Places everything it ought to be. Hot Potato users not only shared locations but social objects as well, such as TV shows, movies, foods, and so on. This type of sharing adds a dynamic that does not currently exist within the apps that focus on physical locations. GetGlue offers similar social object sharing, but does not offer physical location sharing. By combining both, Places has the potential to become the one-stop application for all forms of location sharing, which is undoubtedly Facebook's aim.

The likely roadmap for Places is to encourage users beyond the early adopter group to start sharing their location with a familiar app (Facebook) and then introduce new features to them as they become more used to checking in (see Figure 6.25). Given the size of the Facebook user base (some 500 million worldwide) even a two percent adoption would put them ahead of all the other apps in terms of users. This alone makes Places a very compelling app to watch. Add to this all the other features that Facebook can roll into Places, such as geo-aware advertising, geo-tagging of pictures, cross-posting of pictures with Facebook business pages, facial recognition for auto tagging of friends, auto-check in of friends from pictures, and so forth, and Places starts to not only look like a serious player in the game, it becomes the dominant player overnight.

Figure 6.25 *A Facebook Places check in appears in a user's Facebook stream as a wall post.*

Does this mean that the other apps will simply wither and die? Absolutely not. We might see a shake up because of the introduction of Places, but it is unlikely to be the end of Foursquare, Gowalla, SCVNGR, or Yelp. These are secure apps that have proven themselves to their devotees, and those users are unlikely to abandon the apps in favor of Places unless the apps themselves stop evolving. In addition, Foursquare and SCVNGR have both opted to integrate their apps with Places, and no doubt Gowalla and some of the others will follow suit (if they haven't already by the time you read this).

Overall, Facebook is attempting to become the infrastructure on which the social web is built, so providing both an application and the capability for others to integrate with that app moves this aim forward. This combination will really decide the future of Places. Either it will be the infrastructure on which other apps rest, or it will be a standalone application.

As with other Facebook implementations, privacy was an immediate concern, especially the ability to check in friends without their permission (though this setting can be changed). This feature seems to have very little use in its current implementation; however, I believe that future functionality will have a significant role to play in the evolution of Places.

After the privacy issue is overcome—or at least a comfort level is reached among Places users—the potential to check in with other users (in the same way that SCVNGR does via its Social Check-in feature) opens up Places users and businesses to offer a richer method of interacting. Marketers should be more interested in location sharing if they are able to see how many people frequent venues as parts of groups, or at the very least share a social connection with other customers. This type of data will enable the tailoring of social media campaigns to a level of detail not currently available.

Where Places has to really prove itself, either as an infrastructure environment or as a standalone social location sharing application, is in the business realm. Without the addition of some serious game play, rewards system, and a method of communication that enables businesses to engage with their customers, Places will fall short of meeting expectations.

However, I can easily see a version of Facebook where Places is fully integrated into the existing business offerings available in Facebook, such as adverts, business pages, community pages, and the expanded inbox. It is not too much of a stretch of the imagination to picture that a Places user who "likes" a business on Facebook would then gain additional rewards when they check in at that business in the real world and vice versa. Users could check in at a business that has a business page and be prompted to "like" them via Places for an additional reward.

It will be interesting to see how much data Facebook exposes from all these interactions directly to businesses. The current offering via business pages is improving gradually. How much more powerful would it be to have the check-in data also available in the business page? This could potentially allow a business to see not only the page interactions but the real-world interactions of those who "like" the business page. These complementary data points add a richness to any marketing communication that is currently available only through the use of third-party development and the extraction of data from multiple sources.

Google Hotpot

www.google.com/hotpot

In late 2010, Google released Hotpot, which is tied to its Places app. Hotpot works in lockstep with Places to help you rank and recommend local businesses.

Note

If you thought it was confusing that both Facebook and Google have apps
named Places, you'll be even more confused by the fact that the name
"Hotpot" is quite obviously similar to Facebook's competing app called
"Hot Potato."

So what does Hotpot offer? As you can see in Figure 6.26, its interface is extremely
easy to use.

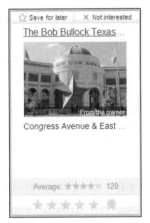

Figure 6.26 *Hotpot's interface is clean and simple.*

Simply hover your mouse pointer over the stars at the bottom of the venue you
want to review and choose a rating. Doing so flips the venue detail over so that you
can enter a text review of the location (though a text review is not required). If the
venue is a café, restaurant, or bar you can further rate the important elements of
these locations, namely, Food, Service, Atmosphere and Value in a simple binary
rating system depicted by a smiley face or a frowny face.

From a marketing perspective, Hotpot will now become the customer facing side of
Google Places. Hotpot is very similar in nature to Yelp's rating and review pages. The
difference between Google Places and the other location apps is that the business is
responsible for setting up the business page within Places. If the business page doesn't
exist, users are not able to create them as they are able to do with other apps.

Where users do come in is with Google Maps. While there is no check-in process,
users of Google Maps can integrate places that they visit with their Google Latitude
account. Latitude is a location sharing service that allows users to add comments
about the location to Google Buzz. Users also can make the location a "starred"
location so that they can find it quickly when they return to the map. Also, because
Android phones are powered by Google, all of these features and those of Hotpot
are immediately available to all Android phone users.

With Google's importance in terms of directing traffic to venues of all sizes, Hotpot does have the potential to create the missing link between social location sharing and search engine optimization. For marketers, this is a tangible benefit that they can show to the C-Suite. Whether this will actually happen remains to be seen. However, given current Internet user behavior—which is to use a search engine (usually Google) to find just about anything including locations—Google's entry into social location sharing cannot be dismissed and should certainly be a part of any marketer's consideration as they plan their campaigns.

Yelp

www.yelp.com

Yelp launched in 2004 primarily as a ratings and review site for consumers. Yelp basically took the secret shopper model and opened it up to the public it so that anyone could enter a review for any business. Yelp has faced some legal issues in recent years and currently faces a class action lawsuit over some of its advertising sales practices.

Those issues aside, Yelp has a very interesting model and differs from the other social location sharing sites in that it has built a community of users that are not only location sharers or reviewers but identify themselves as "Yelpers." This more than anything else separates Yelp from its competitors, and they have continued to grow this affinity base by implementing a special status of "Elite" Yelpers in some cities.

An Elite Yelper is a volunteer position that Yelp reviewers are able to apply for and be selected for, though not all applicants are selected. Elite Yelpers gain a distinct status among other Yelp users and are courted by Yelp themselves. Yelp is also the only app to have successfully broken away from the online only model and hosts parties in its Elite cities for the Elite Yelpers and others to attend, share stories, offer tips on review writing, to network, and also win giveaways.

Yelp describes the qualities needed to be an Elite Yelper in the following way:

As having a lot of reviews that are seen as insightful, engaging and personal. In addition they have profile pages that standout from the crowd and that have a strong appeal to other users, most importantly they must have a picture of the reviewer on the profile page as well as their real name.

No other social location sharing app has a status within its environment that requires an application or that requires specific criteria to be met outside of participation in the game itself. This prior history as a purely ratings and review site makes Yelp something of an oddity in social location sharing. Yelp's mobile app now includes check ins as well as the capability to find businesses, by category, that are near your current location.

When checking in, a user can rate the venue and create a draft review that can be posted later from the website. The capability to create a review while at the location adds a degree of urgency and immediacy that means reviews on Yelp can carry a certain heat that other review and rating sites do not. That they cannot be posted from the mobile app gives the reviewer the opportunity to pause and reread the review, as well as make grammatical corrections that might be due to typing on the keyboard on a mobile device.

One of the most useful features of the mobile application is the Monocle feature, which is Yelp's augmented reality viewer. It activates the camera in the device and then overlays the view the user has with the names, star rating, and number of reviews of the various venues that are within a set radius of the user and are in the direction the mobile device is pointed (see Figure 6.27).

Figure 6.27   *Yelp's Monocle feature is one of its most useful.*

This gives users access to an incredibly rich information environment that definitely empowers them (reread the introduction to this book to see where the ideas for that technology came from) and can directly impact their purchasing decisions. This makes Yelp a serious app for marketers to consider when exploring social location sharing and social location marketing. Having a high number of reviews and a high star rating is more likely to drive traffic to a venue. This rating system provides marketers with something closer to traditional and more tangible metrics than the other apps. This is important for many organizations when considering early steps into social media and in particular social location marketing. Being able to show some form of improvement before the bottom line is impacted is something that most marketers struggle with, and demonstrating this to the C-Suite has long been a challenge.

The Yelp website is more developed than other social location sharing sites and the personal profiles are more detailed. The profile page includes information about the user, the user's recent reviews (which are also shown on a map) and six avatars of the user's friends.

Users of both the mobile application and the website are reminded when completing a review of a location of their recent check in and asked to complete reviews of those locations as well. This is a simple and effective way of increasing a user's number of reviews and so increasing the amount of content available through Yelp. See Figure 6.28 to see how users can use Yelp to share their experiences.

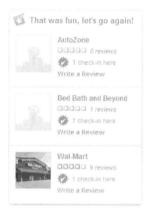

Figure 6.28   *Got something to say after an experience out on the town? Yelp about it!*

Yelp does not allow business owners, employees, or immediate family of business owners to become Elite Yelpers. However, they do provide a complete suite of tools for business owners to monitor their businesses on Yelp.

The first of these is the actual business page. As a business owner or a marketer, it is important that you claim your business on Yelp and set up a business page so that potential customers can find it and leave reviews. Considering that setting up your business's page is free, it's a good first step toward establishing a presence in both social media and social location sharing.

Yelp provides a very useful toolset for managing your business page. These tools differentiate Yelp from the other social location sharing apps and make it worth your time to set up a business page, because the tools offer more than the capability to simply update the business information or create offers.

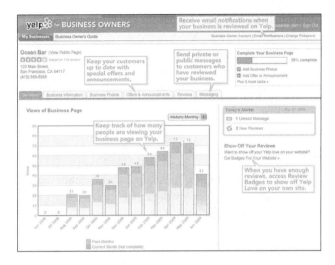

Figure 6.29 *Yelp provides powerful tools for business owners to manage their businesses.*

As Figure 6.29 shows, the business owner can do the following:

- Access the number of page views
- Create offers
- Make announcements
- Add photos
- Read reviews
- Send messages to customers who have left reviews

Whether good or bad, reaching out to reviewers, acknowledging their reviews, and if appropriate, offering to fix a problem is a great way to close the loop in social location marketing. Building a reputation for listening is much more likely to increase the number of positive reviews that you receive.

Reading the reviews of competitor's locations is also something that can aid a business. If your competitor is getting better ratings than you, take a look at why. If someone leaves a complaint, look at what that complaint was and how that relates to your business. Is the reviewer complaining about something that might or does happen at your locations?

Overall, cultivating the Yelp community is a very simple, easy-to-manage entry into social location marketing allowing you to

- Make compelling offerings
- Use the announcements feature to promote specials
- Respond to reviews

All of this can be managed by both the single venue business and the multiple location organization without a need for a large resource base. Getting involved in anything that will result in a major drain in resources is usually the major barrier to any organization getting involved in any form of social media. With tools such as Yelp, it becomes as easy as dealing with email and completing other business tasks that they do every day.

The Others

In this chapter I have covered four of the main social location sharing apps in what I trust is enough depth that you as a reader can get started using them to benefit your business. Many other social location sharing tools are available, and below I list some of those and explore them in a much briefer form. There are many reasons for this—time and space, for example—but also because they are somewhat lacking in features that aren't truly usable by marketers. I provide further details on each app in the upcoming sections.

MyTown

Some people will question my not featuring MyTown in more detail. I have two reasons for not including them in the preceding section.

- The first is that MyTown is available only on the iPhone. While I understand the focus of Booyah in making their application available only on the iPhone, I believe it is so restrictive that it will hurt them in the long run. Android has already over taken iPhone sales and is going to consolidate its dominance in the mobile phone operating system market. For a marketer to consider an app seriously, it has to have the capability to not only reach the intended users but also the marketer's target audience.

- The second reason for not including them is the lack of an open application programming interface (API). Foursquare, Gowalla, and, shortly, SCVNGR all have open APIs. The importance of this for marketers is the growth of third-party applications that can assist them in their social location marketing efforts and the capability for those tools to be integrated into existing systems.

Although MyTown has run some partnerships, they are primarily rich content partnerships rather than marketing opportunities (with the exception of H&M). Those partnerships have a closed platform, which means that Booyah controls the development, and that increases costs for running a campaign. Only very large organizations are likely to be in a position to leverage MyTown in its current iteration. Local businesses (where a bulk of social location marketing takes place) are not likely to be able to utilize this tool in an effective way.

Whrrl

Like MyTown, Whrrl is available only as an application on the iPhone and Android. Although an Blackberry application have been promised for more than a year, nothing has yet emerged. Whrrl is available via the mobile web, and this version works in an acceptable way, but it lacks the ease of a native application and the menu options that come with applications. So for the same reasons as given for MyTown, Whrrl isn't a major player and thus has been excluded from the main section of this chapter.

Whrrl has some excellent features, and its focus on photo sharing and building stories and "societies" makes it very appealing, especially to female users. However, it, too, does not have an open API and so suffers from a lack of third-party applications and the potential to be integrated into other tools. The combination of both these factors again makes it of limited appeal to marketers at this stage.

Whrrl also lacks a real sense of game play or other incentives for users to return to the application after the initial wave of enthusiasm has worn off. Without the sense of urgency and a focus only on checking in and sharing pictures, Whrrl is unlikely to be able to compete with the second generation of social location sharing tools already appearing and the new generations of those that already dominate the market.

Brightkite

As discussed in Chapter 4, Brightkite was one of the early players in social location sharing and is still active. They have a strong focus on SMS technology, which, given all the smart phones and growing size of the applications market, might seem counterintuitive. However, SMS is still the number one method of nonvoice communication used on cell phones. So this focus should not be dismissed. However, from a marketing perspective, it is hard to recommend this app given the direction social location sharing is going.

While Brightkite was an innovative app, it seems to have become mired in the social location sharing arena as it was 2–4 years ago, and failed to maintain its lead. Certainly apps such as Foursquare, Gowalla, and others have left them behind in terms of adoption and buzz.

Brightkite does benefit from being available on most phones, either as a native application or via a third-party interface (on the Blackberry). However, it doesn't seem to have capitalized on this. Certainly its native applications lack the appealing interface of its competitors, and it has been commented on that the interface is confusing to new users and lacks the intuitive nature of the others.

Loopt

Loopt, as outlined in Chapter 4, was one of the first serious players in social location sharing. Loopt continues making changes that are good indicators that it is not done yet. Loopt has rebranded the application and introduced other variants specifically for the iPad and one that focuses on profile exploration.

In addition, Loopt has created a few marketing partnerships with larger brands, such as Burger King, Paul Smith, and so on, showing it does have the capability to support marketing campaigns. However, with the lack of an API, third-party apps, access to data, and the inability for users to create or add to the social location sharing experience, Loopt's efforts seem to be only a hat-tip toward the real needs of marketers from all sizes of organizations; therefore, Loopt isn't a major player in the social location sharing game, in my opinion.

Summary

The apps outlined in this chapter are definitely the major social location sharing players at the time of this writing and are likely to continue to be so for the next few years. As social location sharing matures, marketers and developers will start to figure out new and interesting ways that the apps can be used, and we will see some of the smaller sites start to disappear or be acquired.

Even those that get only a passing mention are still worth watching. As social location sharing develops, marketers may find a niche audience that exactly matches what a particular marketing campaign seeks as a target. At this point, the whole social location sharing space is still emerging, making it difficult to pick a clear winner or even predict if there will ever be such a thing. Ultimately, social location marketing is most likely to be wrapped into the broader social media efforts made by organizations.

For this reason alone, it is essential that marketers pick their apps carefully and ensure that they develop a feel for the entire social location marketing arena and not focus on one app alone. Four years ago, there were several micro-blogging apps to choose from. Now there really is only Twitter. Had marketers invested a lot of time into just one of the others, they would have had to reinvest all that time into Twitter, which leads to the general social media advice of learning the communication method and don't focus on the technology. Certainly, this approach will future proof any strategy built around social media in general and social location sharing in particular.

Case Study: How Listening and Teaching Improved the Café Business

Venue: AJ Bombers—Milwaukee, Wisconsin

Participant: Joe Sorge

Venue Type: Café

AJ Bombers is a small café in Milwaukee that has become a well-known model for both the use of social media and social location marketing. However, this wasn't the case just 18 months ago. The first six months that the café was open, sales were hovering at a variance of +/- 10%, which is pretty much a flat line in the hospitality industry.

Joe wanted to do something different that would attract customers and at the same time mark the café as being customer-centric. He was already using Twitter, so he decided that Twitter would be part of the solution.

He started the AJ Bombers account and started using it to promote daily specials. What he hadn't thought about was that Twitter is a communication tool, not a broadcast medium. While the account was busy sending out specials, it wasn't attracting much in the way of response. This got the team thinking.

They decided to change tack and elicit some feedback from customers about the menu. What did they like on the menu? What didn't they like? What would they like to add? This started the buzz rolling. Here was an establishment actually reaching out to the community and asking for opinions about the menu. Although this doesn't sound all that risky, if you have ever worked in the food industry you can imagine the potential for, if not for disaster, at least some awkward feedback.

However, the gamble paid off and customers started to engage with the café about the menu. Emboldened, the team decided to take it one step further and run a competition. They asked customers to create a new menu item. The winner would have the menu item named after him or her. This is a great example of how to use social media to both generate conversation and improve your business.

Around this time, Joe became aware of the potential for using Foursquare to supplement the Twitter activity. He became a Foursquare user and then started to explore the business potential. Again he wanted to do something that would be a little different; rather than offering a free drink to the Mayor, he wanted to get the local social media community involved in whatever he set up.

He contacted the Foursquare team to see how he could go about setting up a special badge for AJ Bombers and quickly found that it would be outside of his budget. So the creativity had to increase if he was going to do something that stood out among the others that were starting to leverage Foursquare at the time (early 2010). He decided on creating an event that would leverage the existing badges that are a part of the normal use of Foursquare.

After doing some research and confirming how the badges worked with Foursquare, he settled on creating a "Swarm" event. The swarm badge (shown in Figure 6.30) is awarded when 50 or more Foursquare users check in at the same location at the same time.

Figure 6.30   *The Swarm badge.*

AJ Bombers decided to host an event so that their customers could all earn the Swarm badge. The team also recognized that not all their customers were familiar with Foursquare, so they decided that they would hold a quick training session before the actual event so that those that weren't currently using Foursquare could get signed up and be a part of the swarm.

Little did they realize that this would take off so well. They signed up 56 people during their training event—effectively earning the swarm badge before their actual swarm took place an hour later. They had more than 100 people attend the swarm event, so everyone got a swarm badge and AJ Bombers became part of social media legend.

Following the success of this event, they planned to hold a Super Swarm event (250 users checking in). After all, why not build on the success and excitement from the original event? This is a great example of using Foursquare in the way that users can immediately relate to and understand without having a complicated campaign set up around the use of Foursquare.

It also gave the users something they wanted—the opportunity to collect a badge that was (at the time) difficult to achieve. So the promotion became more about the customers than the business. Like the Twitter menu competition I discussed earlier in the chapter, this competition was customer-centric.

On the day of the swarm event, AJ Bombers saw an increase in sales of 110% over the same day in the previous year. In the six months since they started engaging in social media, they have seen a 50% lift in sales.

Oh, what about that Twitter menu competition? The winner was Kate Berry and the menu item is the Berry Burger.

7

Marketing to Social Location Sharers

In this chapter we are going to explore how social location sharing platforms can be used to create marketing communication campaigns by businesses of different sizes. The principles of all of these types of campaigns remain the same:

- *Know your customer*
- *Understand what will motivate customers to take part in your campaign*
- *Understand how that fits with the platform you have decided to use for the campaign*

These principals hold true whether your company is a mom and pop corner store or a multisite national chain. The first principle of knowing the customer cannot be overstated. The level of "knowing" tends to differ depending on the size of the operation, though not always. It is a common myth that small businesses are better at knowing their customers. Chains—while managed from a corporate headquarters—are often operated at a local level by staff who want to retain a local feel.

For example, a local Starbucks coffee shop may well be operated by staff that gets to know their regular customers and their preferred orders. This is a national chain operating at a local level. In this situation it becomes increasingly difficult for the locally owned businesses to differentiate themselves purely on the basis of "knowing" the customer.

Knowing the customer is more than being aware of his or her favorite coffee choice, though. It involves understanding what motivates your customers to choose you over your competition. Given the amount of choice available, knowing the answers to the following questions is critical:

- Why do your customers choose to shop your location over the competition?

- What do you offer that your competition doesn't?

- How are you currently differentiating yourself?

- Would your customers switch if your competition changed?

Answering these questions gives you a better understanding of your customers and a better appreciation of them in terms of loyalty. Would your customers switch if your competition changed?

If you know what differentiates you from your competition, is that difference based on only one thing? For example, are you in a location that offers free parking, whereas your competition suffers from having no parking nearby or only paid parking? Convenience is a strong attractor for many consumers. If this situation changed and suddenly your competition was able to operate on the same basis as you, would your customers find your competitors more convenient and switch because of other factors?

Meeting the Needs

Differentiation, at least to achieve customer loyalty, must be multifaceted. In the 1940s, Abraham Maslow published his "Hierarchy of Needs," which outlined the order in which human beings meet their needs to achieve satiation and satisfaction in life. Differentiation for customers—especially the social customer, who has a broader network from which to draw referrals to alternative products and services—must operate on a similar basis. Figure 7.1 shows the different levels of Maslow's Hierarchy of Needs, this combined with the following sections, explain each of the needs outlined by Maslow and how you might apply that thinking to your social location marketing efforts.

Physiological Needs

At the most elementary level, Maslow's theory explains that humans have basic physiological needs—breathing, nutrition, and so on. Obviously, if these physiological needs are not met, the human body ceases to operate. So, if you were to compare

Maslow's theory to your work in social location marketing, you could compare Maslow's basic physiological needs to the consumer's need for the proper environment. Does the environment in which your location operates meet the basic needs for your customers? For example, if your company is a food outlet, consider things such as temperature, seating, access (including disabled access), washrooms, changing rooms, and appropriateness of size. These elements all differentiate your venue at a physiological level that affects the consumer in a sub-conscious way. These elements help your customers get a "feeling" about your venue—one that either engenders comfort or one that makes them uncomfortable.

Safety

The next level in Maslow's hierarchy is safety: personal, financial, health, and the provision of some type of safeguard—insurance if you will—against misfortune. Consumers need to know that

- Doing business with you is a wise choice—that they can trust you.

- Your product or service will not endanger them or their loved ones.

- They can trust that your credibility is not in question.

- Should they have an issue, you are likely to deal with them in a fair and honest way.

The social consumer acquires this information in several ways:

- Asking members of their social networks

- Reading reviews of your product or service

- Watching how your brand interacts with others on various social media platforms

- Finding blogs that either talk specifically about your brand or talk about the industry in which your brand operates

The social consumer has a wealth of information about your products and services available to them from which to make these decisions. A lack of interaction with customers, a bad experience that has gone unresolved, or product recalls that are not then addressed in the social web are things can damage a brand's image and therefore make the social consumer question whether selecting your product or service is a safe choice. Similarly, it's important that potential customers see that you already have a community of avid—possibly even passionate—consumers that regularly choose the product or service your brand offers. Doing so reinforces to the social consumer that choosing your company's products or services is a safe choice, and that others have made this choice before them and have been rewarded by having a good experience.

This is almost a herd experience. We all know the adage "safety in numbers." Many social consumers do not want to be the lone wolf. Instead, they want to be a part of the herd. Being part of the herd allows consumers to follow where others have gone before them and had safe shopping experiences with brands that communicate, resolve, reward, and generally act in a way that the social consumer is rapidly coming to expect. To be a part of the consideration cycle that we discussed in Chapter 1, it is important that a brand seek to meet these expectations through the use of both traditional and social business practices.

Belonging

Maslow's next level in the Hierarchy of Needs is "belonging." The social consumer wants to be a part of the brand community. They want a sense of community, to feel included, and to feel special. In the general human sense, this is the need that drives us to seek the company of friends and family, and to seek the sense of being loved and accepted. Without these feelings, human beings can suffer anxiety, depression and feelings of rejection.

In some cases, it is even possible that the need for "belonging" will overcome the two previous needs in the hierarchy—physiological and safety. Actions displayed by members of a cult are often the result of this type of situation—the willingness, for example to take part in mass suicide. This example shows just how strong a driver this need is for human beings. Social businesses should view the need to belong in this perspective. Being social isn't just a new marketing craze—a technology-enabled addition to available communications channels—it is a basic human need.

So, when thinking through a social communications campaign, whether at the higher social media level or at the more specific social location sharing level, it is important to think through the aspect of the campaign that meets this particular need. Does the campaign make customers feel like they belong, that they are a part of a community, that in some way taking part in the campaign includes them in a broader way than if they don't take part?

A campaign that shows social consumers that they are part of a community of participants and encourages interaction with them will go a long way to meeting this need. Leveraging that aspect of the social location sharing platform that shows other participants' actions to each other, which is common to all of them, is going to be key to a successful campaign that seeks to meet this need.

Esteem

The next level is esteem—the desire to be valued and accepted by others. Human beings need to engage in activities that give them a sense of contributing to something and in doing so receive the esteem of others.

Maslow actually noted two levels of esteem, higher and lower:

- The lower-level esteem is based on the need for people to feel that others recognize their value and their status within a group or groups.

- The higher-level esteem is derived from a need for a sense of self-worth, self-reliance, strength, independence, and freedom. This is ranked as the higher of the two because it is obtained through experience and self mastery.

The need for status, for the opportunity to contribute and to receive the esteem of others, can be seen at work on social media platforms all the time. Those who gain what is commonly referred to as "influencer" status are often those who share information most often. These influencers are viewed as "in the know" or having access to information that others do not. Those who provide insight to situations, technology, news, and so on are also seen in this way.

If a person can provide information that the group perceives as having value, that person's worth increases, and thus, so does the esteem in which that person is held. Many social media app users are driven to achieve this status because the ability to share in the social media world is greatly amplified over their ability to share in the real world. This desire for esteem is partially responsible for what has been observed as the social media echo chamber effect. This can be best described as the constant repetition of the same information, regardless of whether that information has already been shared. This occurs because the desire to be seen and to share useful information is greater than the potential downside of repeating information and being seen as a part of the echo. Also, some people will often re-create content based on the posts of more popular creators in an attempt to attract attention to themselves. This is known as the "me too" concept. This type of content adds nothing to the conversation because the concept is not extended or developed—it is simply rehashed.

This need for esteem is also one explanation of the "self-promoter" type in social media. Self-promoters want to share useful information and share information about themselves in a way that—rightly or wrongly—gives others the impression that they have more influence than he or she actually does. For example, some self-promoters will share pictures of themselves with true influencers at events. These pictures are posed in such a way as to make others think that the self-promoter is close friends with the real influencer. Another technique is to conduct one-sided conversations on Twitter, in which the self-promoter talks "at" the influencer with no response, but continues the conversation as though the influencer has responded.

It is important for marketers to understand the need some people have for appearing to have influence. More importantly, the marketer must be able to see the difference between those who actually wield influence and those that only provide an appearance of doing so. In social location marketing, having a truly influential user share his or her location and a recommendation about that location can be a huge win. However, the truly influential are few and far between. The mid-tier influencer is a better target for social media marketers because these people not only have a degree of influence, but they are striving for greater influence. That means if you provide those people with opportunities to meet their own needs for increasing their status with their peers/user groups, your campaign is likely to see a greater return on investment.

Self-Actualization

Maslow's final stage in the hierarchy of needs is self-actualization, which is the process of becoming everything that a person is capable of becoming. Of course, the ideal self for each individual will vary for each individual over time. For example, a young man might see his ideal self as a career-orientated, high-achieving businessman. However, as he grows older, perhaps marries and has children, his ideal self might change to become an ideal father. Therefore his steps toward self-actualization will also change.

This process of self-actualization is important to the marketer because your marketing campaigns will be much more powerful if they can speak to the individual at a level that connects with the consumer's path to becoming his or her ideal self. When it comes to social media, many users want to be—or at least want to be perceived as being—more influential. Therefore, a campaign that helps these consumers realize this goal will resonate with them and is more likely to be adopted. Again, this is why knowing your target audience is so important. By identifying and speaking to the goals of your audience, your campaign has a better chance of success. Although it is still important to retain the genuine nature of the message, this shouldn't limit the creativity of your campaign. A good example of this is a deodorant campaign aimed at young men whose ideal self is one that is successful with the opposite sex. The campaign plays on this in a humorous way, by implying that the use of the product will have every woman within miles running to them. Even the most socially challenged young man will realize that the claims are not real, and that they are in fact meant as a joke. However, because this campaign is targeting the ideal self of that audience, the message still resonates.

The Needs of the Social Consumer

Social consumers add a layer of complexity to self-actualization because they have both real-world needs and social web needs. Although these needs are usually in sync, social consumers—especially those who are using the social web to express themselves—often will find it easier to realize some of their ideal self goals through the use of social platforms than they would through the use of more traditional real-world platforms. For example, a person might see herself as one day being a published author of a book for children. In the real world, this person is overwhelmed at the prospect of having to find an agent, a publisher, a designer, an editor, and so on. However, by using social web tools, this person can connect with others, establish an online relationship, and find assistance for meeting that ideal. This person can even self-publish the book and promote it via social tools. The point is that this person's ability to reach her particular self-actualization goal has become easier through the use of the social web.

Marketers must understand how self-actualization goals are more easily met via social media than they would be through more traditional, real-world methods. This understanding is crucial if you are to truly build effective campaigns that meet the needs of, and create engagement among, the social consumers that form the user base of social media in general and social location sharing tools in particular. Although a person can be a social consumer and not use social location sharing tools, it is not true that a person would be a user of social location sharing tools and not be a social consumer. So marketers aiming to use social location marketing must understand the needs of the social consumer first.

Figure 7.1 shows how Maslow's Hierarchy of Needs can be translated to the needs of the social consumer and how those individual needs fit into the increasing scale of needs. A campaign is unlikely to meet all of these needs at the same time. In fact, trying to do so will likely confuse your audience. However, meeting these needs at the appropriate time is much more likely to achieve success.

For example, consider a campaign that speaks to the cleanliness of a food outlet that is run at the time the food is purchased. If the social consumer is buying food, we know what physiological need is being met and therefore which of the corresponding social consumer triggers the consumer is most concerned with and therefore most likely to comment on. There is little point in trying to get the consumer to comment on the feelings of community at that point. That need will be met later in the purchase cycle after the food has been consumed.

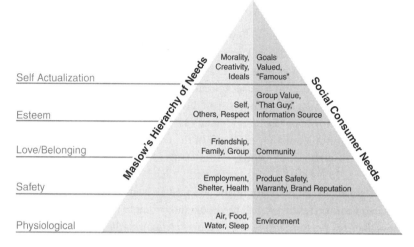

Figure 7.1   *Comparing the needs of social consumers to Maslow's Hierarchy of Needs.*

Social Customer Relationship Management or Customer Information Management

Companies that leverage social location marketing are likely to encounter social customer relationship management (sCRM). Your company's experience with information management and what you're already doing to collect customer information will determine just how deeply you go with sCRM. Social media, in my opinion, is changing Social CRM into Social CIM (Customer Information Management). With respect to social location marketing, this is perhaps the better term to use.

Many organizations have attempted to impose CRM disciplines and systems onto the social media engagements that they undertake without considering first if the applications that they are going to be leveraging will actually supply them with enough data points to enable this.

Social location sharing apps (Foursquare, Gowalla and so on) are not sufficiently developed at this point to provide enough data points that would allow you to fully integrate them into a CRM system. However, they do provide enough data to supplement customer information that is already being captured and further extend customer engagements into the social web; thus, Social CIM is more appropriate.

The difference being that a fully evolved CRM system would allow for the tracking of each engagement point across the social web. Currently, there are no fully integrated systems that allow for this kind of detailed tracking. However, the data provided by some of the tools does allow for information to be captured about a customer. For example, while it might not be possible to find out what other pages a

Facebook user likes, it is possible to collect the information that they "like" your business page. This isn't a complete picture, but it's useful information nonetheless.

The type of customer information that a business should be collecting at various touch points includes the following:

- Name

- Address

- Telephone number

- Email address

These pieces of data are the very minimum that should be collected. However, you might not—and quite probably should not—collect all this information at the same time. The intention here is to get some usable data from the customer, not to bombard them with questions that end up acting as a barrier to them completing the engagement. So, start with the email address and the corresponding name, and then add from there. There are various ways to capture this type of data from a customer. A customer loyalty program is perhaps the easiest and most straightforward. Other than some printed index cards and a pen, no technology is required for the most basic system. Have the customer fill out the form, give it back to you, and when they come back to the venue, give them some kind of reward in return.

Adding technology to the mix can be as simple as entering the collected information into a spreadsheet, or if you are slightly more advanced, a contact database. If you are going to use social location marketing, you will need this more advanced approach, but even this is still very basic compared to cumbersome CRM systems, and it is usually a lot more manageable by a resource challenged organization.

The data provided by social location sharing apps varies from app to app. For example, at the time this book was written, only Foursquare and Yelp have dedicated dashboards for business owners that provide any kind of metrics. However, all the apps show the check ins at venues. That data collected includes who, when, and where information. For a single location venue, this is the type of data that will add to any other information that you have already captured from other sources that will go into your sCIM system—whether that is software or paper based.

Included in this who, when, where data is one very important piece of information: your competitors. You can start to see when your customers go to your competitors' venues and then cross-refer that to what your venue was doing on that particular day.

Is there a menu change needed? Are your opening hours different? Were you short staffed that day? Is there a deeper pattern to when your customers prefer your competitors to you?

All this takes time, both to acquire the data and to analyze it. For some this will be beyond their resources; for others this will provide valuable insight into how their business is operating and where there are opportunities for improvement. As with all data, it is important that you use it in a way that does not cause analysis paralysis; that is, the business is not so overwhelmed by the data that it achieves nothing with it. It is equally important that the business not make major decisions based solely on location sharing data. Rather, this data should be used to inform the business about performance and give indicators of areas of improvement, customer loyalty, and opportunities to reward customer loyalty. It should be tempered with other data points, verbal feedback, visible responses, and so on. Social location sharing data is going to be only a small percentage of the data available to any business.

Incorporating customer information capture should always be a part of the strategic thinking that goes into the design of a social location marketing campaign. While the outward appearance of the campaign may well be to provide a fun experience for your customers and potential customers, don't forget the business aspects of the campaign and miss the opportunity to carry the engagement beyond just the initial contact.

I have seen this done on many occasions with companies both large and small who have missed obvious opportunities to capture customer information in either a discrete, piecemeal fashion or in a more overt manner. Remember that the customer can always say no when asked to share information, but if you never ask them you will never receive it. It is hard to reward customers you don't know. Capturing that customer information does bring with it the responsibility of privacy and safeguards, certainly something that all businesses should be aware of and have proper procedures in place that control access to and use of customer information.

With organizations from banks to Facebook making the headlines for accidentally leaking customer information, your organization doesn't need to join the ranks of these companies and have to handle that type of PR nightmare. So before you start capturing and using customer information, make sure you have the capability to secure it and capture only the information that you believe you are really going to need, not just everything you can get hold of. For example, if you don't need the name of your customers' children's' school, don't capture it, even if they do check in there (not something I advise people to do).

It is important to think through the information you are going to need from a customer and decide the best route to obtain that information. For example, if you are going to ship them a prize, you will, at some point, need an address to which to ship the prize. However, you won't need that before you award the prize. But if you want the address so that you can send direct mail, you will need to find a legitimate reason for the consumer to give you that information. The social consumer is unlikely to part with information simply on the off chance that they might be shipped a prize. This is where the transparency demanded by the social consumer comes in. If your intent is to send them product information along with some offers in the form of money-off coupons and so on, and you want to send them in the mail, tell them that is what you want to do.

Yes, it is likely you will capture fewer addresses this way, but the ones you do capture are from consumers who have decided that they want to engage with you through this medium; you have provided them with the choice and they have recognized that. It has become a conversation about how they, as a social consumer, want to be communicated with; this shows them you are valuing their preferences and considering them as part of the conversation. The social consumer values this highly in brands with which they choose to engage. This is part of doing social business.

The same process applies to other information that you capture about your customers. An email address given as a method of identification—for example, used as a login for a personalized experience on a website—is not the same as giving permission to be emailed with offers. Be clear about how the information is going to be used, both at the time of exchange and in the future. Think about the occasions when you have handed out a business card at a meeting, conference, and the like, only to find yourself added to a mailing list for products or information you are not interested in. This is a common theme at conferences: run a competition, put a fishbowl at the conference stand, ask people to drop their card into the bowl for a chance to win. No disclosure that the company is also going to use that business card and add you to their customer information system or that they are going to follow up with you to see if they can sell you something.

At conferences this practice has become so common that it is almost expected. There is a tacit agreement that if you put your card into a fishbowl at a stand, there is a good chance that someone is going to email, call, or write to you about that company's products or services. With that known, you decide to take that risk in the hopes of winning an iPad, or a vacation, or whatever gift the company is offering as an inducement.

This does not work with the social consumer. The social consumer has higher expectations and a lower tolerance for their information being used in ways that they were not expecting. When Facebook changed its terms of service, there was a huge outcry. People threatened to delete their accounts over it. Campaigns to boycott Facebook were organized. Facebook rethought their approach (though truth be told, not that many accounts were deleted, and the furor died down after a few days). However, the point was made. Social consumers are very savvy. They like to control their information and how it is handled by third parties.

They are increasingly less likely to hand over their information for the proverbial free cup of coffee. They value their information more highly now and see it as part of their social capital. Even more so, they are starting to recognize the value of their social networks and the value it has to marketers, so granting access brings with it an even higher expectation in terms of a value exchange.

In the past, consumers were all too ready to promote a store or product, sometimes unwittingly, sometimes because of the cachet that being associated with the brand brought. Store bags with the name of the store are still a common site in any shopping mall. Customers become walking billboards for the places where they shop. They do this because they are already customers, they are advertising their taste in a particular product line. They are showing the world that they made a purchase choice and in some cases are attracting the social capital that goes with making that choice, especially when it comes to premium brands.

The online marketer has long sought to find a method of leveraging the "store bag" marketing experience. When a consumer makes a purchase through a website, that purchase is closed—no one knows about it except the consumer and the seller. There is no bag to walk around with the product in, no one else to share with at the time of purchase. Social location marketing is one step to filling that void, enabling the marketer to receive the kind of promotion that the real-world store gets from providing a bag and allowing the social consumer to attract social capital associated with a purchase.

Because many users of social location sharing apps link their accounts to their other social media accounts, such as Twitter and Facebook, the promotional value of their check ins is increased. This is the social consumers' version of walking the mall with a shopping bag (which they might well still be doing in the real world). Now, not only strangers see their preference for a place of purchase but those with whom they share some commonality and perhaps even exert some influence over. This makes the social consumer more powerful than the traditional consumer and therefore more valuable to the marketer.

"I shop here, you should too" is the message the social consumer is broadcasting. This relates back to our discussion earlier in the chapter of a sense of community and of safety in numbers. Human beings seek reassurance in their lives that they are making good decisions. Receiving affirmation and confirmation of their decisions, in even small ways—such as knowing that they are buying a product from a location that has been recommended by a family member, friend, colleague, or even a network connection—provides that reassurance.

Because of this broadcast nature of the social check in and because the social consumer is aware of this, the marketer engaging in social location marketing needs to be aware of the value that the social consumer places on broadcasting a message.

This value will vary from social consumer to social consumer but at the very least has a perceived base value among that particular social consumers' network. They know what they are worth, or at least what they feel they are worth. Some of this is being driven by sites that now place monetary value on social network exchanges—

those that tell users how much their tweets are worth. Other sites, such as Klout, assign scores to users based on their social capital and ability to influence others. Although the true value of these sites is still being debated, what is beyond doubt is that they have awoken in social consumers the recognition that when they share a brand name, product, or service with their network, it has worth; it has a value, whether in a financial sense or in the form of some kind of reward, consumers know that they are entering into an exchange system.

With sites such as WeReward that are enabling marketers to pay users for check ins, and others that are translating social capital into everything from free hotel rooms to upgrades on airlines, the social consumer is fast displaying the signs of "entitlement." This is most commonly displayed in their decisions to choose a particular brand, product, or service not based solely on fit, price, or even just service, but also on the ability of that brand to increase the consumers' social capital or reward them in some way for making the purchase.

The social consumer is viewing the exchange as a two-tiered barter system. At the first level is the monetary exchange that we are all familiar with. I give you a certain amount of real-world currency in exchange for your product or service. At the secondary level we are witnessing an almost barter-like system, where I, as the social consumer will perform some kind of social action on behalf of the brand; in return, the brand will provide me with something that I value.

As with prices for goods and services, the cost of the secondary exchange fluctuates from social consumer to social consumer and from brand to brand. Some are willing and able to reward social consumers who are considered to be influential to the brand's intended audience with high value (in a financial sense) rewards. Others are either less willing or less able to make that exchange. This new economic model is so nascent that as yet it is difficult to see whether it is sustainable, and if it is, at what level. That is, will it follow a preexisting economic theory, or will a new set of theories have to be written for this? (For an introductory discussion on this type of exchange system, I recommend *The Whuffie Factor* by Tara Hunt).

Sustainable or not, the reality is that this system is here now and it is increasing in its use. Any marketer planning a social media marketing/social location marketing campaign in the next 12 to 18 months would do well to ensure that this element is baked into their plan so as not to be caught out by the expectations of a social consumer base whose sense of entitlement is growing.

What are you prepared to exchange in return for social consumers using their social capital on your behalf? What is your likely return on investment for them doing so, and what is the likely lift going to be? These are the usual questions asked going into any campaign. Where it becomes problematic for most organizations is that they have no data on which to base their judgments. When making a media buy, an organization can look back at its previous media buys and set expectations based on those, but with an exchange based on social capital, there is so little public data available. For most companies, no previous data means it is very hard to make a real-world estimation. With stories circulating of people like the television celebrity Kim Kardashian being paid $10,000 for a single sponsored tweet but no resultant data released regarding the lift produced by that tweet, it is hard to put this into traditional media buying terms.

What might an actual social location marketing campaign look like? Next I'll propose a few ideas that cover single location venues, multilocation venues, using social location marketing without a location, and business-to-business campaigns.

Elements of a Social Location Marketing Campaign

Regardless of the size of the organization or the number of venues that you have, certain elements will be core to any campaign if it is to be successful. These elements are app agnostic and will fit with the features that each provides.

Fun—One of the main points of a social location marketing campaign should be to avoid "check-in fatigue" among your customers. To ensure that your customers actually want to join in, there needs to be an element of fun. Checking in at your location should not be a chore. Rather, it should be enjoyable.

Measurable—Don't do something you can't measure. So many companies embark on campaigns for which they have no means for measuring success. I am really baffled as to why they do this. They come up with a great creative but they give no thought to how they will measure if their wonderful creative had any positive effect on the business.

Repeatable—When people hear about your fun campaign, they will want to join in—or at least that should be the intent. Make sure that your campaign is repeatable—meaning that return customers can repeat the positive experience, and new customers can have the same experience that they've heard others have had.

Shareable—The key is word of mouth, so the activity and the reward should be something that participants want to talk about, want to share with their networks, and want to encourage others to take part in. A Facebook post or Tweet that says "I just got XXX from Company Y" is something that will catch the eye of a user's network and provoke questions.

Creative—By this, I mean do the unexpected, different, or nontraditional. Remember that the audience for this type of campaign is largely made up of early adopters of new technology. These are the people who specifically seek out the new and unusual. They are easily bored. Think hip-hop guinea pigs selling cars, not insurance salesman.

Focused—Don't make the campaign too broad, because this will lead to confusion among the audience. Your audience should recognize immediately what the campaign is about. Focus the campaign and the rewards around a particular product, service, or event. The product, service, or event that is the focal point of the campaign can always be used to promote other offerings that you have. This is much better than trying to fit your entire catalog of offerings into one campaign.

Reward—Ensure that the reward fits the campaign theme, as well as the audience and the effort that the participants have to put into earning it. Making the participants jump through hoops is allowable if the reward for doing so is perceived as worthwhile. Again, the days of the free coffee being a sufficient reward are over.

So now that we have a better understanding of who we are marketing to, and the ways in which we can plug into their needs, what does a campaign actually look like? What are the elements that go into a campaign for different types of businesses and how do those fit into the greater marketing communications strategy?

In the upcoming three sections, we consider the various types of social location marketing campaigns for businesses that have a physical location, and also consider how a business without a physical location or one that is not open to their customers can still join in the social location marketing space.

What is important to consider with these ideas is that they are not meant as blueprints, but as suggestions drawn from experience with the tools, conversations, and interviews with businesses already using them. I've included my own thoughts on how best to leverage the platforms. If you try out any of these and have success, please feel free to contact me with your story (contact details are in the last chapter of the book). I'm always looking for case studies. If you try them and they don't work, please contact me as well, just not through a lawyer!

My recommendation is to read through the ideas, think about how they apply to your business and your audience, and then adapt them so that they make the most sense for you and your organization. Most of all, however, have fun with them. As I have said before, with social media in general and social location marketing in particular, given the low cost of giving social location marketing a spin, you aren't risking the bank when trialing these campaigns—or at least you shouldn't be. Remember what works or doesn't with one app might well work or not on another. That's the beauty of the diversity that currently exists with social location sharing apps.

Single Location Businesses

Single location venues were the first to recognize the usefulness of social location sharing apps in terms of marketing. These early adopter businesses had little or no marketing materials to work with and had only one opportunity to offer a reward—when someone became Mayor (see Figure 7.2).

Figure 7.2   *The earliest attempts at social location marketing were pretty basic.*

Since then, businesses realized that they have to offer more to their customers (see the A.J. Bombers case study at the end of Chapter 6 for an example) if they are to really get engagement. With the advent of new apps, businesses are now able to offer their customers more.

Let's consider an imaginary coffee shop that for convenience we will call Bob's Brews. Bob's Brews wants to use social location marketing as part of its broader social media efforts. It has one location positioned in the downtown area of Everytown, a small city with a population of a few hundred thousand. Most of its current business comes from passing foot traffic. Bob's Brews offers a limited food menu and an extensive coffee menu.

In this imaginary city, there are a total of six coffee shops, including two outlets from national chains. So Bob's Brews has to compete not only with local competition but with the marketing budget of national chains. It is looking to social location marketing to offer some form of differentiation in its marketing campaign because none of the other coffee houses are using it at present.

Bob's Brews is going to need to ask itself some questions before it embarks on its campaign:

- How much do we want to spend on this type of marketing?
- What do we already know about our customers?
- How are we already reaching them through social media?
- Which platform will we use?
- What will we offer as rewards for loyalty?
- How do we make this fun for the customer and profitable for us?

Given that Bob's Brews is a small outlet and a single venue location, we will assume that it does not have thousands of dollars to spend on a marketing campaign. So we will, for the sake of this example, assume that whatever is spent has to be under $500, including promotional items.

In this example, we are going to accept that the staff of Bob's Brews are fairly proficient at recognizing regulars to the coffee shop and know a few of them by name. However, that is as far as they have taken their Customer Information Management to date. In other words, the Social CIM resides in the heads of the staff and not in a system anywhere, which is a fairly common situation for a lot of small businesses.

So far, Bob's Brews has set up a Twitter account and has a Facebook page. However, it doesn't have a strong grasp on how to use either of these tools and makes only occasional status updates, usually with special offers. It occasionally gets replies on Twitter, but these are few and far between.

Originally, Bob's Brews thought that offering a free coffee might be the direction to go in for a reward, but it has since realized that it needs to offer something a little more compelling, and so it has decided to offer an escalating scale of rewards. The first level will be a reusable travel coffee mug; the second level will be two pounds of the winner's favorite coffee; the third and final level, which will be awarded to only one winner, will be a blend named after the winner, which will be added to the Bob's Brews coffee menu.

To win these prizes, Bob's Brews decided to limit the campaign to a one-month duration and to award the prizes based on frequency of visits, some form of interaction with the venue, and finally the best suggested blend of coffee beans for the new menu item.

What it has yet to decide on is which app to use to promote this campaign. To make this decision, it is useful to step through a process similar to that outlined in the decision tree shown in Figure 7.3.

The tree shows us that the more flexible we make the rewards system, the greater the options are in terms of the apps we have to select from. Conversely, the narrower we make the reward system, the fewer our choices.

This tree covers only 5 of the 10 or so apps that are available at the time of writing. However, these five apps offer the most in terms of flexibility to offer a reward system to a small business. This is especially true for small businesses looking for a method of using the app that is free or very low cost to them.

Given the nature of the campaign that Bob's Brews has decided on, and following the tree, it quickly becomes apparent that SCVNGR is the most applicable choice of app for Bob's Brews to run their campaign on.

That is not to say that it should ignore the other platforms. For example, it should definitely claim its venue on each of the apps and ensure that the information on

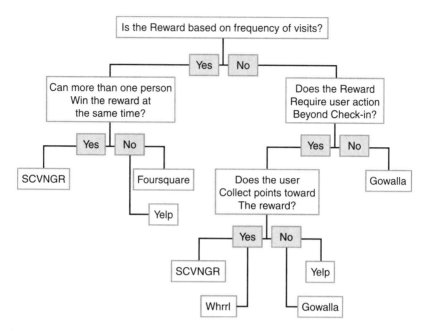

Figure 7.3 *A decision tree can be helpful when determining which social media app is the best fit.*

them is correct and up to date. In particular, when it comes to Yelp, Bob's Brews should ensure that it has set up a Yelp page and logged in to the business dashboard to ensure that it does not have any unanswered negative reviews.

All this should be done in parallel with running a marketing campaign. Remember that social media, including social location marketing, is a two-way communication channel. It is not just there for a business to push out a message but is often used by customers as a way of communicating, either directly or indirectly with the business.

SCVNGR, as discussed in Chapter 6, offers a progressive gaming experience for users and allows business owners to create different challenges within their venue that the user can complete to receive points. These points can be accumulated toward a specific reward.

By making the campaign time constrained, Bob's Brews decided to run it for only one month; it will need to ensure that it communicates the campaign through the use of their other social media channels, such as Twitter and Facebook. This is an overhead that the business needs to recognize at the outset of the campaign. These campaigns do not run themselves. They require involvement throughout the process. It is essential, for example, to ensure that all members of staff know what the campaign is and how it works. Starbucks was embarrassed when it partnered with Foursquare to offer free coffee through the app, only to find that not all store managers had been briefed on the campaign and were turning away customers who were requesting their reward. They subsequently pulled the campaign. Doing so not only cost them a marketing opportunity but made them seem incompetent—not something any business wants.

So having decided what the campaign will consist of, which app it will run on, and how the rewards will be made, Bob's Brews is ready to enter the world of social location marketing. Given SCVNGR's options for challenges, Bob's Brews can offer its customers the opportunity to interact with the environment that they are in. For example, it can set up challenges as simple as getting customers to take a picture of their favorite brew. However, the app gives the flexibility that if the company wanted, it could do something a lot more complex and fun. For example, it might set up a "Barista" challenge, where customers get to be the Barista as part of a challenge.

The actual challenges will depend on the creativity of the team putting them together and the constraints of the environment they find themselves operating in. Obviously, customer safety is paramount, so that has to be considered when putting these challenges together.

As you can see from this example, it is a fairly easy path to go from no social location marketing to having a full-blown campaign. The important element of any campaign is to know why you are doing it. In this case, Bob's Brews wants to achieve a level of differentiation from its competitors. By running these challenges, it is very likely to gain a reputation as being a "fun" place to drink coffee and certainly a different place to enjoy a brew.

Multiple-Venue Businesses

Cohesiveness is key with multiple-venue businesses when it comes to marketing communications, whether those are social media based or not. Although regional variance is allowable and often encouraged to ensure a more "local" flavor, offers that are available in only one area or at certain venues are more likely to frustrate customers than attract them.

If a consumer is a customer of a brand in one location and encounters that brand in another location, the consumer expects a similar experience. The Marriot Hotel chain recognized this many years ago and goes to great lengths to ensure that their facilities are almost identical anywhere in the world. The closet always contains an ironing board and an iron, for example. This provides a level of reassurance to its customers. So it is with marketing communications and marketing campaigns.

If I am a customer taking part in a reward-based campaign at one location, I have the expectation that I will be able to continue taking part at other locations as well. This comes down to even basic customer reward programs like loyalty stamp cards. If I pick up the card at one location and then make a purchase at another location, I still expect to have the card stamped for my purchases. What I don't expect is to be told that the card is valid only at the original location. I point this out because surprisingly this still happens.

Marketing communications is not just a customer-focused activity, it must be an internal activity as well. All locations must be involved in the activity and be aware of the campaign and how it applies to their location.

One advantage that the multiple venue business has over the single venue business is the capability to build in an element of "bread-crumb" game play. In this form of campaign, the idea is that customers can take part at a single location, but they can achieve a greater reward by playing at multiple locations—by completing a challenge/task at one location that leads them to a follow-up task at the next location, and so on.

This type of game play is better to suited to a longer-term campaign. With this type of game play comes the additional requirement to provide progress status to the players. They need the system to keep track of how close they are to their reward. This acts not only as a reminder but as a motivator to keep them interested in continuing to play the game.

Multiple-venue campaigns are, by their very nature, more complex than those operated at a single location. There is no reason why a business that operates multiple locations cannot operate the same campaign at each of its locations, with the caveat given earlier, that the rewards are collectible at each location rather than just the one where the user commenced playing.

This is certainly a good starting point for businesses with multiple locations; it allows the organization to ensure that all staff members are given the same information and that they all understand the concept. As the organization gains experience with social location marketing, it can build in the more complex elements that incorporate variance in the location.

For example, a business that has outlets in different regions of the United States might want to have an overall theme for its social location marketing but have regional variations so that the campaign has a local flavor and is therefore more appealing to local customers.

The basic principles of a social location marketing campaign do not change, and the decision tree given earlier is just as applicable to the multiple-location business as it is to the single-location business. One key difference is the volume of data that the campaign generates, and this should not be underestimated. Again, there is no point in running a campaign without clear metrics in place beforehand and a clear understanding of what those metrics will mean. What part of the business operation will they impact, and who will collate and report the data captured?

A multiple-location business operating a well thought through social location marketing campaign has the potential to generate a considerable amount of earned media (blog posts, traditional media coverage, and so on), which goes a long way to meeting the ROI questions posed by the C-Suite. These side-effects of utilizing what is still considered to be a new and innovative marketing channel should not be underestimated when contemplating the use of social location marketing. The very fact of being first in an industry, or just in a particular location, to use these types of campaigns can bring a considerable amount of brand awareness beyond the actual campaign.

Marketing Without a Location

This seems counterintuitive. How can you possibly use social location marketing if you lack the key element of a location? This is a question I am asked frequently at presentations I give on this topic. It applies equally to the business-to-business arena as well as those businesses that operate only in an online capacity.

If the public can't check in at your location, how are you going to use these apps as marketing communication channels? The answer is surprisingly simple: use someone else's location. I am not suggesting here that you simply take over someone's store as though it was your own. But the use of familiar and popular landmarks as a focal point for the location piece of your campaign works very well. In fact, when it was first launched, this was exactly how Gowalla promoted the service. Obviously, it didn't have people checking in at its offices in Austin. Instead, Gowalla focused its marketing campaign around popular locations such as the Golden Gate Bridge in San Francisco, the Empire State building in New York, and other popular landmarks.

As we discussed in Chapter 5, Coca-Cola, who has no retail locations, successfully utilized social location marketing campaigns by simply having a promotions team member appear at various locations throughout a city. This not only provided a set of locations around which to base the campaign, but it increased the game play of the campaign because players had to also track and locate the promotions team member.

Several other companies have used this same model. Interestingly enough, even those with locations where the public can check in have found this type of campaign to be effective.

Landmark locations do offer the opportunity for a greater level of interaction than those of a store or other type of retail environment, if for no other reason than they make for better pictures, which can be uploaded via the app. This comes with the usual caveats of making sure that whatever you are challenging people to do is actually possible and legal. (Getting them to spray paint your logo on a famous landmark might well get you brand awareness, but not in the way you want!)

Another option for a business without a publicly accessible location is the use of the trips feature within Gowalla, SCVNGR, or Yelp. By setting up a series of locations in the app that are in some way connected, and listing them as a recommendation by your business, you get brand awareness without any campaign.

I did this for our company. We do not have a location that has visitors, so I created two trips in Gowalla—a coffeehouse tour and a restaurant tour, both in Austin. As people check in at the locations I listed, they are notified that they just checked in at a spot that is part of the Incslinger Coffeehouse Tour or the Incslinger Restaurant Tour. When they complete the tour, if their Gowalla account is connected to Twitter, it sends a tweet announcing that they completed the tour, which gives me the opportunity to reach out to them via Twitter.

Simple, effective, and free. No location needed. This type of mini-campaign is more suited to brand awareness but there is no reason you couldn't attach a free offer to the tour for the person who completes it first; you can also promote that via other social media channels.

The point is to ensure that you know why you are doing it and what you are looking to get out of it, which brings us to the next section of this chapter.

Getting to the ROI

As I've mentioned throughout this book, knowing what you are going to measure is crucial, not just to social location marketing but to any form of marketing communication. It's critical that you understand how you are going to track ROI before you start a campaign, not after it's already live. Thinking about ROI early allows you to design your campaign so that you actually have a means for measuring success. If your campaign is designed to raise brand awareness, how will you measure that? If it is designed to support a product launch, how will you judge that it was successful?

Whereas traditionally ROI is measured in dollars and cents, you can use other measures to estimate the effectiveness of a campaign. However, ultimately there is no reason why social media marketing in general and social location marketing in particular should not have a financial element to it. Why shouldn't it drive sales? Why shouldn't it increase revenue? Campaigns that do this tend to be more creative and more engaging, and for many their biggest obstacle is getting past the technology.

Don't use this as an excuse not to measure and not to push the metrics into the realms of revenue. The closer a campaign gets to showing true ROI, the greater the support from the C-Suite. Giving away free products doesn't have to lose you money. Though many marketers factor this loss into the budget for the campaign, they fail to factor in the sales that they expect to generate from the campaign. As discussed previously in this book, part of the reason is they have little or no reliable data from the social location marketing efforts of others on which to base their assumptions.

One of the easiest ways to get to the metrics of a campaign is to use social media monitoring tools such as those from ViralHeat, Lithium or Radian6. All these tools provide data regarding the volume of conversations being undertaken about a particular set of terms, which might include your organization's brand, product names or services, across social media sites such as Facebook, Twitter, as well as various blogs. In addition these tools also provide an analysis of the sentiment of these posts and conversations.

Before starting your campaign, take a baseline and measure what people are already saying about your product, service or brand. Run the campaign and see what the impact is of that on the level of conversations, the places where those conversations are happening (blogs, Facebook, Forums, Twitter etc) and then measure again after the campaign. This provides a very tangible set of metrics that can be used to illustrate how a particular social media campaign impacted the organization.

That is why my recommendation is always to start small, figure out the friction points within your organization and within the delivery mechanism of the campaign, and then build out from there. This methodology will provide a much better basis for a marketer to make more educated estimates of return for a campaign.

Case Study

A Shaggy Dog Story

Venue: Austin Dirty Dog

Participant: Blair Smith

Austin Dirty Dog is a five-location organization centered in Austin, Texas. They provide a very popular dog wash environment, where dog owners can choose to either bathe their dogs themselves or have it done by professional groomers.

Austin Dirty Dog was an early adopter of social location marketing, having noticed that some of their venues were already being entered into the Foursquare database by their customers.

The first step for them was to edit each of the venue pages to ensure that the information about each location was correct and update things such as telephone numbers, Twitter accounts, and so on.

Having completed this process, they decided to work out a series of "Mayor Specials" that they would use to promote the use of Foursquare at their venues and to engage their customers.

They completed the paperwork and submitted it to Foursquare only to be told that at the time Foursquare was only supporting specials from food and beverage outlets, places where they felt people gathered to be social. Obviously they were not regulars at the dog wash!

Eventually, Foursquare opened up the specials functionality to other businesses, and Austin Dirty Dog continued to use it. They put some signage at each location and after a few weeks were excited to get their first "Mayor."

After they had been running their partnership with Foursquare for a few months, I checked in with them to find out what their results had been. I asked Blair Smith, co-owner, what impact partnering with Foursquare had on the business:

"I honestly haven't seen any impact on our business—at least directly. Dog grooming/washing isn't something that people generally do on a whim. However, when people check in and post it to their Facebook/Twitter accounts, we may get new customers from that. However, I've never been told that directly."

To date they had not had anyone redeem the Mayor offer. They hadn't seen any increase in revenue that they could directly attribute to the use of Foursquare, and overall it had become something that they had no real sense of worth from doing.

They decided to try and work with Gowalla, but after contacting them and not receiving a response for over two weeks, they were not hopeful that Gowalla was going to be any better an app for them than Foursquare had been.

Was this the wrong type of business for social location marketing? Was Austin Dirty Dog just too early to the game? Overall I feel that they were too early to the game in some ways, in that Foursquare was not ready for them as a type of business. I also think that with a lack of focus on an actual campaign and the accompanying metrics, this methodology was not going to work.

However, I think this is a valuable lesson for all small businesses to learn from. Don't expect the new medium to do the work for you. For every new method you try, there will be additional work for the business to make a success of it.

I also think that as much as all the app creators want to be available to all businesses, they are focusing on those that will generate most revenue for them as companies, which is to be expected. Certainly Foursquare and Gowalla are now rolling out more of a "self-serve" model for marketers who do not have the large budgets to partner directly with these app creators, but who want to still be involved in a way that makes them different from their competitors.

8

We're Here All Week—Event Marketing with Social Location Sharing Apps

Events are a great opportunity for businesses with no physical location or for those that are not accessible to their customers (manufacturing companies that do not have public facing offices, for example) to engage in social location sharing. Whether your organization will have a booth at a major conference or your small business has one person attending a local seminar, each situation presents its own opportunity to use social location sharing apps for marketing.

Companies that are either sponsoring an event or organizing an event have even more to gain from using social location sharing apps as part of their marketing mix.

This is because they get a greater degree of control over how the channel is used for that type of communication. As a sponsor or organizer, a company should expect to have branded elements used as part of any social location marketing campaign for the event.

Event marketing, or at the very least attending events, is the point at which a lot of organizations—especially those in the business-to-business area—meet their customers face-to-face. Although social media has become the "darling" of marketing departments around the world, face-to-face meetings are still where business becomes real. The customer is no longer a voice on the phone, an email address, a Twitter account, or a "fan." After you meet in person, that customer is now a living human being and it is this point of interaction that can make or break a brand. It is a constant surprise to me that so few brands see the value in this part of their marketing. People buy from people, they don't buy from brands. Of course there are some caveats. You could argue, for example, that commodities are bought on price not because of the person at the register taking your money for a can of beans. But if you receive bad service from that person, chances are, all other things being equal, you will buy your can of beans from a different store the next time. So even with a commodity, the personal interaction can still affect the buying experience.

Whether it is a large conference in Las Vegas, or a local high-tech happy hour, attending events is the point at which a social media strategy becomes reality and where the cohesiveness of your messaging is put to the acid test. This is one reason why some companies are apprehensive about getting involved in events—the real-world form of marketing. Some companies are concerned that their employees will speak in a way that is "off message." Cost is another reason some companies don't participate in events. Purchasing booth space, the cost of the collateral, and the cost of the booth itself can easily run into the tens of thousands of dollars for even a modest booth. Both of these concerns are valid. However, events don't need to be this source of stress and fear for organizations. There are many ways in which they can achieve excellent engagement with their customers and prospective customers without encountering either off-message communications or huge bills.

Arming Employees with the Right Message

Equipping employees with the right message—one that is both truthful and relevant—and having them attend conferences as attendees (rather than as booth puppets desperately trying to get other attendees to put business cards into a fishbowl) can be a much more rewarding experience for both the employees and the other attendees.

By putting the social media practices developed by the company into operation in the real world and actively engaging other attendees, you are more likely to generate quality leads rather than just a glut of irrelevant business cards. You might even go as far as organizing a small gathering while at the conference.

This is the major issue with conference booths. Unless there is something very compelling about them, conference booths tend to have a very low return on investment. Given that the physical booths cost several thousand dollars to purchase and several hundred just to rent—not including the cost of having the booth graphics and other materials created—a company must seriously consider what type of return they are looking for with this level of investment.

Conference attendees wander past, trying to avoid eye contact. They take the free giveaways, perhaps drop a business card off and leave. The team operating the booth has little or no chance to have any meaningful interactions with the majority of booth visitors and no real opportunity to follow up with them until after the event is over. That follow up tends to come in the form of a generic email sent as part of the overall follow up, most of which will solicit no other response than to have the opt-out option exercised by recipients who have long since forgotten exactly which fishbowls they dropped their cards in anyway.

Ultimately, the business cards simply add to the general clutter of unvetted leads that bloat a CRM system and skew the activity metrics of salespeople. The use of social media—and in particular social location marketing at events—can reduce this clutter. Although it will mean that the number of business cards brought back from an event is greatly reduced, it will also mean that the number of meaningful leads increases, which is much more likely to increase the ROI on attending the event in the first place.

There are caveats—the organization must have a compelling story to tell in the first place. You should also have a product or service that someone actually wants to buy. If you do not, social media will not fix this. In fact, using social media in these situations is only likely to highlight these failings rather than hide them. So for the rest of this section in the chapter, I am going to make the assumption that your organization has already faced these challenges and overcome them appropriately. I am also assuming that you are attending a conference or other event because you have a compelling story to tell about your product or service and that the people who are attending the same conference or event are the people who would be among your prospective buyers.

The principles that I am going to discuss apply equally to large conferences as they do to small events. The key is the interaction with the other attendees, because social location sharing relies on the fact that the person checking in is actually present at the event. This is what makes social location sharing so compelling as a marketing tool at events. You already have some indication of who is present because you have a form of virtual introduction (when the customer checks in). This is not something that you would normally have at an event because most event organizers guard the attendee list closely (and rightly so).

Simply trying to broadcast your message to social location sharers—as we have discussed in other chapters—is not something that is either advisable or welcomed by the users. The messaging has to be subtle and yet also prominent enough to attract attention.

One of the most straightforward ways to leverage social location marketing apps at a conference or event is to use the Mayor feature in Foursquare. Set up your booth as a location in Foursquare, place appropriate signage at the booth inviting people to check in with Foursquare, and award a prize to whoever becomes Mayor. There are limitations to this:

- First, the conference or event has to take place over a period of more than one day.

- There will be only one winner.

- Participants must have to have their Foursquare accounts linked to their Twitter accounts so that you can reach out to them.

This use of Foursquare is certainly a simple and easy option for using social location marketing and less intrusive than a business card in a fishbowl. However, it is not particularly engaging. But if you are new to social location marketing, it's a good first step, and it's much better than not attempting anything. I recommend that you at least try this—just to have the experience of setting up a simple campaign and seeing it work.

For a slightly more complex campaign, try using Gowalla or SCVNGR to set up a trip based around the conference or event environment. This kind of campaign can be a much more engaging experience, although it does require some additional work. You will need to select the venues ahead of time and make sure that they are already entered into the spot database or create them. Depending on the type of conference or event you're attending, you can either set up a trip that occurs inside the venue or make use of locations that are close by.

A trip like this provides attendees with the opportunity to get away from the conference or event location and engage with other businesses in the locality. This might seem counterintuitive to normal conference or event marketing. Why would you want to send the people who you are looking to engage with away from your booth and out onto the streets around the venue?

The point is that the last place on the trip is your booth. Customers go out, learn about the environment they are in, and then they come to find you and your team at your booth. There customers learn that you have something to talk about other than just your product or services. You have created an opportunity for genuine conversation. Although your competitors are still trying to palm off a free pen, you are talking about a great lunch spot or an interesting bookstore that is just around the corner.

This makes your business look a lot more interesting to potential customers because you have differentiated yourself immediately from the other companies at the event, and you are much more memorable. Also, those taking part in your trip will talk about you to each other. Your customers will recommend your trip to other potential customers as a way to get to know the locality (because many conference attendees are visitors).

Creating a trip in Gowalla is a very simple process. You will need a minimum of three locations on your trip before it can be published, but other than that you only need a little imagination for the name.

Create a Gowalla Trip

Creating a Gowalla trip is fairly easy:

1. First, create a name for the trip that is both catchy and that includes your company/brand name (see Figure 8.1). You want users to know who is responsible for the trip. Every time people check into one of the locations included in your trip, they will be shown a notification screen telling them that they have completed a check in on your trip. For example, "Get Out & Breathe Bob's Brew's Tour" might be a fun name for a trip that gets attendees out of a conference center and into the local area.

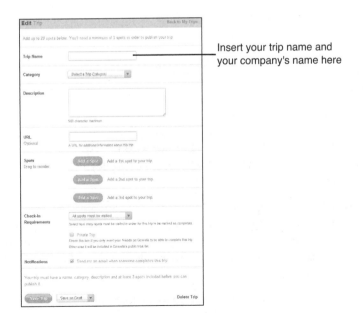

Insert your trip name and your company's name here

Figure 8.1   *Create a name that is memorable, and don't forget to include your company name!*

2. The next step is to categorize the trip (see Figure 8.2). If you are making the trip focused on one activity, such as restaurants or bars, the choice is fairly obvious. However, for something that ties back to your conference booth, you might want to consider a Photo Walk. The reason is quite straightforward. To use Gowalla or any other social location sharing app, the user will have a smartphone. The other element that all smartphones have in common is a camera. Therefore, putting together a Photo Walk requires nothing more than to pick certain places and then have the participants take pictures of them along the way. The user then uploads them to Gowalla as evidence that they were actually at the location and didn't just check in from nearby. You could even incorporate the pictures into your booth competition by having them email them to a competition email address and then selecting the best picture.

Figure 8.2 *Choose a category for your trip.*

3. Describe the trip. This is where you to tell people why they should take part. If you are giving something away to the winner or inviting people to attend a gathering, this is where to put it.

4. Add a URL. As tempting as it might be, don't make this your company website. That seems the obvious thing to put in here, but it's also not very subtle. Instead, why not create a specific landing page just for the trip that is on your domain but is accessible only from this URL? This will give you yet another metric point.

5. Add spots to your trip. Adding spots to the tour involves searching for them by name. Type the search term, and a list of possible selections

containing that term is displayed. Choose the location you want to use (see Figure 8.3).

Figure 8.3 *Add spots to your trip. Keep the number of locations manageable. You don't want to make the trip too difficult or too long.*

 Tip

After you have added the spots that you want on your trip, you can reorder them if you need to by dragging them into the order that you prefer.

6. You then get to determine how a user completes the trip. Do they have to check in at all the spots, or just a few of the spots? Think this through carefully. You want the trip to be fun, you want the trip to be possible to complete, and you have to consider how much time someone will actually want to spend doing this. You also don't want it to be too easy and therefore lack any sense of challenge or achievement. There is a fine balance between these two elements, and knowing the attendees is key to knowing where this balance lies.

7. The final choice is to decide if you want to receive an email notifying you when someone completes the trip. You definitely want that email. It will assist you with your outreach. Check that box and click Publish; you now have a trip that users of Gowalla can use to help them explore the area around the event.

8. Make sure that you copy the URL for the trip. It will look something like this: http://gowalla.com/trips/8736 (this happens to be my Austin

Coffee House tour). You can then promote the trip before and during the event.

So what does a campaign like this actually look like? What results can you expect from it? The next section shows an example.

Chevrolet at the State Fair of Texas

Let's look at a nice example from Chevrolet, which partnered with Gowalla to create a series of trips at the State Fair of Texas where they were conducting a brand awareness campaign. The State Fair of Texas is an institution dating back to the end of the nineteenth century and is distinguished by being the largest annual exposition in North America and the largest of the state fairs in the United States.

Like many annual expositions in the USA, it attracts a particular demographic as its primary audience. One of the things to differentiate it from other state fairs is that it is the only one to host an annual motor show and has done so since 1904. This was one of many reasons it became an obvious place for Chevy to run a social location marketing campaign. The majority of the attendees (approx 80%) live within a 50-mile radius of the Dallas-Fort Worth metroplex area, which means that for many, attending the state fair is a family tradition.

Even with the motor show, the majority of people attending the state fair are not going because they want to learn about the latest vehicles from Chevy—they are going to have some fun with their family, go on the rides, see the fairgrounds, win stuffed animals, and eat fried foods. So how would a car manufacturer approach this group of individuals and create trips that they would want to do?

First, Chevy decided to create four trips focused on different elements of the state fair, each with its own unique pin.

- The Chevy Rocks Texas Challenge, which consisted of four spots: the Chevrolet Main Stage, the Chevrolet Town Square and Test Track, the Go Texan Wine Garden Stage, and the Chevrolet Truck Zone.

- The Chevy State Fair Classics, which consisted of four spots: Big Tex, Texas Star Ferris Wheel, Cotton Bowl, and Chevrolet Town Square and Test Track.

- The Chevy Super-Fan Challenge, which consisted of four spots: Suburban at the Fair Park Coliseum, Chevrolet Town Square and Test Track, Chevrolet Auto Show Booth, and Chevrolet Truck Zone.

- The Chevy Fried Food Challenge, which consisted of eight spots: Fried Beer, Texas Fried FRITO Pie, Vandalay Concession's Texas Fried Cookie Dough, Vandalay Concession's Deep Fried Butter, Yoakum Packaging's

Chicken Fried Bacon, Chevrolet Town Square and Test Track, Fletcher's Corny Dogs, and The Dock's Fried Peaches and Cream Stand.

Without too much searching you can probably spot the one place that was common to all the trips—Chevrolet Town Square and Test Track. This was the main base of operation for Chevy at the State Fair and was where visitors could sign up to test drive the latest vehicles, get information about the new vehicles, and generally interact with the Chevy marketing and sales team. By putting that as a spot in all the trips, they were increasing the likelihood that participants would choose to interact at some level with Chevy staff. When a participant completed a trip, she could go to the Chevy team and show them the pin she was awarded and be given a goodie bag of Chevy promotional items.

So what were the results of this campaign? This is a breakdown of the number of people who completed the individual trips and were therefore awarded a pin:

- The Chevy Rocks Texas Challenge—139

- The Chevy State Fair Classics—202

- The Chevy Super-Fan Challenge—132

- The Chevy Fried Food Challenge—128

That is a significant number of people because the demographics of the state fair attendees does not trend toward the smartphone user as a general rule. In addition, this number does not include the participants who were checking in at these locations but who did not complete the entire trip for whatever reason. Those participants were also exposed to the Chevy branded messaging at each spot, so regardless if they then visited the main Chevy area, they were still made aware of the Chevy brand and of Chevy's presence at the state fair, which was the intent of the campaign. During this campaign, Chevy also received more than 300 new "likes" to their Facebook page, which were directly attributed to this campaign.

These metrics were worked out in advance with their agency to ensure they all knew what elements were going to be monitored as a measure of success and how they would determine if the campaign had actually achieved its goals. Given the environment and that the campaign was run by the corporate communications team rather than an individual dealership, sales was not an appropriate measure to include, and that is perfectly acceptable. There is still a return on investment for this campaign. As I have mentioned before, it is incredibly important to ensure that you are measuring your ROI when putting together a social location marketing campaign.

Interestingly, Chevy opted to do very little in the way of offline promotion for the trips at the state fair. Instead, Chevy relied on users to spread the word. At the main Chevy base, they had one A-board (see Figure 8.4).

Figure 8.4   *This was the extent of Chevy's advertising for the trips at the Texas State Fair.*

As you can see, the ad gives some basic information but it focuses more on Gowalla than on Chevy. The ad provides a hashtag—ChevyTXFair—for people to use on Twitter and to search for more information about the campaign. The ad also includes a landing page hosted by Gowalla where people can find the full details of each of the trips.

The low-key nature of the ad showed that Chevy recognized the true word-of-mouth nature of social location sharing. They understood that the individuals checking in are in fact the best promotional piece for a campaign rather than a multitude of more traditional marketing communication pieces that will only be lost among all the other pieces given out at events like the state fair.

Not all event promotions have to be focused around a single event or conference to be leveraged as part of a social location marketing campaign. Indeed not all are run by commercial enterprises. Because of the low cost of entry that is presented by social location marketing, nonprofits have turned to it as a method of engaging their prospective audience.

VisitBritain: Social Media Tourism Leader

A good example of an event promotion that is not focused around a single event or conference is VisitBritain, which is the online presence of the British Tourist Authority. VisitBritain was created in April 2003 to market Britain to the rest of the

world and to promote and develop the visitor economy of England. It is a department of the British Government and falls under the Department for Culture,
Media, and Sport. The website itself has been recognized as a leading example of
how tourism and visitor convention bureaus can leverage the Internet to promote
their particular areas of interest to tourists. So it is no great surprise that they have
ventured into the area of social location marketing to assist with the promotion of
visitor attractions in Britain.

VisitBritain decided to partner with Facebook Places to create a ranking table on its
own Facebook business page, where it created a new tab called Top 50 Places (see
Figure 8.5). The list of these top 50 places is created dynamically by users of
Facebook Places and is based on the number of check ins that a particular venue
receives.

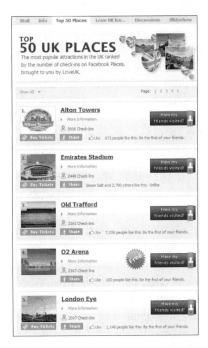

Figure 8.5   *VisitBritain partnered with Facebook Places to create a Top 50 ranking of
Facebook Places.*

 Note

To learn more about Facebook Places, see Chapter 6, "Know Your Apps."

It is interesting that this table counts only those people who have actually checked
in at the location, not the number of "fans" or "likes" that a venue receives on

Facebook. So, for example, if we look at the top five venues, Old Trafford, the home of Manchester United Football (Soccer) team, has received 2,393 check ins but has also received 7,556 "likes." This is 6,885 more "likes" than Alton Towers, a theme park, which holds the number one slot with 3,006 check ins.

Why is this significant? Because check ins are an action that results in revenue, whereas "fans" and "likes" do not. There is only a superficial element of loyalty in a Facebook user clicking the "like" button on a particular Facebook page. However, when a person goes to the actual venue and checks in, there is a much greater likelihood that the person has gone there not just to check-in but to attend the venue as a visitor. Not all the venues that make the list charge an entrance fee. For example, the O2 arena is free to visit, although events that are held there usually charge for attendance. However, even those venues that charge no admission or that are just landmarks, such as Trafalgar Square (number six on the list), generate revenue for the surrounding area.

By creating this list, VisitBritain has not only utilized social location marketing, they have done so in a way that uses the data being provided by their own existing audience to assist in the promotion of venues to their potential audience. The bottom line is that they are using past visitors as promoters to future visitors. The list of 50 top places becomes not only a marketing tool but adds value to the experience for those viewing the VisitBritain Facebook page, which again assists in generating loyalty to the overall brand as a source of information.

If you were planning a visit to Britain, what better way to discover the places that you might want to add to your list than to see those places that get the most visitors. At the very least, the places on this list are implied as being the most popular destinations. Of course, you could also use the list to make sure you avoided those spots that attract the most tourists if you wanted to seek out the venues that are off the beaten path. Either way, this list becomes a valuable resource, especially as over time the venues on it will change. The venues listed, as well as the popularity of each, will change as more users check in and as the seasons change and indoor venues increase in popularity over outdoor venues. Some will swell in their check-in prominence around certain events. For example, Trafalgar Square attracts millions of visitors for the New Year's Eve celebrations held in London, as does Edinburgh Castle. So these types of events will skew the popularity of certain locations at certain times of the year. However, even with these anomalies taken into consideration, VisitBritain has used social location sharing data to create a valuable asset for both their own campaigns and for their target audience.

State of Arkansas Gets Location Aware

VisitBritain is not the only tourism body to see the potential that social location marketing offers their particular areas of marketing. The State of Arkansas became the first state to partner with a location app provider in September 2010 when they selected Gowalla. The State Tourism board had looked at several of the app providers and decided that the Gowalla model of trips was best suited to the type of communication that they wanted to achieve with their visitors.

In a campaign that was similar in its scope to the Chevy State Fair of Texas campaign, the state of Arkansas created five trips for visitors to the state to use as part of their discovery of the different aspects that the state has to offer.

- Haunted Arkansas—This trip has 10 spots that form the trip:
  The Crescent Hotel
  Basin Park Hotel
  Fort Smith National Historic Site
  King Opera House
  Mount Holly Cemetery
  The Empress of Little Rock
  Rush-Gates House
  Peppersauce Bottom
  Gurdon Light
  The Allen House

- Historic Arkansas—Another 10-spot trip, consisting of the following:
  Fort Smith National Historic Site
  Waltons 5-10
  Arkansas Post National Memorial
  Bill Clinton Birthplace Home
  Toltec Mounds Archeological State Park
  Louisiana Purchase Historic State Park
  Little Rock Central High School
  Potts Inn Museum
  Historic Arkansas Museum
  Arkansas Museum of Natural Resources

- Arkansas Float Trip—A trip comprising six spots:
  White River
  Spring River
  Little Red River
  Buffalo River
  Caddo River
  Ouachita River

- Billgrimage—A seven-spot trip made up of the following:
  Bill Clinton Birthplace Home
  Hot Springs High School
  Clinton House Museum
  Arkansas State Capitol

Arkansas Governor's Mansion
Old State House Museum
Clinton Presidential Library and Museum

 • Arkansas Traveler—A 15-spot trip comprising the following:
Clinton Presidential Library and Museum
Big Dam Bridge
Fort Smith National Historic Site
The Lodge at Mount Magazine
Dickson Street
Basin Spring Park
Blanchard Springs Caverns
Hemingway-Pfeiffer Museum
Arkansas Wine Country
Bathhouse Row
Crater of Diamonds State Park
Arkansas Museum Of Natural Resources
Delta Cultural Center
Arts and Science Center
Arkansas Welcome Center Lake Village

What is very different from other organizations that have created this type of campaign is that each of the trips stands alone. There is no common spot to them and no obvious intent to drive traffic to a particular destination. Also, the tourist board opted to not require users to visit all the locations to complete the trip. Four of the trips require a user to check in at only three of the locations to receive the pin, and just one trip—the Arkansas Traveler trip—requires the user to check in at five of the locations.

Choosing to not make people check in at all of the locations follows the advice I mentioned earlier in the chapter—make the trips fun and achievable. If users had to check in at all 10 venues on the Historic Arkansas trip to get their pin, they might well give up before starting. Because the trip might be part of a family vacation, not all the family might want to spend their entire vacation in historic locations.

The trips serve more as a value add to the visitors than an obvious marketing ploy. However, by positioning its campaign in this way, similar to the way VisitBritain positioned its campaign, the Arkansas Tourist board is positioned as the de facto destination for information on how to get the most out of visiting the state.

Keep in mind that a campaign of this size is created for the long term and not for a shorter engagement. This kind of campaign must become a part of the broader marketing communication efforts that the board undertakes. Unlike the Chevy campaign, which had only a five-week window in which to operate, these trips are available year-round. At the time this book was written, only one of the trips had been completed by a user, although all the trips had spots that had some check ins.

(The campaign had been active for a little less than three months when this book was written).

The metrics for this type of campaign would be very different from the Chevy campaign. If the same measures were applied, this campaign would already be considered a failure. Instead, and with the longer term vision in mind, appropriate metrics would be the increase in visitors to each of the venues that correspond with the check ins that take place. In addition, follow-up communication with the users who check in might yield recommendations and feedback on how to improve those venues.

Intel Inside

Consumer marketing organizations and tourism are not the only types of companies to leverage social location marketing. Intel partnered with Foursquare to reach the audience at the 2010 Consumer Electronics Show (CES), in Las Vegas. Despite the name of the event, CES is in fact a trade-only show and not open to consumers. Rather, it is an opportunity for Original Equipment Manufacturers (OEMs) to display their latest products to their customers—the retailers who will be selling them.

Business-to-business has long been the red-headed stepchild of social media marketing. It is hard for this particular sector to leverage the viral, word-of-mouth glitz that consumer-focused campaigns attract. However, Intel managed to appeal to its target audience at CES by creating a competition that required visitors to CES to follow Intel on Foursquare (www.foursquare.com/user/intel) and then check in at various locations in Las Vegas during the convention to unlock various Intel inspired "To-do's." The partnership with Foursquare also included three special-event badges, known as Intel Insider badges (a play on the company's famous tag line—Intel Inside). These badges were awarded to users who checked in at specific events during CES.

- Intel Badge—Awarded for checking in at the Intel Insider Core Kick-Off event held at Sushi Samba in Las Vegas.

- Work That Core Badge—Awarded for checking in at the Intel CES booth during the conference.

- All Ears Badge—Awarded to users who checked in at the Paul Otellini's Intel CES keynote.

For each badge that users unlocked, they were entered into a prize drawing to win an Intel-powered netbook. So there was an incentive to unlock all three badges and therefore be entered three times into the prize drawing. Over the course of four days, Intel had more than 500 entries into the competition. The audience at CES tends toward the tech savvy early adopter, which is a perfect fit for social location marketing. This is a good example of a company knowing its audience and understanding what would motivate them to take part in a campaign of this nature. With more than 100 entries per day, Intel definitely did a good job of putting together a compelling campaign and getting a very good level of participation.

Intel isn't the only business-to-business organization to leverage its presence at a conference as an opportunity to use social location marketing to communicate with potential customers.

Lotus Gets Social on a Boat

At the Enterprise 2.0 conference in Boston, IBM's Lotus division decided to host a party on a boat during the conference. While on the boat, attendees were given the opportunity to see demonstrations of the Lotus Social Computing, Collaboration, Mobile, and Web Portal offerings. Lotus subject matter experts were also on hand to answer questions about the products and provide a more personal experience for the guests.

 When IBM decided to utilize social location marketing, the Lotus team saw an obvious opportunity to partner with Foursquare, which already had a badge that was very relevant—the "I'm on a boat" badge. This badge is usually awarded to users checking in at a venue that has the tag "boat"; not all these venues are in fact boats. Some are restaurants at marinas or boat docks; others are simply boat-themed venues such as the Pirates of the Caribbean ride at Disney World.

So why not use this existing badge for an event that was taking place on an actual boat? This is where a little creativity and some user knowledge go a long way. Had the Lotus team not already been aware of this badge, they might well have missed this opportunity to use something that preexisted as a tie-in to their event. This reinforces my mantra that before you start using these apps as marketing tools, you first get to know your users.

Given that Lotus had limited space available on the boat (a maximum of 300 people could attend) they needed a way to limit the party. First, guests had to be full-ticket attendees at the conference. Second, guests had to check in at the Lotus booth at the conference for ticket giveaways. This is a great example of using social location marketing to drive booth traffic while providing an incentive to the user to take part.

So Lotus drove traffic to its booth and they were able to drive guests to attend their offsite party on the boat and ensure that these were highly engaged individuals with whom they could have meaningful discussions about their products. This level of interaction is not always achievable at a conference booth.

This campaign shows that social location marketing efforts can be very targeted with extremely narrow goals and yet still contain the elements necessary to drive engagement—fun, achievability, and measurability.

Gowalla Calendar

Gowalla offers another method of promoting an event at a location: the Gowalla calendar. Currently available only for Austin, New York, and San Francisco, Gowalla is selling dates for 2011 that will receive a custom stamp designed specifically for the location or the event.

Purchasing a date gets the organization three major pieces of marketing collateral:

- An original Gowalla passport stamp—This appears in the user's passport as well as on Facebook when a user's Facebook account is connected to a Gowalla account or checks in via Facebook Places (see Figure 8.6).

Figure 8.6   *An original Gowalla passport stamp.*

- Featured Event or Venue status—This appears on the date of the event, which puts the event or location at the top of a user's list of nearby venues when using Gowalla.

Figure 8.7   *Featured Event or Venue status means your event appears at the top of the user's nearby venues.*

- A set of two 5×7 window clings—These clings feature the custom designed passport stamp for the venue to display and promote the event in advance of the date purchased.

Figure 8.8   *Use the custom-designed window cling to promote your event.*

By late 2010, January 2011 had already sold out (see Figure 8.9). The cost varies for each date, and interestingly, the pricing model that Gowalla has adopted means that the further into the future your selected date is, the more expensive it is.

Jan	Feb	Mar	Apr	**May**	Jun	Jul	Aug	Sept	Oct	Nov	Dec	2011

Sunday	Monday	Tuesday	Wednesday	Thursday	Friday	Saturday
1 $605 USD Buy	2 $610 USD Buy	3 $615 USD Buy	4 $620 USD Buy	5 $625 USD Buy	6 $630 USD Buy	7 $635 USD Buy
8 $640 USD Buy	9 $645 USD Buy	10 $650 USD Buy	11 $655 USD Buy	12 $660 USD Buy	13 $665 USD Buy	14 $670 USD Buy
15 $675 USD Buy	16 $680 USD Buy	17 $685 USD Buy	18 $690 USD Buy	19 $695 USD Buy	20 $700 USD Buy	21 $705 USD Buy
22 $710 USD Buy	23 $715 USD Buy	24 $720 USD Buy	25 $725 USD Buy	26 $730 USD Buy	27 $735 USD Buy	28 $740 USD Buy
29 $745 USD Buy	30 $750 USD Buy	31 $755 USD Buy				

Figure 8.9   *Booking too far in advance will cost you more money.*

The example shown in Figure 8.9 shows the increasing price of dates in May 2011 for Austin. It can be seen that the cost rises by $5 per day as you progress toward the end of the month, and this price rise continues throughout each month until December 31, 2011.

This is an interesting move by Gowalla; I would guess it is designed to see how much interest there is by marketers in purchasing specific dates. I would certainly expect to see the pricing model change for 2012 so that specific dates in the calendar become more valuable than others. For example, Super Bowl Sunday is likely to be more desirable than an ordinary Sunday for a bar in a particular city if they are holding a Super Bowl watch party.

App developers, such as Gowalla, who are rolling out easier and lower-cost methods for marketers to enter the social location marketing arena, will only encourage more adoption by businesses. One of the criticisms of social location marketing by the media at present is that the use of it by business outstrips the demand for it by consumers. They cite the fact that only 4% of online adults use social location sharing apps. In 2008, the same number was true for users of Twitter, but two years later that number had quadrupled. Many marketers have learned their lesson from missing the early ride that Twitter provided. They are coming to grips with the concept of social location marketing now, before the consumer becomes more adept at it than they are. They are testing what types of campaigns work and what appeals to their particular audiences more.

By doing this now, before the apps have their big shakeout, marketers who are already engaged have a competitive edge over those who have yet to try this form of communication. By the time the platforms consolidate and the offerings are streamlined, it will become increasingly harder for marketers to make an impact with this type of communication—just as it has become with Twitter.

Facebook Deals

In 2010, Facebook announced Facebook Deals as part of the Facebook Places app—a merchant program that is currently being rolled out to a limited number of participating merchants. The program allows merchants to add offers to their locations that are redeemable by Facebook Places users when they check in at the location. The offer might be something as simple as 50% off the price of a cup of coffee or a more complex offering that is part of a bigger reward.

There is nothing particularly special about the Deals program; in fact, it mirrors the early deals programs that were offered via Foursquare and Gowalla. The concept is very similar in nature to the Foursquare Mayor offers that first started the idea of social location marketing a couple of years ago.

Facebook provides an example of a deal which is 50% off a cup of coffee—plugging into the expectations already set by other social location sharing apps.

However, Facebook Deals has immense potential because Facebook has an audience of 500 million compared to Foursquare's 4 million, and Gowalla's almost 1 million. Facebook Places Deals is very likely to bring to the attention of the mainstream online community that there are bargains to be had for simply sharing their location and helping to promote their favorite locations.

This, in turn, will increase the pressure on brands, companies, and organizations to offer incentives for users of these apps at their locations, events, and conferences. The social consumer is having the expectation built for them by the creators of the social location sharing apps that they will be rewarded for sharing their location and promoting a business. The social consumer is no longer satisfied to tout your business, event, product, or service for you by carrying around your logo unrewarded.

Summary

When using social location marketing at an event or conference, think about how the campaign will add value to the audience experience at the event or conference. Will they learn more about the conference? Will they find out useful information about the area around the event location? Will they win a valuable prize?

Your decision about what type of value you are going to add to the audience experience will then help you decide which of the apps you are going to use to run the campaign. As we have already seen, each of the apps has different capabilities and lends themselves to different types of campaigns.

Set clear metrics about how the campaign will provide additional value to the company above and beyond what has been seen before when attending a conference or event. What have you brought back in the past? What will you bring back with the use of this campaign that is different, and how will that benefit the greater organization? This has to be something of greater significance than simply increasing the number of "likes" on the company Facebook page. Focusing on the capability to provide higher quality leads to the sales force is a much better way of ensuring internal buy-in.

Remember that as a marketer you are selling the idea internally as much as you are trying to sell it to your prospective customers.

Socially Speaking: The Social Business

The most common reason that businesses fear social media is that those companies believe the audience will criticize them. Worse still, those companies believe they won't have an appropriate response. This fear is as common to large multi-outlet retailers as it is to a mom and pop corner store. No one wants bad news, and no one likes dealing with people who are perceived as "difficult customers." Yet all businesses must face one inescapable reality at some point—it is impossible for a business to provide a product, service, or customer experience that meets or exceeds every customer's expectations, every time. In a social media world, that means those customers now have an instant platform for sharing their experiences—both good and bad—via social location sharing and social media apps, such as Foursquare, Gowalla, Twitter, and Facebook (not to mention reviews on online shopping sites).

Ignoring social media is not the answer. People will post comments about your company, your products, your services, and your brands, regardless of whether you participate in the discussion. If your company is really unlucky, those comments will spread virally—far and wide—regardless of whether they are justified. With the recent rise in popularity of social media tools such as Twitter, many companies have learned this lesson the hard way.

By that, I mean that because people can post from anywhere with a smartphone, it's easy to get caught up in the heat of the moment. This "heat" is the measure of the immediacy of the post. Some social media comments are made worse by the "heat of the moment" in which they are made. For example, let's say you're waiting to for a sales associate to assist you in a home theater store. After waiting for what you think is too long, you whip out your iPhone, fire up Twitter and in just a few seconds, you've written a scathing comment about how !$#@#! angry you are about how long you've been waiting for a sales associate to help you at store X. Now, you might've been waiting too long, but are you really that angry? Does the store deserve that kind of harsh criticism that could cost them business? Could you have toned it down just a touch? Would you have made the same comment if you had to wait until you got home to make that comment?

Prior to the advent of smartphone-enabled microblogging tools such as Twitter, we would be forced to put time and space between us and the incident that had incurred our wrath. In the pre-smartphone days, if we got angry while out and about, we would have to wait until we got home and in front of a computer before we could tee off. Often, that meant we had time to simmer down and either we forgot about it altogether or our once hot-headed post became much tamer. Not so much now. Now we can write a review as it happens, and that level of immediacy means that the full "heat" of our ire is communicated in our posts. If we are eloquent, if we are well connected, or if we simply hit on a hot topic, the chances that our posts will be commented on, reposted, and generally spread are much higher.

However, if your company is involved in social media, you have an opportunity to respond, apologize (if appropriate), correct inaccurate information, and in general, interact with customers and potential customers in a way that you never could before. If for no other reason, the capability to correct misinformation should be why an organization monitors social media for its brand(s), products, services, and company name on a regular basis. Without knowing what is being said, how can an organization possibly respond or correct misinformation? The simple act of correcting misinformation can mean the difference between a customer gained and a customer lost.

Information is not always maliciously incorrect, either. It could be a simple typographical error regarding the opening times of a store. Perhaps a visitor entered that your store closed at six (when, in fact, it closes at 9) simply because he or she pressed the wrong key. Not much of a difference in terms of content, but those three hours in the hours of the store operation could mean a few lost customers. Why lose them when a simple edit can remove the inaccuracy?

This should not be mistaken for content control. Participating in social media doesn't mean your company can stop the flow of bad comments or have them removed. After those comments are out there, they are out there forever. The inability to maintain custodial control over what is said in social media circles about your brand, product, or service is a common fear. However, in reality, have you ever been able to control what your customers say about your brands, products, or services? Companies have never been able to control the conversations of customers and potential customers. Phone calls, water coolers, airplanes, letters, emails, bars, and hundreds of other media have long enabled the content creator to pass judgment on products, services, and organizations.

The primary difference is that social media means that you are now privy to those conversations. Now you can see exactly what is being said about your company (as can everyone else, including your competitors). Perhaps for many organizations, ignorance was bliss, but social media has removed that ignorance. Brands can no longer claim they were unaware of customer viewpoints, desires, or needs.

Whereas libel laws still apply in the blogosphere, opinion is not covered. So provided a content creator (any kind of online content—blog post, tweet, Facebook comment, Amazon review, and so on) is not posting blatant lies about an organization, he or she is free to share his or her opinion. This is why this part of social media is often handed over to the part of the organization that handles customer service. In reality, however, customer service is a major part of any social media activity, and it should be a constant focus for the social media team. This is especially true with respect to social location sharing tools, such as Foursquare and Gowalla.

The users of these tools are the social media equivalent of secret shoppers, with one valuable (at least for the organization) difference—they don't remain secret. Although many organizations, especially in retail, still retain the services of secret shopping companies to test out their venues and get feedback on customer experiences, nothing can compare with real customer feedback. This is where social location sharing tool users come in. They are the organization's real customers. These customers post comments, tips, observations at the point of purchase, comments about the use of the service or product, and more. This "heat"—this immediacy— makes their comments valuable, whether they are good or bad.

Feedback from social location sharing users is unfiltered. SLS users are not trying to reach a quota, they are not editing for appropriateness, and the only axe they have to grind is the desire to share their thoughts with their network and to become perceived as a valuable asset to that network. It is important to understand that last motivation. Being an asset to their networks is an overriding concern to many SLS users. The most common way Foursquare users, for example, increase their net-works, and therefore their influence, is by providing good content. Good content is that which provides value to the network of content consumers. So by providing timely, relevant information to their networks, Foursquare users increase their own value and generate social capital.

If your company learns to leverage this motivation, you can both assist the SLS user and work toward meeting your own marketing goals. After all, the content creator needs content. Your company wants information posted about you to be accurate and reflective of your products, services, or brands. This can lead to a synergistic relationship between your company and the content creator.

However, your company should be wary of falling into the trap of buying content. It is all too easy for an organization to view this as an appropriate solution, in the same way that they might contemplate any other form of media buy. Simply paying content creators to generate positive posts about an organization will quickly back-fire. First, the Federal Telecommunications Committee has laid out guidelines for content creators, whether they are bloggers or TV producers. Second, when the "real" customers' content appears at odds with the paid content, it can become rap-idly apparent that the paid content creator has sold out. This wrecks the paid con-tent creators' reputation and can quickly lead to a loss of audience and influence, rendering them no longer useful to your company. Also, your company, will lose whatever credibility it had by not acknowledging the real content and trying to cre-ate content that will at the very least have the impression of being "fake."

Creating fake content will only harm a company should it actually have to deal with a post that requires addressing tangible issues with its customers. Being transparent, genuine, or "real" is often the advice given to organizations about how to conduct themselves in social media. However, the reasons for doing so are often not out-lined. The potential for being remembered as the organization that created fake content at some point should be at the forefront of the reasoning to be genuine.

The very minimum response for customer-created content, whether good or bad, is an appropriate acknowledgement, such as "Thank you" for positive comments and "We're sorry" for a bad comment. For the positive comment it is, for the majority of cases, the only response that is really needed, provided that the comment doesn't include recommendations for improvements or contain a question. In those situa-tions, a more detailed response is required.

For the bad comment, the "We're sorry" response should be considered only a stop-gap response, something that lets the content creator know that your company has seen his or her post and you are following up on it. The follow up defines how the relationship between the content creator and your company will be established or changed. The follow up is best handled by whoever has responsibility within your company for customer service/relationship management. This won't necessarily be the same person or team that handles social media, but at this point it is appropriate to hand off the situation to ensure that the situation is resolved properly and in line with the your company's policies. How this handover is completed can be a complex process for some organizations, but to the content creator it should be seamless and invisible.

As previously mentioned, customers do not care about internal organization structures, they care about good service. They don't want to be handed off to different departments or told that the account that they have reached out to or that has made initial contact with them isn't going to follow through. So in setting up the process, a good deal of thought and attention should be paid to this particular part of the process. Often the most appropriate method is to maintain a single point of contact who becomes an issue project manager as issues are discovered. The issue project manager is empowered to hand off the issue but not the contact relationship. However, this can often cause frustration internally when the department tasked with handling customer service/relationship management perceives that they are losing ground to the marketing/pr/tech support department because they are the ones charged with handling or managing the social media accounts for the organization. This is where the social media strategy comes into its own. Recognizing these types of issues before they arise is crucial to providing a good social customer service experience. It is also where an organization has the opportunity to provide a level of service that becomes a differentiator in the customer experience realm.

More Than a Twitter or Facebook Page

Social business is more than having a Twitter account. It is more than accumulating hundreds or even thousands of "likes" on your company Facebook page. The reason for becoming a social business should be driven by a desire to achieve and maintain a competitive edge. Given the increasing number of social tools available and the consumers using them, becoming a social business is a commitment that must go beyond simple participation.

The social business utilizes social tools (Twitter, Facebook, Foursquare, Gowalla, and so on) as means for communication with customers and with each other. This means that the social business democratizes the company and opens the way the company does business for all to see.

For most companies, this is a daunting—if not downright scary—prospect and one that meets with a lot of resistance. However, many companies are already taking the appropriate steps to move their businesses to this model and are reaping the rewards.

By becoming a truly social business rather than just being an organization that has a social media department, an organization can demonstrate that it is truly customer focused. In recent years, shoe and clothing distributor Zappos has made an art of social business. Zappos incorporated the customer perspective into everything from its tag line to its company ethos. It has paid off in more ways than anyone could have imagined and has been central to the company's success. For Zappos, being social wasn't something that was confined to one part of the organization. It wasn't a function of the marketing, PR, or customer service departments, because the entire organization was a customer service department. Building an organization with this perspective is a lot easier than realigning an existing one, and certainly the fact that Zappos started with this perspective cannot be overlooked as a contributing factor in the company's success.

However, if your company truly wants to embrace social media and social location marketing, becoming a social organization that does social business is and should be the ultimate goal. If your company is founded or aligned on the concept of doing social business, you will find it easier to handle customer complaints regardless of whether they are received through social media. In fact, to a social organization, social media is just how business is done.

So, when deciding whether your business is going to take the social business plunge, you have a couple of things to consider:

- Do you believe your company model is already aligned with or can be aligned with social media and social business?

- Do you believe in the social media/social business concept strongly enough to make the investment to change those areas of your company to allow full alignment with the customer-driven social business reality in which all organizations now find themselves?

A social business will find social media a more natural fit than a nonsocial business will. This statement seems obvious when written out, but it is a constant surprise to me that so many businesses that are not social in any other aspect of their marketing communications expect social media to be a natural fit for them and wonder why they find it so difficult to realize real results from their efforts. If the business normally restricts itself to the type of one-way communication that is more broadcast than communication, then social media is obviously going to be a struggle. Companies that broadcast—that is, send offers and new product information, but aren't interested in customer interaction—are going to find social media daunting.

These companies have dealt only with outgoing communications and have no method in place for dealing with the inevitable influx of inbound communication that will arrive (prompted or not). Customers and potential customers will start communicating both in response to offers and with complaints, observations, suggestions, recommendations, praise, and so on.

All of this will happen on multiple apps (Twitter, Facebook, Foursquare, Gowalla, to name a few) and all in a free-form manner, some of which will be directed at your company and some of which will be a part of broader conversations. The first challenge for your company is to find these conversations, posts, comments, and so on. The second challenge is to apply some form of triage and to sort this information into buckets—at the very least positive and negative—so that you can decide which to respond to, who will respond, how you will respond, and which to let go without a response.

For an organization that is used to and perhaps established on the concept that customer communication, at least in the normal run of things, is a one way activity that happens in clearly defined spaces and at predetermined times, social media will seem a daunting prospect and is often typified with Wild West Frontier clichés.

If it wasn't overwhelming enough already, social location sharers armed with smartphones can post comments, write reviews, and upload photos on-the-fly. This information has the potential (depending on the phone and the app the person is using) to include an exact location and timestamp, called a geotag. This could be bad for your business if someone saw an embarrassing incident at a retail location and uploaded a photo—the photo would contain a geotag forever tying it to your business.

Social Customer Relationship Management Database (sCRM)

The social business doesn't struggle with leveraging social media apps such as Foursquare and Gowalla because these apps are simply part of everyday business. Just as most businesses have incorporated websites into their communication plans, an increasing number of businesses are incorporating social media apps into their communication plans as well. What does this mean for the way customers will interact with organizations in the future?

Primarily, the shift toward social business will allow for a more integrated marketing communication strategy to succeed. Instead of looking for media buying opportunities, online ad placement positions, Twitter campaigns, or PPC campaigns on Facebook, the organization will have developed a Social Customer Relationship Management (sCRM) database that allows all the interactions across all platforms with the customer to be held and reviewed at any point. sCRMs are already available, though most do not yet capture all communications on all apps. As sCRMs become increasingly common, it will be possible to identify a customer's preferred social media channel, the preferred delivery mechanism—web, mobile, out-of-home, email—and the type of information that they are more likely to react to. Not only will this provide the marketer with the capability to provide a totally tailored experience on a customer-by-customer basis, but it will also appear to the customer to be less intrusive. This means that campaigns of the future will most likely be shorter and more focused but have higher action rates than we currently see.

Is Change Inevitable?

While social business and the ensuing sCRM databases that follow sound like a marketing utopia—at least for marketers—its realization will depend on how integrated social media becomes to businesses today and how quickly they move toward adopting the social business model. Many businesses will resist this transition. Many will resist because they do not believe in the social business evolution, believing that the status quo works and seeing no reason to change. Not until their competitors start to see results will these reluctant businesses make the transition to this new model. This has always been the case and mirrors the way in which individuals adopt new technology. If this were not the case, it would not be possible to still purchase VHS players, even as Blu-Ray and digital media downloads seek to replace DVDs.

This resistance, of course, comes with an opportunity cost that many will not be able to afford. By allowing competitors to gain an early start in the transition to a social business model, an organization risks losing not only time but also market share. The new social customer wants and expects a higher degree of integration and multichannel communication. The customer no longer expects to receive only a money off coupon in the mail, or via email. Instead, customers want to see these coupons incorporated into their Facebook interactions from friends. They expect to see them in a Twitter stream and they expect to find them provided automatically when they share their locations via Foursquare or Gowalla. If your company is not embracing social media on multiple levels, you will find a diminishing number of social media interactions with your customers and potential customers. Those customers will seek out other companies—your competitors—who are embracing the new model of doing business and have recognized how customers are seeking communication.

A clear example of social business marketing is the partnership between 7-Eleven stores in the USA and Zynga (the software company responsible for the Facebook games Farmville, YoVille, and Mafia Wars). Farmville, while annoying to many, has (at the time of writing) 10 million more active users than Twitter. It is primarily played by women who enjoy the collaborative nature of the game. Coincidentally, a large contingent of the 7-Eleven customer base is composed of women. By partnering with this popular game, placing digital objects into the game, and then running traditional OOH campaigns at 7-Eleven stores and gas stations to promote the objects, 7-Eleven has recognized where its customers are and what they are likely to be doing online. This is perhaps the most important step in transitioning to becoming a social business.

Choosing the Right Social Media App

If you don't know where your customers are spending their time online, it's extremely hard to define a social marketing strategy. This may seem like basic common sense to most, but it is surprising the number of social media campaigns that are started by businesses that have not done their research first. Many businesses assume that because there is a sufficient amount of "buzz" around a particular app, such as Twitter or Facebook, that is where they should conduct their campaigns. But nothing could be further from the truth.

This is just as true for social location marketing as it is for any other social media channel. No one app fits all customer profiles. No one app fits all company types. And just because there's buzz about an app, that doesn't mean it is worth spending your marketing budget on it. Buzz would have told 7-Eleven that Twitter was the social media tool they should use (based on number of users), because Farmville is just a game. 7-Eleven, however, did their homework first and realized that buzz is not a market research metric.

Given the number of social channels available to marketers, it is understandably bewildering to identify where customers and prospective customers might be. Indeed it is likely that some apps will provide some crossover for certain customer profiles. Campaigns that take this crossover into account are more likely to succeed than those that don't. This is where choosing the right style of social media app becomes important to the social business. The goal here is to choose a social media app that will appeal to the audience your business caters to. So with that in mind, consider the following:

- Facebook is a community focused app.

- Twitter is a short-term communication app.

- Foursquare appeals to the more competitive among the social location sharers.

Which of these styles best suits your company is an important question—one that might be a lot more complex than you might at first imagine. First, is your company trying to communicate an entire company impression? Or is your company trying to communicate a brand awareness? Are you creating a particular product promotion campaign for which this will be one of several vehicles? Social location sharing has to be placed into context, not just of the app itself but of the device (smartphone, iPad and so on) and how it's being used.

This contextualization is ultimately the defining framework for the content that is to be transmitted. For example, a commercial that will be viewed at an IMAX cinema has the capability—because of the scale of the environment, the type of technology, and the shared nature of the experience—to be used in a way that is not possible or necessarily desirable from within an app such as Gowalla. Apps such as Gowalla are used on smartphones, which at best have palm-sized screens and are used by single users and in a very focused manner. The available screen space is extremely limited. Worse, however, is that the user will also be subject to a multitude of ancillary inputs—whether it is a member of the wait staff in a café taking an order, a group of friends clamoring for attention, or the start of a sporting event.

Therefore, any messaging you create for a social location marketing campaign must take these factors into account. Failure to do so will almost certainly result in—at the very least—a low action rate and at worst, complete failure of the campaign.

This is a real challenge for marketers who are accustomed to being able to repurpose a campaign message to almost any environment. Banner ads can utilize the same taglines as OOH. Even Twitter posts can be constructed, with the right writing style, to form part of a broader cohesive messaging campaign. SLM messaging, however, does not work this way. There are a couple of reasons:

- First, as we have seen, the apps themselves do not allow for much creativity outside of bought space, which is almost identical to any other online ad space.

- Second, what space *is* available is primarily meant for the users of the app to share information about the experience. So coopting this space has to be done in a way that is seen as beneficial to the users of the app. If it's seen as intrusive or as an attempt to spam them, your marketing will fail.

Repurposed marketing collateral that is shoe-horned into this space intended for the users of the apps will not be welcomed by that community.

Information that will be considered beneficial will vary from customer to customer and will vary even further based on whether you're marketing to a casual music shopper or a serious medical supplies purchaser, for instance. Again, this is where knowledge of your customers or potential customers is essential if the nonintrusive goal is to be met. What is certain is that simply adding comments or tips that are out of sync with the pre-existing content will not work. Yelp ran afoul of this and faces a class action lawsuit over its somewhat unscrupulous management of content and reviews.

Note

> Yelp currently faces a Class Action lawsuit over their attempts to increase
> their sales of advertisements from businesses that had received bad
> reviews. They allegedly made offers to have the bad reviews removed from
> the site if those businesses signed up for advertising packages or
> increased their advertising spend with Yelp. There were some allegations
> of threats to have bad reviews posted where none existed. This case has
> yet to come to court and Yelp has certainly done a lot to remove this
> stigma and show a greater level of transparency in recent months over how
> reviews are managed.

Equally, offers made through SLS apps that don't "speak" to the users' experience will also not be seen favorably. For example, an offer that encouraged customers to vote for their favorite bartender and receive free entry to an event in the near future might be a campaign utilized by a bar; however, if the bar is unpopular or has a reputation for bad service and low selection, then chances are people won't take part in the campaign. SLS, like any other form of social media, isn't a way of papering over the cracks of a bad operation. What it will do is enhance an already good environment and take good customer service to the next level by bringing the customer and the organization one step closer together.

Achieving this level of alignment will make campaigns more attractive to users, increase participation—and therefore conversion to action—and provide a level of sustainability for the organization.

However, if you choose the wrong app on which to base your SLM campaign, none of this will happen.

Deciding which apps to partner with is just one of many big decisions you will need to make as you determine how social media in particular and social business in general will be incorporated into your company.

For a larger enterprise, transitioning an entire business model to a social business structure is something that will take a lot of time and energy. At the time of this writing, there are no real examples of large enterprises that have decided to make this transition. However, there are many that have incorporated a social business model into their method of doing business. Dell, Comcast, and IBM are good examples of large enterprises that have built successful social business models within their organizations.

Smaller businesses may find that transitioning to a entirely social business model is an easier path than trying to operate two distinct business operations. However, even the small business shouldn't underestimate the radical nature of the change.

What I want to explore next is what this social business—the part of the organization that operates in the social world—actually looks like. Who works there? What do they do?

Who Owns Social?

So who should be doing the choosing? Who in the organization decides what the social media campaign looks like and who will actually execute it? This is a difficult decision for most organizations when they first start to explore social media. The most common option is to place it with PR/Marketing and use the existing communications resources that the organization already has.

But is this the right decision? If your company really wants to become a social business, it might not be the right way to approach things. If the marketers in your company are focused on creating one-way communications instead of conversations, or if they haven't built a social brand before, you are probably going to find the conversion to a social business much more difficult.

Many schools of thought exist on what exactly the profile of a social media person looks like: what their background is, what experiences they have had, and what type of work they have been doing prior to joining the organization.

Let's look at a few of these profiles. What follows are extracts from real job postings for social media positions at various companies. By examining what the market currently looks for we can examine them for the commonalities and see how they fit into the creation of a social business.

Job Description One:

Minimum five (5) years of experience with major social media campaigns and addressing social media issues.

Ability to be available/accessible during non-traditional hours when/if needed.

4-year college degree in Communications, Journalism, English, Public Policy, International Relations, or related major. Advanced degree (MBA or Communications).

Experience working within a large business/organization.

Experience in developing social media programs/initiatives as well as corporate communications materials.

Proficient skills in graphic design.

Job Description Two:

Works collaboratively within the communications department to utilize content and visual resources to promote the organization via social media.

Create intelligent, sophisticated, edgy, expert communications.

Successful candidates will possess a bachelor's degree in a relevant discipline.

Previous experience in a supervisory role.

Proven record of developing and executing innovative social media programs.

The ability to perform under tight deadlines in a dynamic, multifaceted, and fast-paced environment.

Job Description Three:

Community and social media channel moderation—going above and beyond to ensure all community members have a great experience.

Take an analytical approaching using tools like Radian6 data to know where to engage and improve the efficiency of the community.

Build and run social web campaigns to support key marketing initiatives and feedback insights to internal stakeholders.

Collaborate with internal stakeholders and feedback customer insights from social media channels.

Keep up to date on new social media tools, best practices, and how other companies are using them so we stay the front runner in this field.

Explore ways of expanding opportunities and growing traffic to our social media properties.

Manage the administration and content schedule of all social media channels.

BA/BS degree.

At least 2+ years in technology-related customer-facing role.

Customer service oriented.

Strong marketing background with the proven ability to think socially.

Knowledge of web 2.0 communication tools.

Excellent communication skills (written and oral).

Ability to communicate personably with large variety of individuals.

Passion for social media with knowledge of Twitter, Facebook, YouTube, and LinkedIn.

Job Description Four:

Generate curiosity by the media.

Focus on getting us interviewed or quoted or our articles/community mentioned in the media.

Work closely with our sales department to create programs that tie into goals.

Create and maintain blogs and/or other interesting, leading-edge ways to communicate with prospects, existing customers and others.

Create and maintain an online community for prospects and existing customers.

Help to create, edit, and reuse customer testimonials—both movie and audio clips.

Brainstorm and coordinate live marketing events (webinars and podcasts, etc).

Write articles, perhaps help to get them placed or picked up by press.

Be responsible for newsletters to existing customers—including important information.

Generalist who will love wearing a lot of hats including: social media, Blogging, Community Management, Marketing, evangelizing, perhaps some PR, Business Development and other "hats" as they develop.

Exceptional communication skills.

Comfortable with newest technology—always learning on their own.

4-year college degree (ideally an MBA with a concentration in Marketing).

Job Description Five:

Lead social media marketing for the digital marketing team, including:

Drive 1 yr/3 yr social media marketing plan tied to overall business objectives.

Manage social media campaigns, including overall 'Big Idea' social campaign; Advertising 'Big Bet' tie-ins, Customer Reviews, Facebook, marketing on new apps and emerging media (i.e. Mobile devices, iPad, iAd, in Cinema, Xbox/gaming).

Develop cross-channel online and offline social media marketing plans working with channel managers (Display, Search, Affiliate, Offline Advertising, DR).

Lead cross-functional team to drive mobile/emerging media strategy, innovation and key marketing initiatives:

Test hypothesis and learn how mobile drives acquisition. Drive overall 1 yr/3 yr mobile marketing and emerging media plan working with product development, web team, digital marketing team, segment team, new business initiatives team.

Develop innovation process to help teams drive fast experimentation and learning.

Prioritize year-1 experiments and goals and what opportunities we should go after first.

Work with analytics and research teams to develop key metrics and drive measurement and analysis of social, mobile, and emerging media programs to ultimately prove out how these program drive and support conversion goals:

Define customer engagement and conversion metrics.

Build reporting and dashboards.

Build solid test plans. Manage and hire agencies and vendors to develop creative and infrastructure to drive social, mobile, and emerging media initiatives.

Take an active role in Social and Digital Marketing communities to share and adopt best practices across the organization. Heavily engage in external communities and with thought leaders to help the organization grow fast and smart in the areas of social, mobile, emerging media. Manage budget, forecast for social, mobile and emerging media marketing.

MBA, or BA/BS with 7-10 years relevant experience.

Deep experience in online and social media thought leadership. Strong understanding of social media in relation to the broader media mix; understanding of the interplay between online/social media and traditional media.

Expert knowledge of social agency and consultant resources in social media.

Understanding of social media best practices.

Ability to teach senior executives and marketing leaders effective use of social media.

Knowledge of innovative industry-leading social media campaigns that tie to revenue growth and brand building.

As you can see, these are five different job descriptions, and on the surface, five very different people are being sought out. You would expect this from five companies that all seek to do different things with social media (we'll address that point in a minute). However, they all have some of the same requirements, so let's start there and examine what is common to a social media post regardless of level within the organization. Table 9.1 breaks down the job requirements for a social media position.

Table 9.1   Social Media Job Requirements

Education	College degree
	Journalism
	Communications
	English
Experience	2–7 years of digital marketing/social media
Skills	Prior experience developing and executing social media programs
	Graphic design
	Marketing communications
	Community management
Duties	Developing "cutting edge" communications
	Developing/executing social media programs
	Keeping up to date with social media changes

These requirements, in one form or another, are common to all the social media job descriptions I have seen, not just the ones I have included in this chapter. I have modified some of the language to ensure that the companies who posted the original job requirements remained anonymous; however, the distilled versions retain the requirements that are common:

- Education is focused strongly on communication subjects, with every company agreeing on at least a four-year degree—nothing wholly surprising there.

- Experience is a range, and that reflects the seniority of the position. It is interesting to see job descriptions that require five years of social media execution and then are seeking to put that person into a junior/mid-level role. If you could find someone that has five years of executing real social media programs, trust me you are not going to hire them as a junior. More realistic is the requirement that this person have digital marketing experience. Although this is not necessarily social media, experience here means this person will at least understand the online environment.

- Skills are all focused on ensuring that the person has done this before, which is absolutely a requirement. This is not the time to hire someone who "thinks" they can do this because they have a Facebook profile.

While it is an area that should be open to experimentation, those experiments need to be backed with reasoned thought and a process for execution. Some of the other skill requirements will vary from role to role,
but certainly the ability to communicate, especially in written form, is
extremely important. Peter Shankman, founder of Help a Reporter Out,
repeatedly states that he will pay for his employees to take any writing
class they want, because communication skills are at the core of social
media competency. I couldn't agree with him more.

- Duties also vary greatly from role to role, but the one that seems to be
  common to most is the ability to create "cutting edge" communications.
  I find this amusing for the most part. What one company or organization calls cutting edge, others would run screaming from—or worse, be
  insulted by. In working with numerous clients over the years, I have
  found that the term is very subjective and almost meaningless; however,
  it seems that is the way social media is viewed—as cutting edge. This
  points more to the emergent nature of its use among those companies
  recruiting for these positions than it does to the maturity of the
  medium.

What is missing from these job descriptions? In my opinion, the major thing missing from all but one of them is experience in a customer facing role. The reason it is
missing is the same as the reason all the job descriptions focus on communications
and marketing experience. What these companies are all seeking is someone who
can leverage social media as a marketing communications channel—in other
words, someone who can write in 140 characters or less the company tagline and
make it go "viral"!

When these organizations say they want experience in executing social media campaigns, what they mean is they want to know the candidate can use social media as
a marketing channel, which is certainly an important part of the role, but it also
implies that the channel is a one-way stream of information passing out of the
organization to customers and potential customers who just can't wait to receive it
and share it with their networks. I think we all know that this is a myth.

So what should a job description look like and what does a good candidate for a
social media position actually look like, at least on paper?

- **Education**—Honestly, I'm not a strong proponent of a formal education. I got all mine as an adult, long after I left high school. It's a tough
  subject, especially in the current society where education is a formal
  business and everyone is now told that without a graduate degree you
  aren't worth considering, which is what we were all told three decades
  ago about an undergraduate degree. Personally, when I make hires, I

care less about their formal education and more about what they have achieved in life that fits with the role I am hiring for. I know this is not a popular stance, especially in corporate America, but give me one person who has demonstrated his or her abilities to execute rather than ten people who have a piece of paper from a college that says they might be able to do it if I train them to.

- **Experience**—Here is where the rubber meets the road. This is what, at least for me, separates those who are worth considering from those who are not. What have they actually done that indicates that they can do the role I am hiring for is the main criteria for most jobs, but for a social media position, that should encompass as many of the aspects as possible of what social media will and can mean for the organization. Not just the ability to push out the corporate message, but handling a crisis, creating community, delivering exceptional customer experience and bringing that to the real world. Look for someone who has experience with customers, that could be working in the service industries, sales, customer service—heck, driving a taxi. This is the front line of your organization. If you are trying to build a more social business and a business that will compete and capture the social customer, you need someone who truly understands the demands of a customer communication role and knows how to build value into the relationships that increase the loyalty of those customers.

So where are these candidates that meet this bill, this laundry list of attributes that people want so badly? First, the wrong place to look for them, in my opinion, is job boards. Places such as Monster, The Ladders, and even LinkedIn are all great for finding a general marketing specialist, a PR person, even a CMO, but not if you want an absolutely amazing social media person/team member who will represent your organization in the best possible way.

Strangely enough, the one place to find these people seems to be the last place that recruiters and hiring managers seem to look: the social web! Look for persons who have clearly demonstrated that they can build something, create awareness, have interactions with people in a positive way, and garner support and a following from a community of users. Obviously there has to be a fit with your product/brand/service, but look for those after you have started to identify someone who will make the best social media representative.

My most recent hire for my company was someone I had followed for over a year on Twitter. I watched this person build a business online, and I had even bought a sponsorship slot with this person's business for some of the videos it was creating. This person had what my company needed, but more than this, this person knew how the social web worked. This person understood the dynamic and had been there and utilized it to create something.

If I were to give you an example of someone that I have watched lately, and who I believe would be a great candidate for a social media role with a company, it would be Poppy Dinsey of *What I Wore Today* fame (see Figure 9.1).

Figure 9.1 *Poppy Dinsey is a self-made social media star.*

Poppy is someone I have been watching for about eight months (at the time of writing). She created *What I Wore Today* (www.wiwt.co.uk) as a way of finding new outfits in her existing wardrobe. In other words, she wanted to save money and "shop her own closet." She decided to document the process by posting a picture of her outfit every day. Friends told her that she would never keep it up, but since January 1, 2010, she has not missed a single day.

More than this, she has actually generated thousands of page views each week on her blog by simply posting a picture. These pictures are not risqué, they are not salacious in nature, they are simply her outfit, be it a pair of jeans and a shirt or a summer dress or even an old dressing gown (on a day she was sick).

Why do I think this is a person that would be good for a social media role? First, she understands what drives traffic. Second, she interacts with people on Twitter when she gets feedback on her outfits. She engages her audience and reacts to them in a human way. In June, I asked her to post a picture for my birthday and she did. There was no reason for her to do so, other than I made the request. She did this just because I was a follower and I made the request. This shows that she reacts to her "fans" and where appropriate, follows up.

Last, and perhaps most important, her work has gained her attention. She now has a column with MSN. They noticed what she was doing and invited her to write a fashion column for them. She was spotted by Vodaphone using an iPhone in her pictures. When the new iPhone was released, they sent her one to try out as a replacement for her old one. When London Fashion week rolled around, Vodaphone, which was a major sponsor of the show, reached out to her again and asked her to be their blogger for the entire event.

All this from someone who decided to post a picture of their outfit online every day. Oh, and the fact that she kept it up even when she was sick also speaks volumes about the type of commitment she shows to a project.

You can't find these details in a resume. You don't find them in educational certificates. This is the real thing. This is what a social media person looks like. Someone who can actually do the job, not someone who thinks they can or has a piece of paper that says they might be able to do it with the right support.

I asked Poppy what advice she has for companies looking to hire a social media person; here is what she replied:

"Really research the work they've done in the past and make sure it fits with your company's brand. I've turned down work when people have approached me knowing my style and then a few meetings down the line they say they don't want me to do X/Y/Z which they *know* is a big part of my personal brand and how I work. Different people have different approaches, so you have to make sure you find the right person. And there are A LOT of charlatans in the world of social media, so as I said before, really research the work they've done in the past."

All sound advice. Note especially her recommendation that you research their work. Recruiting is a costly business. Most of the cost comes from the time involved and yet organizations want to be able to post a job ad and fill it in a matter of weeks, maybe a month. With social media, I say you should start a year before you think you will need someone; draw up a list of likely candidates, put them on a watch list, go to events and meet them, see how they interact over time with people online, and think about how they might fit into your organization.

This sounds like a lot of work. That's because it is. What you are hiring is not a marketer, not a PR person, not a community manager, not a social media specialist. You are hiring someone who will breed loyalty in the community of social consumers, and loyalty isn't cheap.

So this is what your point person in the social media function looks like. In anything larger than a small enterprise, you are going to have other roles in the social business function that will be providing social media capabilities to your organization. These include blogger outreach, social media monitoring, and internal liaison. Some of these roles are going to overlap with existing functions within an organization. For example, blogger outreach might well cross into the PR function within the organization and encroach on the territory of a media list owner (I have seen this in Fortune 500 companies), and social media monitoring may well cross into the realm of corporate communications and customer service, depending on what is being monitored and what is found.

It is important to recognize the roles that are created by the adoption of a social business model. Equally important is the recognition that while these roles are mostly tactical, there needs to be strategic leadership for these roles. This hire or appointment, if you are moving someone internally, will provide the direction and ensure that the role achieves both the organizational goals and does so in a way that can be shown to the C-suite to have had bottom-line impact. Ultimately, this is where the criticism of social media and the social business model is aimed. Having someone who has experience at a senior level of creating meaningful metrics and tying those to bottom-line performance will ensure that the organization not only pursues the model actively but continues to do so as campaigns roll out.

It is unlikely that one person is going to embody all these skills (though there are a few out there), so the most likely path for any organization is to establish a social business team within the organization that not only provides the skills the organization needs for the social consumer, but also provides the education needed internally for the organization to adopt social practices in other parts of the business.

The closer an organization gets to having a social business team, and gradually expands that ethos throughout, the closer the organization becomes to being a fully socially orientated business.

But what are the drawbacks? First, the time and investment of restructuring an organization is never a simple or inexpensive undertaking, and for an enterprise-sized organization, it is almost certainly something that will not spread throughout the entire organization. What is important is that the social business part of the organization becomes integrated into the strategic decision making that directs the organization and how the organization interacts with the social consumer.

Second, the frequent transitions that senior management, especially in enterprise-level organizations go through. There needs to be an adequate bench within the social business area so that these transitions have a minimal impact on the ethos of operating as a social business.

This bench is especially important if the organization opts to have a "face" of social business. For example, Ford has Scott Monty, who not only leads their social business endeavors but is the recognizable face of those endeavors. If your organization seeks to emulate this model, ensuring that there is a second and third "face" available not only helps spread the load in terms of giving voice to campaigns, but it makes transitions easier and more seamless to the people who matter, the customers.

These "faces" are the loyalty point for the brand. In the past, the logo or other imagery was the loyalty point, but for the social consumer, the person that they associate with the brand has become more important. This is understandable; human beings are sociable by nature. The opportunity to meet the face of the brand is much more compelling than the opportunity to simply hang out in a branded area at a conference.

The social consumer wants to build an affinity with an organization based on human traits: trust, communication, honesty, reciprocity. These are the same traits that they look for to build relationships with other human beings. This seems very "touchy feely" to some organizations, and certainly there is an element of that involved in social commerce, but that should not cloud the organization's objective, which, unless it is a nonprofit, is to deliver value to the customer and the owners of the organization.

The new model of social business is still evolving. How the communication will evolve is still being experimented with and will continue to be, driven both by the realization of what can be achieved and by the new waves of technology that enable increasingly closer proximity to the customer.

10

Plan, Plan, and Plan

If you have been reading the chapters in this book somewhat in order, you have seen us explore a variety of topics. We've tackled why you should even bother with social location marketing and where SLM fits into your broader social media strategy. We've discussed what the different social location sharing apps are capable of. We've learned how to construct campaigns for different types of venues—and even for organizations that have no venue. We have explored the social business, how to introduce the concept to an existing organization, and how to hire the right type of person for a social business.

Now we are going to take everything we learned in the previous nine chapters and put it into practice. As this chapter's title suggests, it's all about the plan. More accurately: it's all about the plan that will eventually be executed.

Before you can execute, however, you need to have more than a social media strategy in place. You need a strong plan—one that incorporates all the concepts that have been discussed in this book.

Identify Your Social Business

The first part of the plan is to examine your existing business and identify those elements that already meet the profile of a social business. Where are you already interacting with your customers in a way that encourages them to provide feedback, ask questions, propose ideas, make complaints, and give praise?

Different departments within your company might already be doing things that a social business does. For instance, your customer service department might already be using Twitter to interact with customers, or your marketing department might already be using Foursquare to interact with potential customers. However, it's entirely possible that neither of those departments know what the other is doing. Your goal is to figure out who's already doing what and then organize those efforts into a cohesive social business plan. You will need to identify the skills your company already has, as well as those that are missing. You will sort through each of your company's existing skills, determining which are social customer focused and which are focused on the more traditional customer.

As we discussed in Chapter 9, Socially Speaking: The Social Business, the key to your company's success as a social business will be in finding the right leadership. Perhaps this person is right under your nose, toiling away in relative obscurity within your organization. Perhaps this person will need to be brought in from the outside. Regardless of whoever is put in charge of your social business strategy, that person is likely to inherit a group of people that have never worked together or have worked together only in a limited capacity. This, again, is all part of the planning process—how to bring those individuals or even entire business units together to achieve one goal. How this is done is going to vary from organization to organization and the time it takes will depend greatly on the degree of buy-in from the C-Suite to make the change.

Books could be (and have been) written on the best ways to achieve organizational restructuring. I am not going to attempt to cover that element in this book; rather, I am simply identifying it as an essential part of the plan.

Where Should You Be?

The next stage in the plan is to identify what elements of social media will be utilized by the social business. It is all too easy to fall into the trap of saying, "all of them." However, rarely is this the right answer. Of course Twitter, Facebook, and YouTube get the media attention, but as I have said previously in this book, buzz is not research. Researching where your audience is currently and being aware of where they might be next is essential to ensuring the success of social media use. This knowledge is especially important when building a social business.

You will need to use all the data you've already collected about your customers to help you determine what forms of social media your new social business will use. Crossing what you know about your customers with what we know about social consumers in general will give you a much better picture of where your audience is and how they prefer to receive information from your company.

The social consumer can usually be identified as possessing most or all of the following traits:

- Multitasker

- Part of a social network

- A smartphone user

- Highly computer literate

- Strong comparison shopper

- An opinion sharer

For example, if you know that part of your existing customer base consists of busy professionals who have previously communicated with you via email, then you have a valuable data point to match to what we know about social consumers in general. This exercise helps you avoid the "build it and they will come" myth that so many fall into. The social consumer needs a very good reason to visit your website. For example, many organizations believe that putting a forum element on their websites will have their customers flocking to the site providing them with an endless source of people to which they can push messages about their latest marketing campaigns. The reality is vastly different. If social consumers already belong to a community that focuses on their particular interest, and it is built and run independently of providers in the space, why would they be willing to either move or replicate their membership to come to this new community? Social consumers generally come to new sites only when there is some type of content that is available only at the new site that makes using a product or service more fulfilling or because the incentive to do so is overwhelming.

In reality, you need to be prepared to go where your audience is (detailed and well thought out research will highlight where the audience is). It is also essential to build into the plan that the social business team members become a part of the same communities your audience belongs to. It's important that your social business team members also be active in those communities and strive to be a valuable resource for the other members.

This perception of value can lead to some interesting dilemmas for the traditional business. For example, the social business is not adverse to recommending or directing members of its community to its competition for products or services. At first glance, this seems like brand suicide. However, take a situation in which a social consumer is looking for a complementary service or product to combine with one of yours. Traditional thinking would be to ignore them, hope that they don't find your competitor, and carry on with other customers. This type of ostrich-like thinking doesn't work with the social consumer. Social consumers are looking for people to trust, and valued sources of information about a product, service, or vertical.

Recommending a competitor is one way to build that trust. Recommending a competitor shows that you genuinely care and are interested in the social consumer. Further, it shows that you are not just focusing on selling your own products or services. However—especially at the enterprise level—this type of thinking can be seen as disloyal to the company, potentially threatening, and at the very least just bad business practice.

Companies are also learning that consumers don't always use their products in the ways the companies originally intended. In the past, when a company learned this, it would probably try to advise the customer to use the product only in the way in which it was defined for use and that combining it with another product would in fact be detrimental. Companies did this because they believed they knew what the customer needed. In short, the company believed it knew what features were best for the consumer and how the consumer should use them. However, given the megaphone that is the Internet and social media, consumers are able to articulate the fact that they are not interested in features; they are interested in solutions.

It is an old adage that the customer does not want a 1-inch drill bit; what the customer wants is a 1-inch hole. The social consumer is as much, if not more, focused on this attitude. The social consumer is more marketing savvy and understands (and in many cases can see through) brand messaging. That means if your company can provide a solution—even if it involves a competitor—that solution and, in turn, your company is of much more value than ever before. The steps to getting to this stage will vary from organization to organization. However, showing the value to the C-Suite via metrics around response rates to conversations (which by virtue of value will increase) can aid the adoption of what at first glance seems a counter-intuitive strategy.

What You Should Say

It is a constant surprise to me that marketing, PR, and corporate communications departments have no problem creating "information releases" on a schedule that matches events, product releases, financial reporting, and so on. However, when challenged to create an editorial calendar, they often respond with a "but what would we say?" or simply look blankly at me as though I am suggesting something that they have never heard of.

When we conduct social media monitoring for our clients, we often point out to them that we can pinpoint exactly when they have made a press release, without even seeing the press release. Immediately following a press release, there is a spike in social media chatter. This might not be much of an increase (depends on the size of the client and the impact of the news), but nonetheless we can spot it. Shortly after the release and the spike in chatter, there's an immediate dip—or trough—in social media activity. We can spot it without fail.

This is where the editorial calendar comes in. Don't leave all your blog posts, Twitter updates, Facebook posts or other social media communications for those days when you are releasing news. If you are utilizing these channels effectively, they will be used to spread that news anyway. Where the calendar comes into its own is for the time immediately after your news has crested on the social media wave and people stop talking about you. It is then that you want the follow-up posts, status updates, and so on. This helps you avoid having a trough immediately following an announcement.

If you have a social media team in place, you'll be ahead of the game. Having only one person responsible for all social communication would almost certainly be an overwhelming task. However, by having a team of people empowered to create content for social communications, you can create an editorial calendar. The calendar helps you guarantee that there's always something to share—whether it is industry news, product information, how-to's, even opinion pieces. These are all valuable elements of the social communication that will come from a well-organized social business.

Using an editorial calendar means that each member of the team knows when his or her pieces are due. The communications are prescheduled for release, which also means that they can be moved around if necessary as things change. For example, a major announcement in the industry might deserve a comment, observation, or analysis from the team. It would be hard to calendar a sudden announcement such as that in advance. In the normal course of events, the team would be left scrambling to cover it or perhaps have to pass on the opportunity. With the use of a calendaring system, other communications are already covered by the process, so when these unexpected opportunities arise they can be taken full advantage of.

With the peaks and troughs smoothed out through the use of calendaring, the social communications team can focus more on increasing volume, attending to sentiment changes (moving the needle from negative or neutral to positive) and ensuring that the two-way nature of social communications is really working. The team will be responsible for finding new ways of incorporating feedback received from customers and potential customers. Your team also will be tasked with identifying new channels that are either being used by customers, or are likely to be used, and dismissing those that don't fit your customers and therefore don't need to be part of your plan (although you might still watch them). This last piece is extremely important given the ever-changing nature of social media and the various platforms.

As new social media apps appear, they tend to bring with them a wave of enthusiasm. It is all too easy to believe the well-placed and polished hype that comes attached to some of these new apps. ChatRoulette is a perfect example of this. ChatRoulette was going to revolutionize social media and be an amazing tool for marketing communications. However, when people realized it was simply a place for dubious characters to reveal various parts of their anatomy, they soon abandoned it. That didn't stop some marketing agencies from convincing their clients to include it in their social marketing communications. Most, however, avoided it—and rightly so. As I have said before in this book, and will say again, buzz does not equal research. Be aware of the buzz and take a look at those apps that attract it. However, before making any decisions, take a step back and consider them carefully as vehicles to carry your message and spaces in which you can interact with your customers.

When you take the time to do your research, you will find some diamonds in the rough, so to speak. Facebook recently made changes to the way users can organize the information they share and receive with a new feature called Groups (they already had a feature called Groups and decided to launch another feature with the same name). Although initially it would seem that this had no real use for marketers, because the intent was to keep groups small, this would provide an opportunity for organizations to form groups around industry-specific topics and invite key individuals to join as part of a discussion group. Just another way a tool can aid the positioning of an organization; you can interact with your competitors in a way that is less threatening to the C-Suite.

✉ **Note**

The new Facebook Groups feature differs from the previous version in some very distinct ways. Previously, groups were created in a way that was modeled more like a "club." That is, a Facebook group required membership, they were very closed in terms of communication, and it was hard to know who the members were. The new Groups incarnation focuses more on communication. While it is possible to make a group completely private, the default—as it always is with Facebook—is that the Group be public. What this means is that your network can see when you are added to a group. Your network also can see, via your wall, when you post something to a group. The Group also has the ability to hold Group Chats via the Facebook Chat feature and send emails to the entire group. Some users have complained that there is no opt-out feature for Groups and that they have no control over which groups they are added to. Facebook counters this by emphasizing the "social norms" of Group activity, and that users should know who their friends are.

Brands could also use Facebook Groups for focus or testing groups for specific products or services. This could be especially true for longer-term research, because Facebook Groups could be a way to let consumers test something out and share information with each other as well as the brand.

So, some new launches in social media are definitely worth a second glance and can be put to some very good uses—and even provide alternative ways for organizations to perform tasks that they are already doing in a more traditional manner. Social media isn't all about buzz and glitzy ways to utilize gerbils to sell your products. Some of it has practical uses. It's these practical uses that you can use to sell social media to the skeptics in the C-Suite.

An editorial calendar gives the social business the time to discover these new tools, try them out, and read the analyses that any number of social media thought leaders will perform. After all your homework is done, you can decide if a new tool is a good fit for the way your company runs its social business.

The calendar is so much more than just a reminder to get that blog post out.

We the People

One of the things that scares enterprise-level clients that we work with more than anything is when we tell them that social media happens online *and* in the real world. If you want to be a true social business, you have to meet your customers, face to face. For people working in a small business, this isn't too scary because small business marketers are often also the owner, co-owner, or manager with several other responsibilities—not least of which is interacting with the customers. At the enterprise level, however, marketers are often insulated from having to deal with the great unwashed masses that actually pay their salaries. Usually, these marketers are protected by the sales team and the customer service department. If the company is a business to consumer enterprise (B2C), quite often the marketer is insulated from the customers by the store staff as well.

Keeping yourself insulated from the public is bad for business in general, but it's fatal for the social business. First, whatever your business is—whether it's B2B or B2C—make sure that every member of your social business team spends time (and I mean significant time, not just a few hours) meeting and working with the customers in a face-to-face environment. Your social business team needs to shadow field sales reps, work behind the counter, walk the shop floor, or whatever it takes. Get them in front of the customer; let them hear and see what the customer says and does when interacting with the brand.

If you are a direct sales organization, get your social business team on the phones—and I don't mean just on the training line. Get them to take sales calls. Get them on the help line and have them work with customer service. Why? Because unless they actually get to know who their customers are, they are never going to understand how to communicate with them via social media.

The marketers that I have worked with who always struck me as clueless relied solely on research and statistics for their assessment of how a campaign should be conducted. These truly clueless marketers had never actually interacted with a customer. This is all too common, especially in the Fortune 500. It is also ridiculous. Would you want to drive a car designed by someone who didn't have a driver's license? Of course not. Then why let someone who has never spoken to a customer communicate with them? That makes no sense to me at all—regardless of the academic studies they have completed or the real-world experience they have. Unless they have actually mixed with customers, they are not going to be much help to you in your social business.

It is also important for your company to meet your customers where the customers shop and congregate. You could interact with them at conferences, Tweetups, events, festivals, and so on. These do not have to be major events that your company creates or sponsors. The goal is to allow members of your social business team to meet with your customers and interact in a more social way.

While you're attending the larger events, you can organize smaller events that put you into direct contact with your customers. So, for example, hosting a wine-tasting event in a local bar during a conference where a handful of key customers or potential customers are the invited guests can pay much greater dividends than simply running a prize giveaway at the conference booth.

A properly constructed social event gives your guests the opportunity to talk about you on social networks without you having to promote yourself. Often these opportunities are not even recognized by brands. For instance, your company sends a few employees to a conference to staff a booth with the extent of the planned communication starting and ending at the booth. If your employees are part of your social business, however, they can turn the odd opportunity of bumping into another attendee or two at the bar or dinner into a business opportunity down the line. Social organizations make social opportunities happen. They create an atmosphere of social connectedness. This doesn't mean throwing wild parties. It means providing opportunities for the potential or existing customers to establish rapport without being sold to.

It's is important that your employees understand that customers are more than numbers. By bringing back the real-world stories of customer interactions, the rest of the company can get a true sense of how the customer is interacting with the product, service, or brand. This applies equally to the B2C space as it does to the B2B space. Social media is often seen as the darling of the B2C environment (and that is true). Social media, however, should not be overlooked in B2B. It takes a little more creativity to fully leverage social media in the B2B space. After all, the customers in the B2B space are still people, and your organization still wants their feedback and input into how you are performing as a vendor.

Social media channels are as valid for B2B space as they are in the B2C space. Although a gerbil-laden Facebook campaign might not be the direction you want to take your B2B efforts, and the offer of a free cup of coffee for being mayor is likely to seem irrelevant to your business customers, the platforms themselves still provide enough opportunity for them to be a part of any social communication plan.

What is required are two things: a knowledge of your customer and some creativity. Yes I have stated those before, and I will do so again because both of these are at the core of any social media campaign. It is a constant surprise to me how many organizations launch communications campaigns—social media or otherwise—with these pieces so obviously missing. The disconnect between the customer and the marketing department is, in my opinion, why this happens. Bringing the people who are responsible for the marketing communications closer to their audience will in turn enable the audience (customers and prospective customers) to get closer to the organization, which is the overall objective of the social business.

Your social business plan therefore needs to include training for your social business team members that involves them getting closer to the customer in the real world.

They Said What?

At some point, all organizations face the difficult customer scenario. Through the channels provided by social media, organizations are now exposed to those awkward moments—those times when they see a comment about their product, service, or brand that they wish that they had never seen, and yet need to see because without those comments they will not improve.

At the enterprise level, it can be especially difficult to translate some of these into actionable events without more information. For example, if your company receives a comment on a social location sharing app that reads, "the person behind the counter was rude and gave very poor service," but leaves it at that, you have very limited information. You know the location of the store, the date of the transaction, and the approximate time of day. However, beyond those details, you have no real information. This is where a plan comes into effect. By creating a decision tree as part of the plan, which covers various types of interactions and responses that have already been approved by both the legal department and the C-Suite, an enterprise-sized organization can respond with the agility more familiar to the customers of small- and medium-sized businesses.

This decision tree approach allows contingencies to be enacted without reference to senior management and therefore can be delegated across the social business to areas where there are a greater number of resources.

 Note

An example of how a system for responding to social media comments could be set up is available here: http://www.web-strategist.com/blog/2008/12/31/diagram-how-the-air-force-response-to-blogs/

Back to our example: First, you are going to want to contact the customer, because whether the incident happened exactly as described or not, the customer's perception is that this was a bad experience—bad enough that he or she chose to share it with his or her network. It might take a little research to identify the customer, depending on how much that person has shared with, for instance, Twitter or Foursquare. Your first contact with the person complaining should always be an apology that stops short of implying liability. This can be something along the lines of "Sorry to hear you had a bad experience. Let us know how we can make it better." A short reply such as this lets the customer know that your company is listening and is interested in a dialogue that might lead to the situation being rectified.

In the interim, the location in which the complaint was made can be contacted for additional information. You may also start your standard process of analyzing that customer feedback. Again, it is important that the social business does not circumvent these steps in order to simply "quiet" a noisy customer. Some organizations have already had their fingers burned while trying to put a quick end to a public problem. Social businesses should not become victims of their willingness to listen and placate any customer simply because they have received negative feedback. There are those unscrupulous individuals who try to take advantage of businesses for personal gain. Some people do this for nothing more than building their own reputation for being able to make companies jump through hoops.

Your response plan should ensure that both sides of the story (the complainant's and your company's) are heard in a timely manner. This plan also should ensure that your company's pre-existing procedures are incorporated, but in a way that does not impede the response. Remember, in the fast moving social media world, you don't have as much time to react as you would offline, which is why your initial outreach to the complainant is so important. Whereas you once might have had days or weeks to respond to an angry customer who contacted you via mail, you have only hours to respond to a social media complainant. Having a plan in place greatly reduces the amount of time it will take you to react to customer complaints and more importantly, quell customer backlash before it takes on a life of its own in the social media world.

It's Not All Doom and Gloom

Bad news is not the only news. Often companies come to social media expecting that there will be nothing but complaints. They view their social customers as being the vocal ones in their community and—like the squeaky wheel—are the ones in need of oil. This is not the case. In fact, many of our clients brace themselves for their first report only to find that there are few, if any, bad reports about them. Some seem positively insulted that no one has thought to write something bad about their product, service, or brand—as if this were some badge of honor.

However prepared they have been for what they feared would be a deluge of negative sentiment about them, I have yet to find a company that was prepared to handle the flood of *positive* sentiment with anything other than a shrug and a sheepish smile. Neither of which is communicable to the content creators.

Again, the plan needs to incorporate a set of appropriate responses for the positive sentiment and especially where individual employees of the company are singled out for praise. Just as there are escalation paths for negative feedback, so there needs to be escalation paths for positive feedback, depending on much the same criteria:

- Who is providing the feedback?

- Who is their audience?

- How long have they been customers?

- Is their experience repeatable by other consumers of the product or service?

- Is it repeatable by the organization?

- Was it a normal run of business event or an exception?

These criteria are important in determining how the positive feedback is handled beyond a simple "thank you." Of course, saying thank you might be all that is required, but providing more than that is the way to increase affinity and encourage loyalty among customers. A customer is unlikely to share the news that her favorite brand thanked her, but she is very likely to share the news that her favorite brand sent her a gift card as a thank you. This difference in terms of response is how a social business differentiates itself from its more traditional competitors.

If your company's social business plan includes these kinds of responses and your team members are empowered to use them without approval from upper management, you can greatly improve your response time to social media comments, both good and bad. Your company's response isn't the only thing that's important to your social media customers. Those customers also value the speed in which the response is made because the social consumer perceives quick acting companies as being connected to them and valuing their time.

Look Small, Think Big

The often stated aim of companies entering the social arena is to get closer to their customers. However, what they really mean is that they want to engender a feeling more often associated with smaller, more community-oriented venues such as the Mom and Pop corner store. However, when considering a big box store that has more employees than some small towns have residents, it is an almost impossible problem for which to find a solution. The social business enables a move toward this feeling. I hope it is becoming readily apparent to you that the social business plan is central to moving the enterprise in this direction.

As much as we have discussed the enterprise social business plan, you should not think that this type of plan applies only to companies at that level. A social business plan should be integrated into every organization, regardless of size. If your company intends to use social media in any form, you need a social business plan. This will help prevent it from simply become a "fad"—something that was tried once or twice and then forgotten. Your social business plan needs to become integrated into the way your company does business.

A small, single-location business can have a social business plan that's just as effective (even with limited financing and staffing resources) as a larger enterprise's plan. The execution of the plan is where the variance will largely be, but that is true of all forms of marketing communication. Social media does, at least to a degree, level the playing field, and smaller businesses should capitalize on this as much as possible to ensure that they remain competitive with their larger cousins in their neighborhoods. The ability of the small business to "know" their customers—and in some cases, the fact that they are already close to them in the real world—makes it easier for them to get close to their customers in their online world.

Early elements of this part of the plan can be as simple as telling your customers that the business is engaged in social media. Promoting your Facebook page, your Twitter account, your venue page on Foursquare in your business's physical location is all part of this plan. However, a sign that simply reads "Like us on Facebook" (which I have seen more times than I care to remember) does not constitute being social in the real world. Remember social media is part of marketing communications, so why would you have a piece of marketing communication that exists without a call to action? Back to basics—don't lose sight of the purpose of all this social business:

- Increase awareness
- Increase customers

- Increase revenue

A sign that reads "Like us on Facebook—You could win a monthly prize" (with details of what the prize might be) is much more likely to get a response.

Being clever about it doesn't hurt, either. For example, try to create something that gets the interest of customers as they stand in line to check out. If the ad reminds customers that they can connect with your business right then, right from a mobile phone, you increase the odds that customers will take action. The odds increase because customers doesn't have to remember to do it the next time they are in front of a computer.

Figure 10.1 shows how simple the message can be. This ad has a call to action, prompts the customer to respond, has an element of intrigue, and a sense of fun. It has all that, and it takes a few minutes to put together and very little in the way of financial investment to print off a few and place them around the store.

Figure 10.1   *Your message needn't be complicated. This one is simple, clear, and fun.*

This idea is just an example of how to get started. I'm sure your creative endeavors will be sharper than this. What I wanted to make clear was, with all this talk of a plan, don't overthink it.

Don't try to be so clever that your customer doesn't get it or that you get so caught up in the process and procedures that your organization never actually executes anything (I've been there with clients, too). There is a fine line between having a strong enough plan that can be executed and a plan that is so nailed shut that execution has been planned completely out of the process.

Where that line falls will be something that the organization figures out as it develops a plan for its social business. Incorporating existing procedures is definitely something that is recommended, because no one embraces change less than the large enterprise. However, don't let the incorporation of those procedures make the plan into something that can't be executed.

Local Wins the Day

When putting the plan together, it is important to ensure that the organization—whether enterprise or small business—not forget that in real terms, your customers and potential customers are "local" to you. By local, I mean they are local whether temporarily, in the sense of being visitors, or in the permanent sense that they inhabit the same town as your store or venue.

Apps such as Bryan's Local List and TriOutNC are taking the concept of social location sharing and making it hyper-local. Bryan's Local List focuses solely on the Orange County area in California, and TriOutNC focuses solely on the Triangle area of North Carolina.

TriOutNC describes its service as offering a point incentive system as a way to get involved when you are out and about in the Triangle. Points are accumulated on a weekly basis by checking in, posting a review, or rating a location. You can win virtual awards based on your checkin habits, as well as The Key, which is a special honor for being the user who has checked-in the most times at a particular location. Businesses often offer their own specials or rewards for checking in a certain number of times or for being the Key Holder to their establishment.

These apps seek to become both the location service and also the promotion platform for local businesses in specific regions. The idea is that residents like to support their locally based businesses over big box stores and visitors like to gain local flavor.

Certainly there is a segment of the social consumer base for which this is very true. The model that both of these apps follow is designed to make it easier for small businesses to take part in this type of marketing. Small businesses can track results from the shop door to the checkout without requiring an entire marketing department to do so.

Even the large retailer should consider this type of option as a method of promoting themselves to the local populace (though at the time of writing, Bryan's list does not permit large brands to use the site). As hyper-local enters the mainstream vocabulary of marketers, we will see more of these types of social location sharing tools that allow even national chains to act in a more local way when choosing social marketing communications channels, in much the same way as they have done previously with radio or television.

Micropayment Systems

When considering the local focus, don't forget to also include micropayment systems. These have been popular in Asia for quite some time now and are gradually spreading to the United States and Europe with the increased adoption of smartphones. Systems such as Venmo, which was originally set up to share money between friends, are already gaining popularity among merchants who want to enable customers to pay with their cell phones rather than with loose change or by using credit cards for small purchases.

Venmo actually allows for transfers of sums up to $1,000 in one transaction, so conceivably it would be possible to pay for much larger items. (Although I think that the social consumers are not currently feeling safe enough to want to make payments of this size with their cell phones.)

However, paying the tab in a coffee shop or at a bar is a much more reasonable proposition. Austin-based company TabbedOut is designed to solve this type of payment by enabling smartphone users to open a tab at select venues via their phones and close it when they leave the location, without ever having to hand over their credit cards. The dual appeal of this service to users is both the convenience and the capability to take one type of identity fraud out of the realm of possibility. Handing over a credit card to wait staff is definitely one way in which people can have their identity stolen. Using a secure payment system via a phone is, according to TabbedOut, a safer way to make those payments.

I think there is still some resistance to both of these concepts, with the most obvious being, "What if I lose my phone?" The counterargument is, however, that it would be the same as currently losing your wallet. Both arguments are valid, and only time will show if the marketplace and its users are ready to explore a truly mobile world in this way.

Check Out

In closing this book, I hope that you have found the ideas, suggestions, and information useful. If you have, let me know. I'd love to hear from you. If you have questions about the content, please feel free to email me, tweet me, or contact me through your favorite social media channel. I'm pretty easy to find online, as Incslinger. I've listed some of the more popular places to find me on the following page.

I hope that you enjoy sharing your location as much as I do, and that your business finds a way to incorporate this new channel into your marketing communications strategy and plans. If you have any questions about how to do that, you can always contact me about those. If you really have problems, you can just hire my company to solve them for you.

As with everything that goes into these types of books, by the time you read it something will have changed. As far as possible, I tried to future proof the book, either by avoiding those platforms that I thought would not still be around by the time this book hit the shelves or by making sure that the ones I included were stable enough for me to recommend to you.

Find me online:

simon@theincslingers.com

http://twitter.com/incslinger

http://www.foursquare.com/user/incslinger

http://gowalla.com/users/incslinger

http://www.scvngr.com/users/194928 (Yes they need to allow personalization!)

In real life—Simon Salt; come say hi!

Index

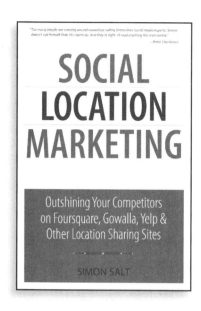

SOCIAL LOCATION MARKETING

Outshining Your Competitors on Foursquare, Gowalla, Yelp & Other Location Sharing Sites

SIMON SALT

FREE Online Edition

Your purchase of **Social Location Marketing** includes access to a free online edition for 45 days through the Safari Books Online subscription service. Nearly every Que book is available online through Safari Books Online, along with more than 5,000 other technical books and videos from publishers such as Addison-Wesley Professional, Cisco Press, Exam Cram, IBM Press, O'Reilly, Prentice Hall, and Sams.

SAFARI BOOKS ONLINE allows you to search for a specific answer, cut and paste code, download chapters, and stay current with emerging technologies.

Activate your FREE Online Edition at www.informit.com/safarifree

> **STEP 1:** Enter the coupon code: UJUVXFA.

> **STEP 2:** New Safari users, complete the brief registration form. Safari subscribers, just log in.

If you have difficulty registering on Safari or accessing the online edition, please e-mail customer-service@safaribooksonline.com